RUGBY'S NEW-AGE TRAVELLERS

RUGBY'S NEW-AGE TRAVELLERS

STUART BARNES

MAINSTREAM
PUBLISHING

EDINBURGH AND LONDON

Photographs © Colorsport

First published in Great Britain in 1997 by
MAINSTREAM PUBLISHING COMPANY (EDINBURGH) LTD
7 Albany Street
Edinburgh EH1 3UG

ISBN 1 85158 917 1

A catalogue record for this book is available from the British Library

Typeset in Berkeley
Printed and bound in Great Britain by Butler and Tanner Ltd, Frome

To Lesley and my parents, John and Joyce

Contents

Acknowledgements

I would like to acknowledge Bill, Peter and, especially, Cathy from Mainstream for their faith, hard work and spirit of adventure. Sincere thanks also to Igor the Gooner and Rusty Cheyne for their magnificent photographic work. It would be remiss of me not to mention my colleagues at Sky, whose infectious eagerness propped up any waning enthusiasm in the dark December days, and, finally, thanks go to all the people whose words and deeds made this book possible.

The Five Nations: The Battle off the Pitch

At 2.30 p.m. on 5 June 1996, the Rugby Football Union, represented by its TV and Media Committee, signed a television Heads of Agreement with BSkyB. The contract was reported to be worth £87.5 million over five years. Of that, £22.5 million would be set aside for the senior clubs. The rest of the world knew these teams as 'professional', but the RFU were still reluctant to utter such obscenities in public.

This still left approximately 1,980 clubs, 3,000 schools and an infrastructure of civil service proportions with quite a sum. The existing TV contracts were worth £4.52 million per season – and a cool £12.98 million a season more was on the table. The downside? Terrestrial television did not have live rights to internationals played at Twickenham. Considering England's Neanderthal style of recent years, a logical person might have regarded this as a bonus. A quick glance at Ceefax and the viewer would know whether to stay in and watch the delayed transmission or head for a quick one at the local.

It was the dream win-win scenario for your average male. He need not purchase a satellite dish. This could result in brownie points with his partner – 'There are more important things in life than sport; we do not need satellite television' – and he could then use the absence of a dish as an excuse for spending Saturday afternoon in the pub. Sadly, forces were at work that failed to understand this very essence of the sporting male.

By the time of the AGM on 12 July, there was crisis in the air. The other Unions had expressed their displeasure at a deal guilty of excessive commercial reality and, inevitably, that heavy-handed touch of English arrogance. The Five Nations, that most revered, if mediocre, of tournaments was under threat. England at home to Wales or Scotland is part of the very fabric of Middle England. They may not be too concerned with falling standards in health and education (a fair assumption, as the majority of English rugby supporters remain defiant Conservatives), but they were prepared to stand and be counted when something as important as a gin-soaked day at Twickenham was under threat. And so a hard-core majority of the 1,980 clubs were opposed to the deal. The Television Committee, like Neville Chamberlain, did not bring peace in their time. Those who cannot comprehend why the RFU struggled so heavily with the mutation from old to new should attend the AGM. No history lesson could ever teach as much about rugby union and its administrators.

The AGM is held annually in the Park Lane Hilton. It offers the regional members a certain exotic taste of power. The foyer of the hotel is a bizarre mingling of military side partings, dressed in blazers, and beautiful Eastern women, who are either bored mistresses of Muslim millionaires or hookers; frequently they are both. Neither group is interested in the other.

It's a big day out for the representatives of the English clubs; for some it is a moment of intoxicating glory. The gin and tonics, the one real luxury on British Rail, are deferred. Feeling good in their blazers, many are eager to swell their chests and reveal their rhetorical skills previously only admired in the local Freemason scene.

On this occasion the air of anticipation was almost tangible: the shires were about to speak out. The meeting was held in the ballroom, the same room where thousands of internationals have been bored to death by a bunch of horn-blowers playing tally-ho music. This crowd would have appreciated it.

The assembled mass faced the top table, where members of the Executive faced their inquisitors. Once the Executive was at the vanguard of the amateur movement; here its members stood condemned as arrogant money-grabbers. John Jeavons Fellows, one of the International Board delegates – once enemy, now friend of the leading clubs – appeared to mutter 'Luddites' as he turned his head towards the audience.

Jeavons Fellows took his place on the top table with Bill Bishop, the happiest man in the room. He was handing the poisoned chalice of presidency to John Richardson, a Warwickshire lawyer and former Navy man – classic RFU committee breeding. The spotlight was on three others that night. There was Dave Robinson, the treasurer (now sadly deceased) who had to defend the BSkyB deal, and Tony Hallett, the secretary widely regarded as the man who drove the game into the twentieth century – a reason for admiration or contempt, depending on the style of your hair and the cut of your blazer. Then there was the chairman of the Executive, the man of the people: self-made millionaire Cliff Brittle. He was perceived as the champion of the small clubs, the scourge of professionalism . . . and, in his own view, the defender of rugby union democracy.

Behind the platform was a wall of three red roses. I closed my eyes and recalled Neil Kinnock's last conference as leader of the Labour Party. This meeting would illustrate unexpected similarities between his Labour Party and this RFU committee. I say 'unexpected' because this gathering would have elected *any* right-wing government on a landslide. Farmers, military and self-made men – even Tony Blair appeared a radical left-winger in comparison.

Bill Bishop, an old-fashioned and decent Cornishman, kicked off the meeting. Anybody who had been on a recent Martian vacation and was unaware of the main topic soon realised what the night was all about and why the media sat with anticipatory smiles, observing from the wings, like twentieth-century vampires. Bishop introduced the new president, with the most genuine of smiles. He then paused, tried to take the pasty out of the accent and delivered his words with the gravest *gravitas*. It was only marginally more authoritative than the dalek's voice of the Moral Major himself. 'I have met with the president of the WRU, Sir Tasker Watkins, and he has given me permission to read this statement: "There is unanimous agreement that the Five Nations is of paramount importance, and ways of ensuring this are to be pursued actively and urgently."'

The ballroom rippled with applause; the English love the Five Nations. While the World Cup is an uncomfortable reminder that England do not rule the waves, the Five Nations has a far more reassuring feel. Since the advent of Geoff Cooke, England have dominated the tournament. To criticise England for winning Grand Slams against inferior opponents without fulfilling their true potential has been regarded as almost treasonable in some eyes. Harmless but blinkered xenophobia is the nature of the tournament and the English love it. In contrast, the Celtic nations are motivated by a sense of national retribution. The ghosts of Owain Glyndwr and Robert the Bruce walk the stadiums of Cardiff and Edinburgh.

Additionally, people who know nothing about the sport attend internationals in their droves. Maybe that is why committee men love the Five Nations. Buoyed by unexpected warmth, Bishop bid adieu to the hot seat, but not before a mention of his dear wife 'Christine, without whom, especially in the dark days, I could not have come through'. And people tell players not to take the game too seriously!

The formalities were over; it was time for the serious stuff. Dave Robinson, by this time already wheelchair-ridden, proved just how much some people do care for the game. As he struggled for words, nobody could accuse him of self-interest. It had been a self-sacrifice to see out the year. By the time of the AGM he was forced to address the audience via a pre-recorded video.

Robinson, weak of limb, was strong of word. The only certain thing was the fast-expanding cost-base of the RFU: they had a syndicated bank loan of £34 million, capital investment in youth was regarded as akin to development policy, etc. etc. It was a rat-a-tat machine-gun explanation of the reasons for the Sky deal. It made commercial sense and it made rugby sense, but Robinson might just as well have spoken in Greek. The moderate mob within the audience were not here to listen.

Robinson sought to allay the rumour that the working party had acted beyond their brief. The mob were told that it was normal for the treasurer and secretary to sign such contracts. As treasurer elect, Colin Herridge, former press officer for the team, had also been party to the signings.

A working group to deal with television and media had been created as far back as 1989. Since inception there had only been two changes in the committee, the crucial one being the progressive Tony Hallett for the more circumspect Dudley Wood. Hallett was the hate figure of the traditionalists. The individuals who comprised the party had been authorised to negotiate as recently as April 1996. Robinson was certain of his team's mandate.

They were told that it was acceptable to meet with Sky on 24 May. By 5 June the Heads of Agreement were signed. Even the president was unaware until he was informed at 5.30 that night. The decision, in Robinson's urgent words, was 'the right and proper decision to secure assets and provide sufficient cash to keep all levels of the game successful'. He finished by reminding the AGM that it had been their decision to throw the game open in March. It was they who had allowed the clubs to become professional and therefore start to exercise their undoubted powers, dormant for over a century. There could be no turning back from tough commercial reality.

That was not the message that the floor wanted to hear. They asked if the committee were aware how the other nations would react. Robinson, belying his frail physique, was strident. 'We have sold our products, now we have done what I think we should have done three years ago . . . it is essential to look after our assets.' If he had been talking about a business, he would have received a standing ovation for such a hard-nosed free market stance. And yet he *was* talking about a business – one called rugby union – that the traditionalists and, yes, the volunteers could not bear to accept. We were witnessing either mass stupidity or gross self-delusion, but the floor had the smell of blood. I half expected the tally-ho band to appear with a pack of dogs in pursuit of Hallett, Jeavons Fellows and Robinson.

Voices were raised from the floor. 'What about not seeing the game live with family and friends?' 'Were Sky likely to make a profit?' What sort of questions were these? Most of the rugby has barely been worth watching, most of the questioners found themselves tickets for the match, and I doubt whether their families wanted them around on a Saturday afternoon anyway. As for the matter of Sky's profitability, this stripped bare the implacable hostility to Murdoch. It was more a matter of class and tradition than viewing figures or availability. There was also the small matter of Murdoch's reputation for setting the agenda. If there is one thing that unites a rugby committee, it is a fear of the loss of power. That was the rationale behind the events in the ballroom of the Hilton. A power struggle was being fought out.

The hostility towards the Executive stemmed directly from this feeling of growing helplessness. One man alone was perceived as the saviour: Cliff Brittle, the man elected as chairman of the Executive in front of John Jeavons Fellows, who had been the choice of the Executive. Brittle stood on the mandate of the floor who had elected him. The papers saw the battle between the Executive and the rest as a personality clash between him and Hallett. It was Kinnock against Benn. The Kinnock/Hallett figure was the pragmatic reformer, perceived as a betrayer of the cause in the name of power. In Hallett's case, power could be substituted for money. Kinnock argued that Labour needed change to survive; Hallett thought the same way about the RFU.

In opposition was the feared figure of Tony Benn, the loathed figure in the Parliamentary Labour Party because of persistent reminders to Kinnock that the party constitution, not the PLP, made policy. When I drew this analogy with Brittle to the man himself, he spluttered in good humour: 'Not Tony Benn.' This came as no surprise. Few self-made millionaires are flattered by a comparison with Benn. But there are similarities. Both are reviled by the establishment – the players think Brittle 'vulgar', to quote one famous England international – but both have a sturdy love of the fight.

Brittle, tanned and with the sort of grey hair that would win him a role in *Dynasty*, spends much of his time as a tax exile on the Isle of Man. He summers near Cannes and he appears totally convinced of his own position. When a voice from the floor asked Brittle if he had been sidelined and, if so, how he could progress in his work, Brittle stepped forward. The question was a clear set-up. While the rest of the Executive stood and spoke from the top table, Brittle walked to the dais; the man was joining his people. 'I had expected difficulty; instead it [his role] has proved almost impossible.' He confirmed that he had been sidelined in certain issues, that he could not go forward in his role. Displaying a rare streak of aesthetics in a businessman, he quoted Oscar Wilde: 'If one tells the truth, then sooner or later the truth will come out.' The voice in the Executive wilderness claimed affiliation to 'you' at all levels: 'I consider my position still rests in your hands.' Brittle was winning the PR battle with ease, but the floor were so set in their ways that they would probably have cheered Hitler had he attacked the BSkyB deal.

One of the most telling statements from the floor accused the RFU of forgetting their biggest assets, the supporters. Who exactly did he think these supporters would have left to support without the very real, commercial necessity of finance? Clarity? There was more in a glass of port.

And so the attacks rolled remorselessly over the Executive. Silence was short-lived when a lone voice of support queried enigmatically, 'Where else would the money come from?' Robinson smiled, but the mob barely registered the voice in the wilderness. What did they care? These people had no concept of professionalism.

Yet they did represent the majority of the RFU. Brittle was, in reality, fighting the battle for democracy. That did not place the Executive in the wrong. To follow the wishes of the members was to revert to amateurism. That was the corporate wish. The clubs with the internationals, representing 0.01 per cent of the constituent body, would have no option but to seek new administration. That also applied to the national team, who were naturally expected to be the most professional of all English teams. Quite how that would leave the RFU and its £34 million overdraft had not been considered. It was perhaps too big a question for some of the mob, who bore a passing resemblance to the posturing court of Jonathan Swift's Lilliputians.

There was almost a state of civil war within the English game. To placate opposition from the floor John Richardson, the new president, had to announce the creation of a working party. The Executive were aware that Richardson was planning this conciliatory gesture, but his announcement at the AGM caught them unawares. Critics saw it as an attempt to end the feud between Brittle and Hallett. That was the perception, but too often we simplify issues. This was not just about two individuals; it was, quite literally, about the state of the union. Brittle himself confided that he was more interested in the big clubs than the small, Europe more than Lancashire. But his role as executive chairman was to fulfil the wish of the constitution. Hallett had similar interests to those for which Brittle claimed covert support, but he and his supporters were certain that direct action was the only way to conquer the cacophony of antiquated words.

The RFU Executive were adamant that their decision to deal unilaterally was out of the blue. In fact the truth was very different. Three years earlier England had emphasised that they needed a larger slice than the equitable 25 per cent. The reasons were the obvious ones: greater infrastructure, more clubs, more schools, more players – in other words, England were the major nation. It was only on the slenderest of votes that England had not declared unilateralism then. The other nations knew that England were unhappy with their 25 per cent share of the terrestrial deal – or, at least, *the Executive* were unhappy.

As for the opposition from the floor, the late John Burgess, a former president and coach of the national team and mentor to the likes of Fran Cotton and Bill Beaumont, launched an impassioned attack. Words like 'alienation' and phrases like 'the forfeiture of moral leadership' (only the English would be arrogant enough to claim such a high ground) poured forth in an unstoppable torrent. Hallett and co. had 'patronised' the members, they were 'out of touch', 'a side-effect of arrogance was deafness . . . which led to their polarisation'. He stated that certain prominent people were openly subverting the interests of the game, that they had sold control of the game and its soul to a TV mogul, and that the *nouveaux riches* were increasingly being given precedence over real rugby people. I waited for him to call them Republicans, Trotskyites, fans of Michael Jackson . . . their crimes seemed legion.

It was great rhetorical stuff: idealistic, passionate and not lacking elements of truth. But it was too late – the sport was professional and Burgess, the ostrich, pissing in the wind, seemed more likely to destroy than save what was left of rugby's now-tarnished ethos. Brittle was cast in the role of the weapon aimed at undermining the progressives within the RFU. His actions would be crucial in the next few months.

The reaction of the floor came as less than revelatory to those involved with the Sky deal. The fundamental reason was the famous English reactionary streak. As one member of the Executive stated, 'The feeling was that no matter how much we tried to tell people, too many had taken entrenched positions and were not prepared to listen to the arguments. There were people out there who had watched rugby on the BBC for the last 30 years; they were purely concerned by change. Firstly, they were concerned that we had gone to a satellite channel and stopped the masses watching, and secondly there was also a negative feeling about Murdoch coupled with the question of why England should go it alone.' The Executive left the meeting feeling they had held their own. I suppose General Custer thought that too.

But if men like Tony Hallett thought they were in for a quiet weekend, they soon discovered otherwise. With the morning sun came news of England's ejection from the Five Nations. The civil war had extended to the rest of Britain, and the legion of tabloids that had neither knowledge of nor interest in the game itself cracked open the champagne bottles. I headed home, via a large and lonely gin on British Rail. Would I ever write about rugby as a sport, rather than a political issue, again?

Hallett should not have been surprised by England's expulsion, according to Wales's daily paper, *The Western Mail*. The paper accused 'certain individuals' within the Executive of 'crass arrogance' for not taking prior expulsion threats seriously. Even the tome's leader column found space to decry England's 'startling degree of greed'. It seemed that Wales were enjoying what they perceived as England's fall from any moral high ground considered by elements of the Rugby Football Union to be the natural home of all decent Englishmen.

The vast majority of threats throughout July 1996 had been emanating from Wales and, in particular, from Vernon Pugh. As president of rugby union's International Board and a highly respected Queen's Counsel, the impartiality of Vernon Pugh is not in doubt, but to a minority of English ears some of his words did appear to draw an iron curtain across the Celtic countries, keeping out rampant capitalism once again. But this time the enemy was Australia rather than America, veiled in the image of the dear old Digger himself:

Rupert Murdoch and his BSkyB satellite channel. Pugh announced Celtic independence three days before America's celebrations. 'There is no way we will abandon Scotland and Ireland because to do so would be to abandon ourselves. We are not negotiating with Sky because there are too many conditions attached to their money. We have invited tenders from other television companies for international and domestic rugby.' Four days later his opposition was even more unequivocal. 'The decision of the RFU [concerning the Sky deal], if not altered, will bring an end to this most cherished of tournaments.' The writing was writ large on the wall, translated into English.

The Welsh AGM almost led to the closing of borders. Pugh's words were pumped with rhetoric of deeply belligerent bent. 'We are in a game of bluff, and we might be playing blind man's bluff, but we are not wearing the blindfold.' His fervour mounted. 'We have been offered a silver knife and are told we can keep it to cut our throats.' It was inflammatory enough to suggest a future alongside such idealogues as Michael Portillo. The war was taken into the enemy camp. 'It would be interesting to discover what the public in England would do if their team were not in the tournament.' Not so much interesting as depressing. Perhaps hidden west of the Severn, Pugh was unaware that Englishmen are only slightly more interested in the fate of others than are our American cousins. England has a fairly deserved reputation for arrogant insularity. We may know that the Germans are arrogant, that the French farmers are unreasonable and that the Spanish fishermen are trying to avenge the Armada, but not much else. How many Englishmen hang out at the Eisteddfod? How many Home Countyites peruse the Edinburgh Fringe? No, it's Glyndebourne or Euro 96, depending on status. The other weakness in Pugh's probings is that most people who watch the Five Nations have little interest in the sport *per se*. The interest is stimulated by England whacking their neighbours. If anyone tells me that viewing figures are linked to the quality of the tournament, I will puke all the way to my southern hemisphere video collection.

Sir Tasker Watkins, the esteemed president, used the old political policy of misinformation. He claimed that England were trapped by the will of the other nations because the deal was dependent on the existence of a Five Nations for Sky to televise. BSkyB had kept a low profile in the debate, but at this a swift statement denying the veracity of Watkins's words was issued. The Welsh efforts to drive a rift between the RFU and Sky had failed, and that line was dropped.

But two days after the Welsh AGM an even more influential voice joined the attack. England's former captain, Will Carling, was apparently intent on maintaining his man-of-the-people image. He praised the quality of BBC and ITV coverage in the past. In terms of match coverage he was arguably right. In terms of commitment to the game, he was wholly wrong. The BBC, especially, cannot claim any durable affinity to the game. The Five Nations were a wow in terms of viewing figures, but what else had the Beeb done to stimulate interest? They showed the occasional second half of the cup final and had a weekly magazine programme tucked away in a discreet late-Sunday-afternoon slot. ITV had at least committed themselves to the European Cup in its first year, along with the World Cup and live overseas Tests, but it could not be compared with Sky's extensive and regular coverage of the game. Admittedly, Sky has the flexibility of being a committed sports service . . . but is that not the point?

Carling argued, 'I fear the benefits of the Sky deal will be short-term and I am concerned about the effects this is going to have on the future of the Five Nations tournament. It will mean losing the interest and the increasing awareness and appeal which rugby has been steadily gaining since the 1991 World Cup.' Like a politician or a member of the Royal Family, Carling was out of touch. It is understandable. England has become a full-time career, and a very lucrative one. On the motivational circuit, Carling's profession, he mingles with leaders of industry, whose sum knowledge extends to the Five Nations. The fact that club crowds were barely growing hardly strengthened his assertions. Terrestrial coverage was *not* spreading the gospel and finding the converts. A comparison with viewing figures at football clubs since Sky's television coverage of Premiership football commenced is even more instructive. Crowds have risen indisputably and the popularity of the sport has soared.

Carling called England's expulsion a disaster for the players and English rugby as a whole. Jonathan Humphreys, the Welsh captain, agreed. Given the national Welsh stance and the control exercised by the Welsh Rugby Union through his contract, this hardly stunned the rugby world. Humphreys announced that there was no room for England to play the three southern hemisphere superpowers on a regular basis, thereby proving that he has a hotline to Murdoch and the governing bodies of the southern hemisphere nations. Humphreys told *The Western Mail* that England 'thought themselves bigger fish than they were'. Unkind critics thought this Welsh fish was out of his depth.

As an employee of the WRU he could take no other position; Welshmen who did asked not to be named. Carling could, quite literally, afford to spurn Sky's millions, but by August it was clear that his views were personal and not representative of his colleagues. Club partner at Harlequins Jason Leonard said, 'I would definitely like to stay in the Five Nations, but I don't think England should compromise too much to achieve that.' Lawrence Dallaglio showed solidarity, adding, 'Obviously we want the Five Nations to continue, but if this is not possible then something else will happen.' Neither guy sounded like a traumatised victim of disaster.

The terrestrial defenders of Five Nations traditions were further undermined by rugby's great visionaries, the New Zealanders. In the season when politicians showed an endearing death wish by thinking the unthinkable (well, they did eight months before the election), it was left to John Hart, the All Blacks coach, to question the future of the game. 'The whole structure of international rugby will change in the near future and in that respect the Five Nations business in Britain might help.' Inspired by the Murdoch money that created Super 12 and the Tri-Nations, people were thinking about world leagues of provincial and international dimensions. England's eviction would clear a path for their entry, leaving the Celtic countries with a second-rate tournament and second-rate finances. Vernon Pugh, Freddie McLeod and Tom Kiernan's defence of their countries' positions were potentially the 'silver knives' to which Pugh had earlier referred.

The fifth column within the RFU were encouraged by resistance on the part of the other nations. Supported by such traditionalists as Bill Beaumont, Richardson restructured the negotiating committee. Tony Hallett, a significant figure in the Sky deal, was the chief sacrifice in the urgent attempt to mend bridges. Ten days after their unceremonious eviction, a representative from the RFU travelled to Cardiff with a new set of proposals to appease the angry Celts. Ireland's delegates arrived late for the meeting. It is unfashionable to accuse any British nation bar England of offensive manners, but this would not be the first time that England received a proverbial hanky in the face.

Nor was it only the Celts who questioned the decisions of the Executive. Shortly after Hallett and the rest of the RFU accepted the Sky offer, it was translated into a legally binding Heads of Agreement. Sam Chisholm, the craggy former king of Sky, attended this meeting. With him were Bruce McWilliam and Jonathon Skyes, Sky's legal man, and Vic Wakeling, Head of Sport. Colin Herridge, the popular penguin-lookalike treasurer, chaired the meeting, and representing EPRUC was Donald Kerr. EPRUC and Kerr would become portable thorn-bushes in the side of the RFU later that year (but that is one office tale too many for this book). Kerr questioned the deal before 'Sam lashed in with a wonderful quarter-of-an-hour speech telling him what he thought of those who didn't accept what was the biggest deal they would ever get in their lives. It rather quietened them.' Not for long.

The Heads of Agreement was put to the Executive of the RFU and unanimously signed – excepting the notable signature of the chairman of the Executive, Cliff Brittle. This was a crucial stage in the breakdown of relations between Brittle and the rest of the Executive. He refused to accept collective responsibility. Brittle obviously leans on the side of the referendum. As one member of the Executive said, 'We went along and voted on behalf of the people we represent' – a sort of parliamentary democracy. As in an ideal Parliament, the individual should argue his or her case, vote and accept the decision. Excluding the dying days of Major's government, any individual incapable of accepting the majority decision would reasonably be expected to resign. According to one of the respected members of the committee, Brittle's failure to do so was 'the main reason why the whole thing became so acrimonious. Hallett and Jeavons Fellows were accused of misleading everyone, which was wrong, of signing without a mandate, which was also wrong, and of signing a bad deal, which most people would say was nonsense.'

The RFU Executive of the time also dismissed as nonsense the rumour that they knew of their impending ejection from the sanctified Five Nations. Concerned by the shelling of abuse from Wales, England sought a truce. On 9 July, three days before the AGM, Bill Bishop organised a meeting with the Welsh delegation at the East India Club. Bill Bishop, Peter Brook, Dennis Fellows and Colin Herridge were other Englishmen present. Representing Wales were Tasker Watkins, Ray Williams, Glanmor Griffiths and Vernon Pugh. They discussed the reasons and the background behind the Sky deal. It is alleged that England asked Wales outright if they were preparing to eject them from the Five Nations and that the Welsh answered in the negative. England also allegedly inquired about their rejection of *any* satellite involvement in principle; again the Welsh purportedly stated that this was not the case. England assumed that 'meaningful compromise was a probability'. Old friendships were toasted and reaffirmed at Shepherd's restaurant. Little did the Executive know that the next day the Welsh delegation were to fly to Paris, where the Four Nations deal was signed and announced without England's knowledge. The Executive were caught cold. 'We expected another meeting with the other Unions. We thought they would respect the fact that we had this contract.'

That proved to be the assumption that made asses of so many administrators. It transpired that the Welsh believed England's BSkyB contract was not binding at this stage, and that a side letter proved the fact. There was no side letter. A touch optimistically, they requested a sight of the contract, a request to which the RFU understandably refused to accede. It is pushing the borders of belief to think that they travelled to Paris on a romantic whim; the plan was surely hatched in advance and only the tearing up of the deal and the tugging of the forelock could have diverted the plane bound for Paris.

The conspiracy theory that fuelled the venom of the rank-and-file members of the AGM stemmed from the rumour that the RFU had been informed *before* the announcement of the Four Nations and before the AGM. The RFU are adamant that those who had sipped their sherry with their Celtic counterparts had been unaware of the decision at the time of the AGM, yet rumours persist that one man within the Executive had been informed. It was becoming dirty enough to be mistaken for real politics.

The AGM signalled the end of the series of meetings. Like Parliament, the RFU take a summer recess. No executive meetings were planned, but Bishop, the outgoing president, arranged a desperate meeting with his recent counterpart, Tasker Watkins. The crisis meeting was scheduled for 23 July.

The English negotiating party included John Richardson, Cliff Brittle, Dennis Fellows and Colin Herridge. Wales were represented by the Shepherd's four. Ireland's president attended, together with two of the amateur code's great names, Syd Millar and Tom Kiernan. Scotland had Freddie McLeod, Charlie Dicken and Alan Hosie in attendance. The French were absent.

It was one of the most acrimonious gatherings held in the Park Hotel. England arrived in a mood of compromise. They were prepared to throw around £10 million of their money into the pot as long as the Celtic nations acknowledged the binding nature of the contract. England also reminded the other nations that Sky contracts were on the table for each of the Unions.

The meeting did not make it that far. The treasurer, Colin Herridge, admits, 'We were harangued to a degree that I could not believe. I've sat in acrimonious board meetings but this was a different level altogether.' The hostility of ancient Saxon–Celtic rivalry surprised the entire English delegation. It acted as a unifying force. John Jeavons Fellows – a man from 'the Sydney charm school', according to one colleague – made the RFU's point strongly. It hardened a perception that England were possessed of an arrogant selfishness, while the English thought it yet another sign of the ancient strife. The RFU left with tails between legs, having achieved nothing.

Money was never discussed. 'Principle' was the word that created an unsurpassable barrier to negotiations. They were averse to England's unilateral dealings and they were unhappy with satellite. The perceived global aspirations of Murdoch were giving them nightmares. The Celtic nations were playing the role of underdog against extra-terrestrialism.

The English delegation retreated to London and a six-hour meeting on 31 July. The antagonism of the meeting in Cardiff was a turning-point. The energies in the civil war between the forces of Brittle and Hallett found a new direction and a common enemy. Even Brittle was reportedly stunned by the antagonistic attitude of the Celts. Those who had previously criticised the contract became immediately more sympathetic when the aborted efforts of the team were explained. There is nothing like an Englishman spurned. Herridge reiterated the financial importance of the deal, with EPRUC a shadow on the horizon. Take away tax and the payments to clubs, schools, overdrafts and the like, and the need for the finances was suddenly revealed. The scales fell from the eyes of many former enemies of the deal.

Money hardly made the agenda of the Celts. They met at a Heathrow hotel on 8 August and again denounced England. Tom Kiernan infuriated England by breaking an alleged agreement not to talk with the media when he announced that the RFU had not 'gone far enough'. The reality was that the RFU were not in a position to fulfil the wishes of Kiernan, even had they had the will to do so. Ireland and the other countries were still demanding that the RFU unscramble their Sky contract. Still they did not realise that England were legally bound. It was a stalemate.

It was imperative for the RFU to change the perceptions of their erstwhile friends if the Five Nations was to be saved. The plan was one based upon an exhausting course of shuttle diplomacy on the part of

Cliff Brittle. In Cardiff he had sought to bring the Celts together with Murdoch's men to find common ground. The alliance were adamant in their refusal, but Brittle was designated as the man to pursue this course once more. Even his enemies within the RFU admired the tenacity of his efforts. The sheer resolve (and possible good faith in a man whose very public disputes with Hallett made him more acceptable) eventually led to progress.

Throughout August 1996, Brittle yo-yoed his way from his French base to Scotland, Wales, Ireland and, allegedly, Sam Chisholm's pad near Paddington. Towards the end of the month, the other nations followed. Compromises were agreed and the Five Nations was saved. England had kept most of their deal intact. Yet in July the odds had been stacked against the Executive winning the day. Perhaps it was always likely to be compulsion that propelled this dinosaur of an administration forward. The sheer necessity of the funds for a game suffering horrendous growing pains forced their hand; the support of players and the likelihood of lucrative fixtures with the southern hemisphere countries were other reasons behind the shift from doddering amateurs to hardish-nosed realists. England were happy to save the Five Nations, but with an alternative back-up they were ready to stand their ground with awful consequences for the future of the less populous rugby-playing nations within Great Britain and Ireland.

England also knew that Wales were financially hide-bound, that a championship without England was 'not much' (the RFU's words, not mine) and, most importantly, that the Welsh knew that England could survive on their high-protein diet of southern hemisphere rugby. The gamble on the rank and file defeating the Executive was lost when those ancient hostilities surfaced, hostilities beyond Chisholm and Murdoch, hostilities that existed when the names New Zealand and Australia were non-existent. England's innate chauvinism came to the fore, and that support offered the safety net which strengthened English resolve.

Brittle finally convinced Pugh that Sky was England's new limit, and progress in the salvation of the scruffy old tournament was made. Pugh drew up an accord. From around 7 p.m. until 2 a.m. the battling nations sat up in the International Board offices, then located in Bristol, to thrash out negotiations. Herridge, Brittle, Richardson, Alan Hosie, Pugh and Kiernan attended, along with legal experts. Agreement was finally reached. The Celts were much more conciliatory; England were delighted. The men in white had won the battle of principle. England had maintained their rights of unilateral signings and their extensive southern hemisphere fixtures. Their contract, the biggest ever secured in the northern hemisphere, remained, satellite's role was acknowledged and England's excessive logistical demands were coolly accepted.

I will not venture into the complicated mathematics of the deal, but England did not expect to lose more than £3–£4 million. By the time the accountants have worked out the percentages and win bonuses, we will be girding ourselves for the next World Cup. Kicked in the head by commercial reality, England will doubtless present a serious challenge in 1999, but the World Cup was the last thing on the minds of the RFU as the Five Nations crisis passed into history. The rumblings of discontent from the newly professionalised clubs erupted. Vesuvius spewed forth more venom, Twickenham was again engulfed. The story of the battle between Sir John Hall and Cliff Brittle, the senior clubs and the RFU, modern values against traditional codes has filled countless column inches of newspapers. Again it symbolised the growing pains of the new age of rugby. To do full justice to this part-principled, part-Machiavellian encounter would leave little or no room for what rugby union really cares about: the game itself. From the office to the pitch.

The Five Nations: The Battle on the Pitch

Come January of every year, the British rugby fraternity unleashes a seismic groan. A rugby Christmas. Supporters, xenophobes, suppressed Celts, arrogant Saxons and those mystifying men from across the Channel carrying cockerels all gather for one of the northern hemisphere's great parties – the Five Nations.

The curtains are drawn on the rest of the rugby world. The eternal superiority of the southern hemisphere is consigned to the back of the filing system as players who would struggle to find a place in either the Auckland or the Natal team are deemed great with hyperbolic abandon. Best of all, if you happen to be English, you normally win it. The defunct Home International football championship leaves the English soccer team with no avenue for trophies; the cricketers perpetually win the surly-and-sad-sportsmen award for sulking, but little else. That leaves Nick Faldo, Steven Redgrave and Tim Henman to provide the rare cherished moments. Yes, English sport and its transfixed patriotic pride is generally in the doldrums . . . until the Five Nations.

Expectations are forever high. The memories are forgotten of last season's interminable bore, when you swore never to watch a Five Nations clash again at Twickenham, Cardiff or, if you are a lucky man but an unlucky or plain masochistic rugby fan, Lansdowne Road. The Home Unions will never admit it, but the whole event is a masquerade. It is as far removed from great sport as John Major is from No. 10. But, God, what a party. The All Blacks and the Springboks may have historical monopolies on the serious stuff on the pitch, but off it they all envy the crowds, the passion and, as the Irish will tell you, 'the craic'. Every other Saturday for ten weeks is a rugby equivalent of Chelten-

27

ham's glorious homage to Bacchus. Yes, even an old cynic like me enjoys the atmosphere.

1997 had an extra edge for the participants. The Lions would be touring South Africa the following summer. A lot of players would secretly be more concerned with their individual performances than the result. Believe me. I, and many others, have been that soldier.

The players' Five Nations starts with selection. On Monday 13 January, my tournament started with a trip across the inspirational new Severn Bridge to Cardiff and the announcement of the Welsh team for the match with Scotland. If the Welsh team could play as well as the bridge looked, they were Grand Slam bankers. Unfortunately, the second crossing was constructed by a French company.

The Centenary Suite of the National Stadium was rather low key in comparison. The concrete bowels of a sports stadium can be depressing places even on a match day, but when a rag-bag assortment of journalists (the majority were the local Welsh pack, as England's media showed their typical apathy with all things Celtic) and the management of the Welsh squad shared centre stage with a pair of tea ladies who bore a striking resemblance to Welsh dolls of folk tradition, well, frankly I wondered what life as a dustman would be like.

The Centenary Suite focused on Kevin Bowring, Terry Cobner, David Pickering and Jonathan Humphreys, coach, director of rugby, emerging team coach and reinstated captain respectively. They sat behind a set which reminded us that Wales were the host Union for the 1999 World Cup. This also reminded me how little time the northern powers had remaining in the countdown to another probable humiliation. The fleur-de-lys of Wales was eclipsed by the insignia of Reebok, for these were the early days of professionalism. There was little professional about the questions from the floor: 'Are you a good watcher, Jon?' (Humphreys had been suspended for the American match the previous Saturday), 'Have the last seven days been frustrating?', 'Does your mother darn your socks?', 'Do you want to travel the world and help underprivileged children?' . . . Miss World is grilled in comparison. This was the grim side of swapping boots for laptop. The most interesting aspect of the proceedings was the way Kevin Bowring handled the media. One tabloid colleague confided that 'He has changed in the last 12 months; he bloody well answers questions with questions'. Very wise. A stupid question lends itself to a misinterpreted answer. Bowring, staring straight ahead, apparently focused on an object on the back wall of the room, gave the press nothing, not a single juicy morsel to mangle. 'Are the front five too slow, Kevin?' he was asked. 'In comparison to what?' Good stuff. Wales were confident. There was no idle boasting, but Wales were quietly relaxed. Cobner and Pickering both mentioned the fact that Wales would have a good chance of the Triple Crown if they could beat Scotland the following Saturday at Murrayfield. Faced with France away, there was no talk of a Grand Slam. But somewhere, deep within the heart of Bowring and Humphreys, that dream was alive – as it was for every other coach, captain and player in the championship. Like Christmas and Cheltenham, the best part is in the anticipation.

A fair degree of both anticipation and trepidation was equally evident in the Scottish capital that week. Edinburgh lacks a Soho area to appeal to the multitude of inebriates, but the Celtic link makes the Welsh far more relaxed in the 'London of the North' – although a good Scot will remind you that London is in fact the Edinburgh of the South.

Whatever, the Welsh were invading. I arrived on the Friday. The British Midland flight from Heathrow was thick with the smell of alcohol as exiled Welsh brokers from the City reclaimed their birthright as they mingled with their compatriots whose exile from the Valleys was more temporary. *The Scotsman* newspaper claimed that 6,000 Welshmen had arrived by plane on the Thursday alone, and that 20,000 would flood the city by Saturday. Those of a taciturn nature were filled with dread; those who owned bars were perusing the most expensive holiday brochures. The Five Nations is a gold-rush for publicans.

Paul was a twenty-something Welshman with cropped red hair. He had travelled north as part of a 74-strong contingent from the Cardiff suburb of Whitchurch. A plain-clothes CID officer, it was his seventh visit to Edinburgh. He had been part of the joyous exodus since well before the legal drinking age – and he a policeman!

We met on a floating restaurant in Leith on the Friday night. He was in a state of high animation. 'Some old man walked into the pub where we were getting pissed, stood in the doorway and shouted, "I've got some tickets; who wants to buy 'em?" So I grabbed the old bastard.' The concerns evoked by the Birmingham four and the Bridgewater case surfaced uneasily in my mind. Serious criminals might be safe, but watch out ticket touts. Still, he had his ticket at the seventh attempt. I assured him that Wales would win with him, the scourge of the touts, as their good omen.

Back in the Hilton, the boyos were conducting a heated argument over the merits of Arwel Thomas or Jonathan Davies. Former internationals were dragged into the debate. In Wales the right number ten is a matter of religious significance. One Welshman asked me if I would sign an autograph for his son, adding, 'His name is Jonathan Davies, like the great man who should be playing today.' Oh Christ, I thought, the rugby bore strikes again.

The excitement was tangible, but there was a bizarre absence of expectation. Welshmen tripped over themselves to be pessimistic, while Scotland's greats – Gavin Hastings and Andy Irvine – tipped Wales. Irvine thought that Scotland lacked hard men in the front five. I felt that the conservative selection of Armstrong and Chalmers, rather than the more quicksilver partnership of Redpath and Townsend, would be a more significant factor against the Welsh.

On the athletics track that surrounds the famous turf of Murrayfield, John Jeffrey, the cult Scottish flanker turned selector, admitted that the mood of the team itself was 'apprehensive'. A stunning admission. At sport's highest levels, psychology is every bit as crucial as ability. I hurriedly phoned my bookmakers to increase my bet on the Welsh. Being a TV pundit and newspaper columnist is a pretty tough way to make an honest buck, but at least there is scope for some City-style insider dealing.

The atmosphere within Murrayfield was as mute as the expectation emanating from either set of supporters. The all-seater stadium allowed the crowds to linger as long as possible in the nearby hostelries or, less agreeably, in the corporate boxes. Twenty minutes before kick-off, barely 5,000 seats were occupied as an obscure pop singer entertained. Until recently it would have been a marching band. The tell-tale signs of the professional age. The spirit of the Five Nations is more likely to be suffocated by the malaise of corporatism than it ever was by the television dealings that had divided Britain earlier that season.

As for the match itself, the first 30 minutes were so tedious that I suspected the corporate punters were asking themselves whether the free malts were worth a day away from the family. Both teams were negative and free of any confidence until Scott Hastings scored a try, forged by a lightning piece of handling by Townsend, playing in the centre, who otherwise looked like a man making the most of a savage Siberian exile. It is tough being the sole artist among a group of artisans.

This galvanised Wales. Suddenly Arwel Thomas, playing with wonderful aggression, fired out a sublime pass to Allan Bateman. He skipped outside a confused Scott Hastings before linking with fellow former rugby league star Scott Gibbs. He then linked with a third league prodigal, Scott Quinnell, who battered his way to a score that lifted a nation.

Craig Chalmers dropped a goal on the stroke of half-time and Rowan Shepherd kicked a penalty to open up a six-point lead early in the second half, before Arwel Thomas made a break as dazzling as a set of presidential teeth. In Wales it is a sacred moment when a fly-half spreadeagles a defence and the Dragons roared accordingly. Neil Jenkins, every bit as comfortable at full-back as he has looked uncomfortable at fly-half in the red of Wales, weighed in with 19 points. Thomas himself – a mercurial figure all afternoon – and the venerable Ieuan Evans both crossed for tries as the final whistle sounded, almost drowned out by hymns and arias. The Welsh Renaissance was once more a talking-point. Scotland mourned their side's efforts, blaming the structure of the administration, the selectors, bad luck . . . it was an endless list. The only consolation was in the words of one Scot: 'At least they [the Welsh] will puke happily on our streets tonight.' And so the Five Nations, despite all the scaremongering of the autumn, was up and running. The night faded into obscurity as rival Celts ended up as closest friends, singing of how the infernal English were the real enemy.

That was the case in Edinburgh. It was slightly more confusing in Dublin, where one Saxon, by the name of Brian Ashton, had just seen Ireland lose to France. Their new coaching adviser would have to develop a slightly more amicable relationship with his Celtic cousins. He would also need a saintly capacity to work miracles if Ireland, so poor against Italy and Western Samoa, were to emerge with anything more tangible than traditional blood, guts and beatings. Ashton had been stunned by the immensity of the task that faced him as he joined the Irish squad for his first training session before the French challenge. He recalls with a grin, 'That first session was quite a culture shock. I assumed far too much and no coach should ever assume anything. I assumed that the Irish players had a command of the basic skills and a general knowledge of how rugby should be played. I found out pretty quickly that some players had no command of basic skills and very few had any idea of how the game should be played at any level, let alone international level.'

Yet for all his trepidation there was a genuine sense of excitement. It was such a different challenge from the one he had left behind in the West Country (refer to the chapter on Bath). He had known the Bath players for seven years and had worked with them on a daily basis. The only knowledge he had of the Irish squad came from those he had encountered in opposition to Bath. He admits, 'I went to an environment about which I knew nothing at all. That is exactly where I love to operate – in the non-comfort zone.' The seeds of doubt existed, but they were short-lived. 'While the players were involved in some drill, I turned around, looked at the skies above Limerick and thought, "What the hell am I doing here?" Then I realised that if I ever wanted a challenge in life, this was it, the very top. [Hindsight makes this a dubious statement.] It would tell me whether I was up to it.' Ashton was ready to bury the 'theorist' tag with which some journalists had labelled his coaching. 'Before the French game I had sat down, looked at what our boys were good at and said, "Right, that's all you will do on Saturday, nothing else," and so we disguised our weaknesses within the framework of a game.'

Ashton talked with regularity about both the good fortune that offered him an international post from thin air and the short-term nature of the four-match appointment. No gypsy teller was needed to reveal that Ashton desperately wanted a win for his team, but he also wanted it for the sake of his long-term appointment. 'I have an opportunity to perform at the highest level, but I need short-term work to help me get that win and secure a green future.' He emphasised the practical side to his coaching. 'I am not a romantic, I'm just interested in player development. I do have a rugby vision, but my prime objective is to win . . . I do not place style before results.'

The Irish players were forming a disorderly line to tell the media what a great guy their new guru was. That is no surprise; Ashton has always been a player's coach. There are coach's coaches and media coaches, just do not ask Ashton what he thinks of these people. As an exceedingly 'non-media' coach, Ashton had to come to terms with the avalanche of interest that surrounded his appointment. 'On the day that the news broke, I received five telephone calls from various Irish newspapers.' The little Lancastrian adopted a worldly indifference to the whole matter. 'It's certainly not the sort of profile that I was seeking, but it was inevitable. It does not bother me that much because I have been with Bath, who have made headlines week in, week out, for good and bad reasons. Life will carry on as normal, here at home.'

Ashton and his wife Monica lead a calm, contented life together. The same cannot be said for rugby union's equivalent to Richard Burton and Elizabeth Taylor's love/hate affair: the tempestuous coupling of Jack Rowell, the England coach, and the English media. Both have been guilty of silly excesses. But Rowell definitely approached this championship in a far lighter mode. It was just as well, because everyone else was gunning for him. One member of the England coaching panel confided that 'Nobody is on Jack's side, except Les Cusworth'. *The Mail on Sunday* had run an exclusive back-page headline predicting the end of Rowell's reign. This was nearly a month before their first game.

Dick Best had also delivered a savage broadside against Rowell, with which, most alarmingly, certain players agreed. In the week of the Scotland match his predecessor, Geoff Cooke, joined in the cat chorus of withering abuse. 'If Jack had shut up and not talked all this mumbo-jumbo about interactive and expansive rugby, it would not have created such a great weight of expectation . . . if you talk things up and don't deliver, it gives the critics more ammunition than they need have . . . I have also been in contact with members of the England squad and the message I am getting is that the players don't seem to know what is expected of them.'

Cooke ironically hit a nerve, but the prime reasons for the communication failures were of his making. If Rowell was guilty of seeming too loosely structured for some members of the squad, it was only because under Cooke they had never taken on the responsibility of making snap decisions on the pitch. Admittedly, Cooke and Carling carried England to a World Cup final, but their inflexibility cost them the ultimate rugby prize. If Rowell was guilty of one massive mistake, it was keeping too many of Cooke's men too long. Will Carling, an outstanding rugby player but a deeply limited thinker on the game, was the prime example. A fear of media savagery, more than any 'mumbo-jumbo', was his prime weakness. His conservative selection for the match against Scotland was an example of his concern not to lose and not to create controversy by dropping Carling (although this backfired, as we hacks rubbished the absence of Jeremy Guscott, sacrificed for Carling and the captaincy qualities of Phil de Glanville), rather than to win. He had a right to worry for his position. The knives were glinting in the dawn, from every press room to the corridors of power within Twickenham. Yes, Rowell had a right to be worried.

This concern revealed itself to astute eyes on the Thursday before the Calcutta Cup clash with Scotland. Drinking coffee after training, he talked with Bill McLaren. One member of the national media swears that 'He was spilling the stuff all over his shaking hands and he barely seemed to notice it – steam as well'. The arch evolutionist of English coaching was wound up and ready to spring like a cuckoo clock.

Rowell may have felt the pressure as match day arrived, but at least the team bus spared him the ordeal of the long walk through the West Car Park, sometimes known as Tory Party Headquarters. There are enough four-wheel drives to suggest that you are about to enter the Kruger National Park and not a rugby ground in the leafiest of south-west London's suburbs. Why are these cross-country vehicles perceived as a status symbol and an upper-middle-class badge? I do not know the answer any more than the gentleman whose car aerial was festooned with the red cross of St George with the words 'Oliver's Army' emblazoned across it knew who the bloody hell Elvis Costello was. Bugger Johannesburg. 'If you're out of luck or out of work, we can send you to the West Car Park.' That will make the scroungers jump off their backsides.

Tony Hallett, the secretary of the RFU, had promised more pre-match razzmatazz to pull the green wellies from the Bolly and into the ground in a bid to generate the atmosphere that had been so evidently lacking a fortnight earlier at Murrayfield. Would it be the cast of *Evita*, or maybe even Phil Collins? Fortunately it was neither, but the answer was almost as bad. Tony Hallett should have asked Peter Mandelson about focus groups; I am certain that the Minister without Portfolio would have warned him that not too many Twickenham ticket-holders were interested in the Essex Dogs Display Team. Terry Cooper, the Press Association's master of the morose, muttered that it sounded like one of the tabloid journalist's former girlfriends. It was the nearest the press box came to a laugh as we thrilled to the pooches jumping through rings of fire. Where were you Johnny Cash?

Predictably, the pre-match entertainment drifted from awful to appalling. The Royal Artillery Band played 'Rule Britannia' as a bunch of poor man's Portillos (remember him?) hollered along behind me in the West Stand. This was followed by 'There'll Always Be an England'. Not everyone singing the lusty tune was so certain, as the European debate rumbled on.

They were replaced by the world-famous Welwyn Garden City and Vauxhall Male Voice Choirs. Instead of 'Cwm Rhondda' and 'Bread of Heaven' we were treated to the delights of 'Jerusalem'. When I hear that sung with such gusto by blinkered patriots, I have an urge to tell these ignoramuses that William Blake's poem was actually anything but a eulogy to industrial England. Still, Willy Whistle and Timmy Try, two Twickenham characters as endearing as a dose of influenza, raised their arms, urging the rulers of the waves to join in . . . and they did. Finally

John Brown's Body mouldered in his grave. From that song it is a logical step to 'Swing Low' and, for me, the puke bag.

Luckily, England were mercifully average for 65 minutes, so the boos outdecibelled the oohs and 'Swing Low' resounded nowhere. In times of angst, the Twickenham anthem is silent. But, when Andy Gomarsall, Will Carling and Phil de Glanville crossed for three tries in five minutes, the cacophony drowned out the Scottish cries of 'déjà vu'. The final score of 41–13 reflected the weakness of Scotland more than the strength of England. The power and the pace of the home team had been a threat rather than a promise. The team were again too cautious in their start. The South Africans and New Zealanders attempt to wrap games up in the first half; England prefer to soften their opponents up. It helps when one team is full of Steve Reeves lookalikes, while the other is made up of boys auditioning for the part of the kids who get sand kicked in their face. But England were relieved with the margin. It was their record score in the championship. There would be little honest self-analysis. Of course, if the captain and coach were being honest in the post-match press conference, then buy me a pair of flares – because England were time-travelling backwards.

Jack Rowell, wearing a blooming red rose, was exuberant. 'We blew away the cobwebs', 'We emerged from psychological bondage' (a reference to Geoff Cooke's ill-timed attack), 'Scotland were heroic' . . . and so it rolled, with not a hint of his deeper thoughts. Phil de Glanville was also in a smiling mood. His England position remained a matter of contention, with Jeremy Guscott and Leicester's Will Greenwood bashing the door down.

You could sense the pressure. He was far more reticent in public. The free-smiling Phil was all caginess. He tried to sound a note of caution. 'We cannot get carried away with a big win. We'll take whatever is said with a pinch of salt.' The fact that most of the media were not particularly impressed with England is an indication that the immediate response to the win from the dressing-room had been one of excess elation.

Scotland's camp was some contrast. Rob Wainwright looked an empty shell. There was no sign of a light in his eyes. Even Gregor Townsend, the golden boy of British rugby, faced the fire. 'We needed to strike a balance between when to run and when to kick.' Townsend, back in his favoured position of fly-half, had tipped the scales all the way to the running side. But with an absence of power in the forwards and no pace in the backs, it was difficult to imagine even a wizard conjuring a Scottish win.

Meanwhile in Cardiff, the man called the Welsh wizard, Ieuan Evans, scored a brace of tries to add to his Murrayfield strike, but the Welsh Renaissance and Triple Crown flights of the imagination crumbled in the face of the Irish. The Emerald Isle proclaimed their own wizard, a man whose powers of conjuring had outstripped even those of Ieuan Evans on the day, the leprechaun from Lancashire, Brian Ashton. In a country where the devout believe that statues move, Ashton's efforts were already being described as miraculous.

In barely a fortnight, the man who described his first training session in Limerick as 'a culture shock', when discovering some of his players had few basic skills and little rugby knowledge, had steered his adopted country home to a famous win against the revived Welsh. Pundits claimed that this represented no shock on the strength of Ireland's record in Cardiff since 1983. Ashton is dismissive of such suggestions. 'I am more interested in what happens tomorrow than what happened in the past . . . it's what happens on the day that counts. I do not believe that historic facts have any relevance at all.'

He must have been more concerned with recent history, however. The night before the match, the Irish team found their sleep interrupted in the early hours of the morning because of a fire alarm that forced the hotel to be evacuated. As the players pulled on some clothes, the Irish committee meandered from their private party, disgruntled with the interruption to their festivities as they smoked their huge and smoke-bellowing cigars. Ashton showed admirable sang-froid by not blurting out in frustration, 'It could only happen to the Irish.' If that was a night of interrupted sleep, the next night was to be one of hardly any sleep. 'It was a good night,' said Ashton with understatement. Ireland had beaten Wales. Ashton had his first coveted win at international level and probably a sainthood to combine with the inevitable longer-term appointment.

It was with relief that he recollected the emotions of those dying minutes as Wales strived for victory, having trailed badly at half-time. 'I had a sense of *déjà vu* with the French game. We had been leading comfortably with 60 minutes to go and suddenly Wales were creeping up on us. If we had played another five minutes we would have lost, no doubt about it. It was purely relief, not excitement. That came later on at the press conference when we realised what we had done: won against the odds away from home and conceded a seven-point start in less than 30 seconds.'

Ireland won the game off the pitch every bit as much as it was won over 80 minutes on it. Before France, Ashton had taken a quiet back seat. He had had little option, probably struggling to fit faces to names. But for this match, the shrewd coach was far more active. It transformed the individuals. 'What was different between the France and the Wales games was that in the latter the players were making positive contributions themselves. That is imperative because a coach should be almost impotent on a Saturday afternoon for 80-odd minutes. I had to gear players to realise that the ball-carrier has the power to be in charge of the game.' Apart from advocating more responsibility from every one of his 15 players, Ashton also used the experience gained from years alongside the master of the psychological game, Jack Rowell. As a coaching adviser it would have been surprising for him to gain such intimate access to players, but after just two games he was admitting, 'My role as coaching adviser is a complete cover [and not a very good one, either]. I am coach. As coach I wanted to change our focus, find Welsh weaknesses, but not attack them if they did not coincide with our strengths; that would be pointless. The physical intensity tones down by Wednesday and then comes the mental battle. I targeted individuals like Niall Hogan. I told him forcefully, "You must be a better player than Rob Howley between 3.00 and 4.30 on Saturday afternoon, and you must believe it." Exactly the same with Eric Miller and Scott Quinnell. We had done the technical and tactical stuff; in the last days it is a matter of psychological strength.' Ashton, tactically, technically and psychologically, had proved himself. (Before your mind races to the débâcles that were to follow, think about Ireland's games before Christmas – progress is all relative.)

The modest Ashton has never been too keen on turning wine into water but, freed from the mental shackles of Bath, he was loving his shot at the big time. The news of Ireland's tremendous result gave every feature-writer his dream for a fortnight later. England travelled to Ireland as Jack Rowell and Brian Ashton prepared to face up to one another. The days of their Bath partnership were a thing of nostalgia.

But there was an intriguing sub-plot, straight from the bard. The big man, the little man and the moment of reckoning. Every newspaper carried the sub-plot until the 'sub' seemed to sink from sight. It was fortunate indeed that February is my month of near-monastic abstinence in the preparation for the excessive hedonism that is Cheltenham's three-day festival of National Hunt Racing. Otherwise, should I have supped a pint for every coupling of the names Jack Charlton and Brian Ashton, I would most surely have been incapable of continuing this tome.

It is an obvious enough analogy. The Englishman who lifted Irish spirits on the soccer field and an Irishman who restored the 'craic' for the Irish, through which the light of hope flooded in at Cardiff as darkness descended on Welsh dreams. Easy assumption, but totally incorrect. The sporting philosophies of Charlton and Ashton are about as far apart as the political philosophies of Tony Blair and Tony Benn.

There was one former Bath coach who did fit the bill, but he was the England coach, Jack Rowell. He is sharp-tongued and gangling like Charlton, and both men are Geordies and, more tellingly, hard-nosed pragmatists. It was Rowell's pragmatic cry of 'Evolution, not revolution' that spurred Bath to unprecedented success. Ashton expected Rowell to be as focused as ever as he prepared his green men for England. 'I have never met anyone with a greater desire to win every day. At Bath, each and every game was a little compartment; the opposition had to be defeated – end of story. We would never look further than the next 80 minutes.'

Ashton's reputation was almost diametrically opposed. Unlike Rowell, he would allow his critics a hearing. 'I have had some criticism, most of it justified, for not possessing the absolute crucial desire to win at all costs, week in, week out.' That is what the Bath old guard were bemoaning as they headed for a barren season. Rowell would happily stoop to conquer, as the volte-face recall of Dean Richards for the game against Scotland the previous season amply demonstrated, but Ashton, not deterred by a lack of inches, was the one who peered beyond the horizon.

These visions occasionally wandered too far from Rowell's less ethereal next 80 minutes. That was partly the reason for the brittle brilliance of Bath in the 1996–97 season – the players must also share the blame. It was never thus with Rowell. In tandem, the pragmatist and the revolutionary were devastating. Alone, there was the question of whether the pragmatist lacked courage and the visionary common sense. The early Irish experiences hinted at an almost Pauline conversion in Ashton. 'At the moment all I am thinking about is winning the next game. When and if I am in a more secure position, I'll think a bit more about the future.'

Rowell would nod a sage, pragmatic head in approval at such sentiments from his old friend, but he would have been less pleased with Ashton's appraisal that Rowell was a much better man-manager than technical coach. Not that Big Jack was turning the lessons of charm school in Ashton's direction. After the Scotland game he was asked

38

about the Ashton threat. His reply? 'Ireland can beat anyone on their day.' He was not heading for Ireland in order to praise this little Celtic Caesar.

Ashton was a wise enough campaigner to know that, ironically, his romance with the Irish had been dented by the success in Cardiff. Expectation is the death knell of sporting romance. And Rowell, so irritable with the media, would remind Ashton that honeymoons are always too brief.

Watching England's match against Scotland on video, Ashton made cautiously optimistic noises. If his team could hold the power of the English front five, and if they could execute a cute tactical game plan that revolved around Eric Elwood kicking the ball into areas where Tony Underwood, Tim Stimpson and Jon Sleightholme were uncomfortable and Niall Hogan snapping at the umbilical cord of the team, the link between eight and nine, Rodber and Gomarsall . . . well, Ireland might just have an outside chance. This proved to be significantly larger than Rudyard Kipling's much misinterpreted 'If'.

The newspapers were full of stories of great Irish wins in recent history. In the previous ten matches at Lansdowne Road, the record was 5–5. That was a considerably better record than any of the more endowed northern nations could boast. Newspapers always write about the elemental fury of a match that makes you think of a game at Lansdowne Road as a similar experience to a descent into hell.

Having played and lost twice there, it is certainly not my happiest of hunting-grounds, but the intimidation of a Cardiff or an Edinburgh is lacking. Paradoxically, this hinders, rather than helps, the English team. When the Welsh crowd roars, or 'Flower of Scotland' sets the adrenalin into overdrive, it is easy to gird the loin, as we lovers of the great sporting cliché would say. As a captain, Will Carling thrived upon this intensity of feeling and used the Celtic anger as a constructive force in motivating the English team. The men in white do not find it as easy to evoke natural rivalry due to that sense of superiority (you remember the Empire, in the days when British meant English – although such misconceptions can still be found today on the green pastures of Surrey golf courses). But Ireland's rugby team and its supporters have a different relationship. During the terrible troubles of the 1970s, it was England who continued to send teams to face an Ireland united only on the field of rugby. The hospitable Irish never forgot, and much as they like to put one over the English, it is not a tribal war. As a result, it is Dublin, of all the away matches, that an English international most enjoys. This does not always equate with the mental preparation needed to win Test-match rugby. This explains why the unquestionable superiority of English teams on paper has not always translated to the only place in which it matters: the field of play.

The romantics dreamed of Rowell and his unsmiling giants being upstaged by the leprechaun from Lancashire, already as popular in Ireland as a pint of Guinness. But romance in rugby is fast becoming a nostalgic memory from bygone days when rugby legends stumbled to their beds at five in the morning before playing the match of their lives. The professional world of rugby union is vastly different – and just maybe diminished.

As if to emphasise the harsh new order of the sport, I awoke to a match day unique in my experiences of Ireland. In the old amateur order, it *always* rained in Dublin on the day of the Test. But not this time. The sky was softly blue as the paper trails of the first planes leaving the venerable gateway to Guinness, Dublin Airport, headed westwards, bound for America. The sun shimmered, creating an aura of tranquillity on Lambay Island, just half a mile from where I mused on the rare experience of sobriety on an Irish morning. This was more a day to read W.B. Yeats than to fight on a rugby field. I found it impossible to suppress a smile and mutter to myself, 'Work, my ass.' This was a good day to earn a living from rugby union.

Even the pitch at Lansdowne Road had a different look and feel to it. It was once the most lush surface on the international circuit, but the advent of the Republic of Ireland using the ground for soccer internationals had transformed the surface; it was cropped almost as closely as a Buddhist's head. It was actually being watered to create softer conditions underfoot. The rainbow that danced through the spray rounded off a weirdly placid atmosphere, which even the presence of Sky Television's private security man failed to diminish. Ulster and the IRA seemed a universe away from cheery Lansdowne Road, with the Dart train that stops beneath the stand and the fairy-tale cottage which doubles as a post-match hostelry.

Only five of the English team had experienced the beguiling 'craic' of this intimate and atmospheric stadium, but on this day of glorious weather there was no breeze to fan an Irish fire. The omens were good for England. At 11 a.m. the Irish team strolled around the pitch, with Brian Ashton joking about the weather. It was an appropriate lack of tradition, as were the comments of Jim Staples, Ireland's captain and full-back. He smiled as he spoke of those distant days when Ireland called on primal forces, punted the ball in the general direction of their maker and chased like hounds from hell. He was confident that this Irish team were capable of much more constructive rugby. I headed for a civilised media lunch in Jury's Hotel – one of the traditional staging posts for the festivities – with one thought in my mind: a confident Irish team are normally a danger to . . . Ireland.

Passing the Berkeley Court Hotel, I collided with the entire contents of the Rugby Football Union committee bus. It was a throwback to ancient times as the blue blazers and grey trousers waddled towards the inviting world of gin and tonics. And the ladies? All seemed to be having a great time. After the traumas of the season for the guardians of our sport's soul, it was wonderful to see normal alickadoo service restored.

In Jury's the media lunch was a riot of salmon and finest fillet of beef (Southern Irish and BSE-free, I was assured) and a little glass of the red stuff. I left the plebeian element, peering in at rugby's good and grandiose, to the dark stuff. The hotel had everything needed for a great party: live bands, slopping plastic pints, carpets that stick to your shoes and a spirit of total hedonism. If there had been an extra 15,000 bar staff and I had not been working, this would have been as close to heaven as this atheist will ever find himself.

Back in the ground, not-so-old acquaintances were being renewed. One hour from kick-off and the new Irish hero, Brian Ashton, was shaking hands with England replacements Jeremy Guscott and Mike Catt: the man surplus to Bath's requirements and the men England didn't need. It was comforting to feel some atmosphere in advance of the kick-off. Unlike Murrayfield, Twickenham or the National Stadium, Lansdowne Road retains the warmth and humour generated by terracing at either end of the ground. These are the stands where people piss on you from behind. It may be a particularly unpleasant trait, but if it keeps the corporate guests and yahoos away, I'm all for unzipping the flies.

It is with deep regret that I admit Ireland are only marginally better than their RFU counterparts in the field of pre-match entertainment. A band from the Garda emphasised just how unfunky the Irish police can be. Forget U2, these guys were in a time warp. The Beatles had just arrived, hot from The Cavern. How we all enjoyed the band's version of 'Ob La Di Ob La Da', followed by two clearly subversive and reactionary tunes from the dying embers of the amateur administrators: 'Money Can't Buy Me Love' and 'Yesterday'. Sweet memories.

As the band played on, it was interesting to note the combinations of

English players out practising on the pitch. Catt and Guscott stroked the ball across the pitch, while 15 metres upfield Paul Grayson and Tim Stimpson did likewise. The bench and the players accept a benign form of apartheid on match days. Although substitutions were now legitimate tactical weapons, the conflict remained essentially one between 30 men. As if to remind us that sport's quintessential appeal is the escape from more pressing problems, as Mary Robinson, Ireland's President, met the two teams, an aeroplane flew over the ground trailing the message 'Stop the ceasefire now'.

There was little sympathy with that message in Lansdowne Road. 'God Save the Queen' was heard for the first time at Lansdowne Road in 60 years. Republican sentiment was not strong in this bastion of the middle class. Once again the feeling of friendship engulfed this cosy ground. Until the kick-off. Brian Ashton, clearly irritated by the 'Mr Nice Guy' image, had his men wound up; they tore into England with serious venom. There was a splendid, if belated, spirit of confrontation. Ireland hammered at England, but after 11 minutes it was Eric Miller, the great white hope from Leicester, who was stretchered from the field. In rugby parlance, we call it the result of a 'bit of a bang'; in medical terms, he was knocked out. Accidents will happen, as Elvis Costello sang.

There were not to be too many more accidental occurrences that afternoon. Irish fire was extinguished by a mighty fire-fighting force called the English front five. Jason Leonard was, as ever, a rock, while Mark Regan and Graham Rowntree enjoyed their best games to date for England. Behind them the combination of Martin Johnson and Simon Shaw were a pair of powerhouses. This must have been immensely satisfying to Shaw. By the age of 22 he had endured more injuries than most players suffer in a career. His knee ligaments snapped months before the World Cup, a tournament for which he was adjudged a certainty to make the England party. He overcame that injury only to suffer the most devastating ankle break. The sight of his ankle twisted through 180 degrees brought a mixture of tears and nausea to that sensitive soul, Mark Regan. That was one hell of a break. But again Shaw forced himself back from despair. The reward was that cherished England cap and days like these.

He was not the only Englishman to enjoy himself. Lawrence Dallaglio and Richard Hill enjoyed 80 minutes of creativity and destructiveness in equal measures. Paul Grayson produced another accomplished performance and Jon Sleightholme added a brace of tries to the one he had scored the previous season against the men in green. Irish eyes do not smile when the Yorkshireman receives the ball. Fellow tyke and fellow winger Tony Underwood also had reason to celebrate; his vibrant two-try performance offered release from the ghost of Jonah Lomu. I hope the money from the pizza advertisement was enough to buy a few tons of mozzarella.

England produced another rousing finale. The match was won by half-time as Ireland succumbed to superior power, but England turned on the style in the last seven minutes, scoring 22 points without reply. This coincided with a brief debut for Austin Healey and the return from the bench of Jeremy Guscott. All of Lansdowne Road rose to acclaim a man whose legend grew with every non-selection for the starting line-up. The match was lost for the home supporters so they allowed themselves to bask in seven glorious minutes of rugby. Guscott was a jewel in what was, eventually, a well-polished, if not regal, performance. The final score was Ireland 6, England 46. The leprechaun found no gold at the end of the rainbow, just a record tanking. Ashton's honeymoon was over, but for Jack Rowell the days of mumbo-jumbo were replaced, as King Midas bestrode the fortunes of his England.

The Irish press conference had the same shell-shocked air as that of Scotland's after the Welsh and English débâcles. Ashton answered questions with as straight a bat as possible, but the shock of defeat filled the air. Even in defeat there were a few barbed comments for the victorious opponents: 'I'm glad they don't start as they finish.' It was a reference to England's excessively cautious approach to the first hour of a match. In their defence, Lansdowne Road is not the place to open the game up and offer opportunities for the home team to make crunching tackles and juice the adrenalin. On this occasion England were a shade cautious, as opposed to their semi-craven respect for the Lilliputian Scots. Ashton reiterated that 'There is no quick fix; it will take two or three years'. The euphoria of Cardiff was entirely dissipated.

Rowell, in contrast, was back to the jocular jester of his glory days at Bath. In his third year at the helm, England were scoring enough points to silence their multitude of critics. In the company of a relieved Phil de Glanville (defeat would almost certainly have cost him both his place and the captaincy), he beamed his way through the minefields of the media. Rowell called it 'very uplifting for England', said that Guscott was 'a prince of centres' (why did we not ask him if that made de Glanville and Carling a pair of kings?) and claimed that 'the front five were giants' – and so the eulogies rolled from the tongue. He mentioned the word 'aspire' on five separate occasions. This was the Rowellism of the moment. As Paul Hayward, surely the best-dressed member of the media, raffishly suggested, 'At least if England keep playing well, he won't be able to keep talking about aspire.'

The press conference ended on a note of levity. Rowell laughed about the lack of pace in the centre; de Glanville accepted it as jest, before answering a question from Terry Cooper – the cynical old bird from the Press Association. He wanted to know the structure of the team to face France. De Glanville took his chance to strike back. 'We'll pick two wings, two props . . .' One for the playing side. In the aftermath of the press conference it was clear just how much pressure de Glanville had been under. As he ghosted his column for *The Observer*, he sighted me heading towards the exit from the ground and the entrance to oblivion. The threat to punch me in order to give me something to write about was not a serious one, but the implications of a mini rant in public were. He was feeling the pressure. I was initially dismissive of him; after all, I had never behaved in such a manner with a critical member of the press. But I had not been criticised by someone with whom I shared the camaraderie of the changing-room. De Glanville might have been England's captain of rugby, but my overwhelming emotions were of sympathy. Even Dr Faustus would think twice before accepting the invitation.

Elsewhere, France beat Wales 27–22 in Cardiff. Kevin Bowring was back in the loathed land of honourable defeat, while France, like England before Dublin, attracted more brickbats than praise in victory. Once again the title was to be decided between the big two, but as darkness set in Dublin and the dark stuff drained into my stomach, that match could have been a millennium, rather than a fortnight, away. It was time to share a pint with the spirits of Brendan Behan and Flann O'Brien.

The serious stuff replaced the dark stuff as the big guns of the northern hemisphere, England and France, turned their guns on each other. The old Napoleonic War rift was duly trotted out, but as the days leading up to the battle passed, the French state appeared parlous to say the least. Their injury list suggested that these boys were veterans of the 1812 Russian campaign rather than rugby players. Missing from the team were some of the grandest names north of the equator: Saint André and Ntmack, two of the finest French wingers of recent times, Castaignède and Dourthe, the poet and the steamer partnership at centre, Olivier Roumat, their most reliable source of lineout possession, and, finally, Philippe Benetton, an experienced open-side flanker. When the England camp talked of their frustrations caused by a niggling injury list which had a detrimental effect on training, few hearts, English or otherwise, went out to them.

The bookmakers took note of France's erratic winning start and the casualty list and installed England as favourites by as much as a 12-point margin. I thought this dubious. England had racked up some Stephen Hendry break scores against Ireland and Scotland, but it would take the generosity of Santa Claus to describe either team as anything other than woeful. England had essentially used their overwhelming power to batter them into submission before unleashing two 20-minute spells of 'interactive' rugby, to borrow a favoured word from Jack Rowell.

Generally the performances lacked the ambition needed to lift England towards the stratosphere in which they would need to be come 1999 and the arrival of the southern hemisphere superpowers in Cardiff for the World Cup. Question marks surrounded the team like the Riddler's costume and yet the style of their coruscating final 20 minutes in the first two games indicated that the players were starting to understand Rowell's message of collective responsibility and dynamism. Indeed, Geoff Cooke's mumbo-jumbo comments were looking decidedly hasty – but France, even with their injury crisis, would be the real test. England were against a team who could stand face to face with them and slug it out. England were unlikely to tame and then tatter France. This was a match that would need more than the bludgeon to secure an easy victory.

The match day dawned. It was more like Paris in the spring than south-west London – and that is one of the most tedious clichés in the game, but what the hell; it was a good day to be alive. Even the Barbours in the West Car Park were not about to spoil the fun. At midday the roads to Twickenham were packed. Traffic moved at about the same speed as Jason Leonard over 200 metres. The place was buzzing. Outside the Sun Inn, Richmond (one of the area's great rugby pubs in which Jason Leonard can occasionally be spotted recuperating from those 200-metre runs), the gathering group of revellers swayed as if it was midnight, not midday. The sun dappled through the pints of bitter transporting all nostalgic English alcoholics back to a world where John Major wanted to be. Twickenham and its environs may not be my favourite place on earth, but at least it is safe on a match day. The only danger to passers-by would be low-flying vomit.

Inside the ground the atmosphere was less *laissez-faire*. The bureaucrats were through the gates and one of the finest traditions in the Five Nations calendar was to be the victim. When France play at Twickenham, cockerels are always released on to the pitch. It is as traditional as giant daffodils being carried to the Arms Park; but this year was different. The Cockerel Protection Squad were on the case of those mischievous Frenchmen. They had been warned. Men wearing berets and smelling of Pernod were to be bodily searched before entering 'Twickers'. Any cockerels found on their personages would be taken to a quarantine unit that had been specifically set up for the weekend at Twickenham. How we traditionalists waited and prayed for our little friends to appear, but, alas, the unit knew their business. So, deprived of our colourful interlopers, we settled down to the Welwyn Garden City and Vauxhall Male Voice Choirs.

Twickenham made its move into the modern world of rugby with the arrival of a group called China Black (no, nor have I). They had been well briefed on the vagaries of your average rugby fan. After delighting us with a song that was apparently unknown to everyone bar Andy Gomarsall, they cranked the level of entertainment to fever pitch. The lead singer fixed his sights at row upon row of whiskers and tartan skirts beloved of cosy Home Counties ladies in the West Stand and let rip: 'Oggi, Oggi, Oggi . . .' Fuck me, give me John Brown and his mouldering body any day.

Matters worsened. The tribal stupidity of 'Oggying' over, he handed out our orders: 'I want you all to sing along to this one.' I knew what was coming: 'Swing low, sweet chariot.' The crowd were reticent, so he encouraged them: 'Twickenham, can I hear you?' This request was too much. The song drifted into the changing-room of the French with the game only minutes away. They must have thought, 'What a bunch of prats.'

The singing certainly failed to lift the French for an early assault on England's line. Rowell's men did exactly what they had threatened to do, but had never achieved on the pitch: they attacked, at pace, from the start. It is just as well for Phil de Glanville that the public have short memories. Those members of the media who had previously had the temerity to suggest that Brian Ashton had been right, that England could prove an irresistible force if they stretched defences from the kick-off, had been told that international rugby was not that simple, even though New Zealand and South Africa played in a manner that suggested otherwise. It was another sign of the intrinsic defensiveness of the English character. But Rowell's men were out of their shells on this afternoon. Tim Stimpson counter-attacked from deep in the opening minutes. That set the tempo of the game. On 40 minutes, Dallaglio finally burst through the beleaguered French defence and the retreat from Twickenham seemed to have commenced. Two early penalties from the boot of Paul Grayson carried England to a 20–6 lead on the hour mark . . . and England's best 20 minutes were to come. Abdel Benazzi left the field injured. His replacement was the flaxen-haired Marc de Rougement. 'Swing Low' drifted to the rafters.

It proved premature. France made a substitution in the second row, Christophe Lamaison planted a sublime chip into the hungry arms of Laurent Laflammand and suddenly the pendulum swung violently towards the visitors. England, imperious for an hour, collapsed. Lamaison himself scored, converted, then added a penalty, and south-west London became an extension of the Bois de Boulogne. France had conjured a 23–20 victory from nowhere, and this had been a truly outstanding sporting occasion.

The fanatical French followers forgot about their missing cockerels and forged on to the sacred turf to embrace their heroes, *les sacrés bleus*. No amount of security could stop this invasion. Red, white and blue were the new colours of Twickenham as La Marseillaise bled English hearts white. Gallic passion overflowed like a fine bottle of St Émilion. It had been some afternoon.

Olivier Merle, the French child psychologist represented as an ogre by the British press, cried his huge heart out as he entered the players' tunnel, almost reluctant to leave the scene of triumph. With the departure of Abdel Benazzi, the giant had become a hero. Every restart was claimed, every lineout remotely near him was taken, every charge was flat out, every tackle thunderous. Merle the magnificent. Alongside him, Jean Luc Sadourney and Christophe Lamaison were as effective, if not as symbolic. France were on course for their first Grand Slam in a decade. For once it would not be Jack Rowell and Phil de Glanville who would commence the press conference.

The French press contingent applauded with an understandable display of chauvinism when their management walked into the hollow room which hosts the post-match interrogations. Joe Maso, the French manager, sat smiling; with tight curly hair and round glasses, that most revered of romantic centres looked every inch the mad professor. Alongside him sat the French assistant coach, another man from the world of Gallic dreamers: Pierre Villepreux, the king of Toulouse but until this moment never of the French federation. He wore a tattered hat from a Jacques Tati comedy. He also smiled dreamily. Jean Claude Skrela appeared eccentric for looking uneccentric, while the injured mountain from Morocco, Abdel Benazzi, sat dutifully, ready to answer questions before hobbling to hospital for some X-rays to the ribs. You had the feeling he could live with the pain.

It was Benazzi who kicked off proceedings. 'Did you honestly believe that you could win this game?' was the question. I had seen the French team in an ultra-relaxed mode at training on the Friday and knew he was telling the truth when he said, 'We believed all week we could do it. We came here to win.' But the aim was never to win at all costs, as that great rugby romantic Pierre Villepreux emphasised: 'Today we played very well, but the whole team were collective and we maintained the style we wanted. Even down 20–6 we kept playing and we won only because we continued to run the ball.' Style and flair are the ingredients Villepreux uses to create beautiful and passionate rugby. 'The rugby was played by both teams. It promotes the game. The public were glad . . . it is an emotional game . . . and if we continue to play this rugby we can get to the southern hemisphere standards. England too played rugby I liked and could have won.'

He was not kidding. England had gained more in defeat than in countless one-sided Celtic batterings of the last decade. That does not prevent the hurt that comes with defeat, however, which the boisterous singing from the direction of the French changing-room cannot have dulled.

The media love a guru and Villepreux loves to play the role. We were in the palm of his hand when Michael Humphreys, England's press officer, interrupted with what I considered to be exemplary rudeness, asking, 'Is that it, gentlemen?' The message from the heart of the establishment was clear: England are ready and why do you want to hear from the French? Thankfully the press corps carries a substantial number of Europhiles who rate such xenophobic manners less highly than Twickenham's Tory toffs. The court still belonged to Villepreux.

His final comments were the ones that anybody with enough vision to look beyond the comfortable claustrophobia of the Five Nations had been waiting years to hear: 'If you want to play the style of game to take on the southern hemisphere, you must play with ambition – and you need two to tango. England did it.' Jack Rowell's team may have lost the match, but it was mighty consolation to escape the reputation of being a bunch of morris dancers and to be reborn not only with a red rose on the chest, but with one between the teeth.

The French walked out standing tall, to be replaced by the stooping frame of a man who hates defeat. Jack Rowell looked shorter than Joe Maso. He admitted that 'it was a wonderful victory for France' but could not hide his bitterness at watching a 14-point lead disappear. 'At 20–6 you should be able to close the game down.' He was right. When the pressure had increased, men like Gomarsall and Grayson had failed to raise their game.

Against physically weak teams, strength of body can prove so over-powering that the mental edge becomes irrelevant. It is the story of Geoff Cooke's and, occasionally, Jack Rowell's England. That was the question mark that still surrounded this team, despite their point-scoring frenzies against Scotland and Ireland. Phil de Glanville expounded upon the same theme. 'Mentally we switched off a little bit. For 50 minutes we were in their face, but at 20–6, instead of going for the kill, we eased back.' The real answer is beyond this surface explanation. England had finally decided that the time had come to step way beyond the comfort zone of grinding attrition with a flourish to end. They were, as Villepreux identified, playing rugby with one eye on the future. If they had played the game in the manner of the Ireland performance they might well have won the match, but the evolution towards the World Cup would have decelerated. Some Englishmen who think the world ends at Dover might prefer England to have done just that, but for those who cherish greater aspirations for their national team, this had been a step forward. Until this day there had been a strong feeling that, in the words of Bob Dylan, 'the only thing he knew how to do was to keep on keeping on'. In defeat, the purpose of the plan had become clear. Rowell's mumbo-jumbo was the right course for England. Ironically, a story had broken this very day about the future of Jack Rowell. The man who had received a vote of confidence from Tony Hallett before the Five Nations was explaining that this game might just be his last in charge at Twickenham.

The reasons were clear-cut enough. 'The game is moving forward to outright professionalism and I have other things in my life. It's about finding a balance and the situation has been made more complex by becoming outright professional.' That came from the man who wanted his players together for six days before an international. In reality, Rowell was playing a manipulative game à la Will Carling. Say you may quit so if you are axed you can save face. Play the game on your terms. Those were the rules according to Jack Rowell. As he explained that the whole matter had been dynamited out of all perspective, de Glanville sat slumped, sipping Lucozade in the chair where Skrela had earlier been bolting beer. Winners and losers.

On that subject Brian Ashton was a man of mixed emotions. That week Ireland had offered him a contract to take them through to the World Cup in the year 2003. Days later a weak Ireland team were thrashed 38–10 by a weak Scotland outfit. The contract offered him the security he wanted for his family, but the wonder of Cardiff must have felt a long way away that night in Edinburgh. I didn't know whether to congratulate or commiserate with him on the appointment. His championship had petered out with two dismal days, but for the other coaches there was an immense amount at stake as the tournament steamed towards its tumultuous conclusion.

The venues guaranteed that, in the words of Pierre Villepreux, rugby would be an emotional game. Neither the Parc des Princes nor the holiest of holy rugby stadiums, the Cardiff Arms Park, would ever host another Five Nations international, as giant and probably soulless monoliths arose from their ashes to replace these temples of times past. In Paris, France were on the verge of a first Grand Slam in a decade. Villepreux and Skrela were on the verge of canonisation. What a way to bid adieu to the Parc. Meanwhile in Cardiff, Kevin Bowring's Triple Crown dreams were shattered and his team stood on the brink of another season with just one win. Before the tournament started he had publicly stated that results *and* performance would matter this season. A harsh jury awaited another failure. Jack Rowell was also under tremendous pressure. A Triple Crown achieved in style would constitute a highly satisfactory campaign, for all the agonies of the French defeat. But defeat would probably cost him the job he was not certain he wanted. The tightrope on which international rugby coaches walk is becoming more taut with every day of professionalism.

That high-octane pressure may represent the new face of rugby in its tough commercial mode, but for lovers of tradition, all roads headed straight into the centre of Cardiff and the last ever battle at the Arms Park between Wales and their old oppressors England. The ground has held a quarter of a century of nightmares for England, thanks to Welsh dreams like Gareth Edwards, Phil Bennett, Gerald Davies and Barry John. But England had laid this ghost under Geoff Cooke and travelled to Wales as hot favourites to end the party early and joylessly from the Welsh perspective.

Twinges of sentiment buckled my body as I boarded the 10.26 train from Bristol Parkway. It should have been called the Red Train. That colour enveloped the insides. There was more hope of England being acclaimed Wales's favourite visitors than of reaching the hallowed carriages and a seat, which were only three times overcrowded. The only option was to pretend that the bowels were not so good and lock yourself in the toilet for 20 minutes. You could have a seat too. Alas, my natural aversion to British Rail toilets left me holding my breath and the exit door tightly as men wearing daffodils, yet sounding like Londoners, talked up hopes of a Welsh victory. These must be the Englishmen who share an aversion to the West Car Park and invest their rugby hopes in Celtic upsets. It had been a bad season for these dreamers thus far, but hope springs eternal.

I flew from the train the moment it stopped in Cardiff like a champagne cork from a shaken bottle. The blessed fresh air of Cardiff on a match day. Well, maybe not fresh air, but air smelling of stale beer, burgers and overflowing toilets. Say what you like about romance, but Catherine Cookson would feel pretty queasy walking the littered streets of the Welsh capital on the morning of an England match.

While the Welsh race are rightly famous for their literary sensitivity, I was still stunned to see the prominence being given to some obscure Ernest Hemingway festival being held this day. Every street light and bus stop was covered with a billboard stating 'A Farewell to Arms'. *The Western Mail* even issued a special commemorative spread.

Grown men were weeping, muttering about commerce, money and the loss of soul. Tender thoughts from big, fat, hairy men. None of them were heading to the literary festival, not unless it was being held in the Angel Hotel or The Coach and Horses public house. And why so many bouncers to keep out a bunch of book readers? I could not work out this little conundrum, so I hurried to the Arms Park to prepare for my commentary work on behalf of dear Uncle Rupert. As I was educated in Wales (that is not a contradiction in terms!), my heart secretly yearned for the fairy-tale ending to this wonderful old brute of a ground – until the lady in the press room charged me 60 pence for a coffee. At Twickenham all food and all beverages are courtesy of the Rugby Football Union. Scratch every word I have said about my dislike of Twickenham.

What is disappointing about Twickenham and Murrayfield is the lack of terracing. By the time of the match, Cardiff Arms Park was only left with the East Terrace, but it was from here that the heart and soul of the ground derived. That old terrace, where the plastic leeks and daffodils are higher than any others in the world, was the pulse of the stadium.

To secure a vantage point spectators arrive early, and, knowing about the quality of rugby union's pre-match entertainment, there is little to do but drink . . . and when Welshmen drink, they sing. They were in fine heart because the electronic scoreboard told them that English hopes of a championship were fading fast. The match in Paris had kicked off 45 minutes in advance of this one. Fifteen minutes before our kick-off the score read France 16, Scotland 6. Wales themselves had stunned France and gifted England the championship the previous year; they were in no mood for Scotland to do the same.

Every England player who deemed to stretch his muscles within 20 metres of the terrace was roundly barracked. Fitting for the Farewell to Arms. The military band, every bit as modern as their Twickenham counterparts, tried to lift the tone of proceedings with the rousing songs that any person who knows about rugby will know have been sung a thousand times before. The last 'Bread of Heaven' which greeted England's entry on to the pitch was a real tear-jerker for thousands. 'Calon Lan', 'We'll Keep a Welcome in the Hillsides' and others were all sung passionately, but the real encore was 'Delilah'. Good old Tom Jones. It was just slightly depressing that the passion with which the crowd asked Delilah 'Why?' in the first verse was not matched by that in the second. Now that sort of ignorance really does constitute a lack of education in Wales.

The parachutists tumbled from the sky with the match ball. Huge roars for the lucky man who fluttered the Welsh dragon in the wind; an enormous jeer for the unlucky aerial St George. Smoke wafted across the park from where the marker flares had been planted. This was some atmosphere.

Out ran England. Phil de Glanville would later admit that the sheer emotional intensity raised the spirits of the team. Far from being intimidated, England were inspired. A very Saxon sense of superiority was in the air. Then came that familiar roar. Neil Jenkins ran on to the pitch, winning his 50th cap. (It would prove to be an unlucky 50 as he would later break his arm.)

The television cameras dwelt on one face, that of Jonathan Davies. An injury crisis which had seen the Welsh team decimated by a third had allowed the great prodigal one last shot at glory against the oldest of all Welsh enemies. The script had been written in Welsh. He was to be the fag end of this century's Owain Glyndwr.

As the Welsh national anthem reached a rapturous conclusion, Jonathan Humphreys, the Welsh captain, raised one clenched fist beyond the stand to some rugby Valhalla. It was a sign of unity with the great ghosts of Welsh rugby that so wanted the romance to return one last time.

It was a pity for Humphreys that ghosts are probably a combination of mental fabrication and poetic licence. His team needed some other-worldly assistance. Shorn of such talent as Scott Gibbs and Ieuan Evans (how it must have hurt the latter to miss this finale), the odds were on the side of a team who may have lost to France but who appeared to be growing comfortable in playing Rowell's way. The one giant doubt concerned any sign of fragile psyches in the wake of that last 20 minutes against the French. And Mike Catt was under enor-mous pressure, after being called from the bench to replace the injured Paul Grayson. The last time he had started an international at fly-half the home crowd had jeered him from the field. Seeing his head in his hands, you feared for his future on a rugby field. Not only was he back at number ten, but he was chosen to face the greatest flak of all: he would kick the goals. Worse still, Jack Rowell had panicked and called Rob Andrew from the obscurity of retirement in the North-east as 'back-up' in case Catt cracked. Some endorsement of Catt and some snub for Alex King, the young Wasps fly-half. Jack loves to be enigmatic, but this act of regression did, and still does, appear too perverse for words.

Yet after four minutes, the eyes of the crowd were straining towards the England bench and the figure of Rob Andrew. Catt had missed a comfortable kick with a lot to spare. At that moment Catt's England career was on the precipice. If he collapsed, as he had under the lesser pressure of Argentina, the talented Bath player was finished. That is a heavy burden to carry, but Catt, to his eternal credit, rose to the challenge to such an extent that, come his substitution five minutes from the end (another ridiculous decision by Rowell), he appeared taller than Simon Shaw. He kicked with variety, precision and intelligence, but most importantly he galvanised the midfield. Taking the ball daringly flat, he perpetually committed the Welsh defence. Crisp passing found Tim Stimpson at pace and the unwieldy full-back suddenly flowered from deep.

Only heroic tackling from Jonathan Davies, one tackle on Austin Healey and a stunning stop on Jon Sleightholme as the winger dived for the corner held the tide in Canutish fashion. It was an incredible testimony to the fitness, will and character of a great player. England were in command, but at half-time the gap was a mere three points and so the singing continued. Hope was still springing eternal . . . that is, until a certain Jeremy Guscott replaced the injured Sleightholme.

Out of position on the wing he may have been, but class prevails and suddenly the near misses became glorious tries. Poor Gareth Thomas and Wayne Proctor were left rooted in the famous turf, a pair of revolved corkscrews as Guscott mesmerised them. Tim Stimpson was the beneficiary of one piece of magic, the tireless Richard Hill the other. He had galvanised the team, a man from another rugby world. Carling and de Glanville would be described as 'game stayers' if they were race-horses; Guscott is a thoroughbred with class.

Aided and abetted by Catt's performance, de Glanville's best match of the season and top-quality displays from Tim Rodber and Richard Hill, England romped into a 20–6 lead. The same score as against France with 20 minutes left. An injury-hit Wales were no France, but England had clearly learned their lesson as they kept up their gallop to romp home by the decidedly unromantic score of 34–13. The only consolation for every romantic was the brilliant nature of Robert Howley's individual score in injury time. It was appropriate that the last try on this hallowed stadium should belong to a descendant of the immortal Gareth Edwards, and how right that Jonathan Davies should kick the conversion. England's superiority in every aspect made them worthy Triple Crown winners, but few wanted Wales to drift too tamely into rugby's good night.

This time it was Rowell and de Glanville who started press pro-ceedings afterwards. It was a confusing affair. Rowell was inundated with questions about Guscott's startling form. Would he be selected for the Lions? Rowell was adamant that Guscott would not only be selected, but that he would be a Test certainty. Not surprisingly, a few wondered that if Rowell rated him so highly, why had he only played 44 minutes for England, creating four tries in that short time? There was logic in the answer. Rowell said that the two teams had a different set of priorities; his were for tomorrow and the day after (i.e. the World Cup), while the Lions had to consider the here and now of the South African challenge. Fine, but by that criteria why the hell was he picking Carling, and why recall Rob Andrew? Rowell had finished the Five Nations with considerable credit. England, for the first time, looked a team capable of competing with the best. They may still be a long way from their destination, but at least they are undoubtedly on the right road, which was definitely not the case last season. Yet still the contradictions sur-rounded this complex and contrary man.

Rowell also let his guard down when pressed about the use of substitutes (another area in which he had been slow to react). In the dying minutes, Chris Sheasby, Rob Andrew and Darren Garforth all came on. From ignoring the potential, Rowell now seemed addicted to it. Amazingly, considering he claims never to read newspapers, he justified his actions thus: 'It is your fault, gents. You keep writing about using substitutes.' Despite his front, Rowell is deeply sensitive to press criticism and here he was inadvertently admitting its influence. Rowell was happy enough to claim a 'big step forward this year' – he was right about that – and to indulge in some clichés. Between him and de Glanville, they managed to use the phrase 'that is what rugby is all about' an impressive three times. The captain slipped one 'at the end of the day' in, but thereafter conducted himself well. It had been a hard season for the England skipper. Every pundit thought him the wrong captain, the Lions did not rate him in their best 62 players and even old colleagues criticised him. Good luck to any future England captains; you can keep the financial perks.

The season at international level was a happy ending for the England camp; for Wales it was unmitigated misery. Jonathan Humphreys sat throughout the Welsh press conference with his forefingers placed either side of his nose. Two pinpricks of pain could just be seen, gazing into some far-off world where rugby does not exist. It was the same look of pain both Jim Staples and Rob Wainwright had worn with fortitude in the wake of England's merciless drubbings. Kevin Bowring's hopes of a Triple Crown had long drifted down the Taff, but the end product of one win and three losses made his position appear vulnerable. The Welsh press sounded ominously close to Brutus. He had demanded results and failed. Wales was becoming impatient with the 'we played well and deserved more' line. But my heart went out to Bowring. Wales did perform with grit in Paris, and they did suffer a terrible injury toll before England (which, to their credit, they refused en masse to blame for the hammering). Perhaps the real post-match hero was Wales's director of rugby, Terry Cobner. Suffering was etched in the face of the former Pontypool hard man, but when he looked ready to break down, he sighed, allowed his eyes to wander, and ruefully stated, 'We can't win here, that's why we decided to knock this place down and play all our games away.' You are right, Terry. It's only bricks and mortar, and it's only a game.

In Paris it was a glorious game. Scotland were crushed 47–20 as France, with all their injuries, claimed the Grand Slam. Four wins for

France, a Triple Crown for England and just one win apiece for the Celtic fringe countries. The form book, so gloriously overturned since the inception of this grand old tournament, had been rock solid. Yet, although the rugby in the Five Nations had been of a higher standard than for many years, the first year of professionalism may have sounded a death knell for this beloved, passionate, claustrophobic and most parochial of tournaments.

As has been frequently stated in this chapter and in newspapers that occasionally have the temerity to poke their head above the parapets of English superiority, the appeal of the tournament has been its sheer unpredictability. A few blinkered commentators overcooked its standards, which have generally veered between clumsy and downright appalling. Due to the ignorance of the majority of Five Nations viewers – more patriot than rugby enthusiast, sitting at home in the armchair with a can of Brains, Guinness, McEwan's, Veuve Clicquot or gin and tonic, depending on place of residence – the deceivers in our sport escaped with their façade intact. But not any more. More people are slowly starting to watch the ever-improving standards of club rugby, both on BSkyB and live at grounds. People now realise that Ireland, Scotland and Wales would be light years from filling the first three positions in the Courage League. Indeed, in the hustle and bustle of weekly rugby, where crowds of 60,000 cannot inspire, it is easy to see relegation as a more probable scenario.

Even more damning has been the advent of the World Cup. We can now see the great teams from the southern hemisphere on a far more regular basis than in days of yore. All the Tri-Nations matches between Australia, South Africa and New Zealand are televised live, as was the epoch-making Test series between the Springboks and the All Blacks in the late summer of 1996. This was rugby beyond the ken of anybody bar New Zealanders and South Africans. All the old excuses about Scotland being so inspired by rugby rivalry that England dare not take risks were finally revealed as the hocus-pocus they have always been. There is no greater rivalry in world rugby than that between New Zealand and South Africa, rugby union's two mighty hegemonies. Any talk of the competing standards of the Five Nations was exposed as lies, lies and more lies.

But what the southern hemisphere lacked was the geographical proximity which created a unique atmosphere and underdogs to rewrite rugby history (especially since Australia dragged itself into the big league in the 1980s). A great game of sport can and must have more than mere quality. Romance, passion, shock and sheer heroic bloody-mindedness are all parts of the cocktail. The Five Nations has possessed every one of these qualities in abundance. These aspects are the ones that made me fall for the tournament. But the first year of professionalism has changed it. Look at England's record against the Celts: 132 points and 14 tries scored, 32 and two conceded. That's the equivalent of Jack climbing up the beanstalk only to be flattened by the boot of a 50-foot giant. Where is the romance in that? Even gloating Englishmen will soon become bored with such bloodless triumph. It may be heresy and I truly hope I am wrong, but Wales, Scotland and Ireland might soon not be worth beating. And what about the downtrodden Celts – how long will they be prepared to suffer such merciless crushings? Add the inflationary trend of ticket prices and we are back to the tournament in crisis which Vernon Pugh feared, but for very different reasons.

Do you remember the Home Championship football tournament? That's it, the one where England played Scotland . . . well, Northern Ireland and Wales were also participants. But the monotonous regularity of results eventually led to the public's disinterest and the tournament's dissolution. The Five Nations will suffer a similar fate if the obvious occurs perpetually: France versus England for the title. Apologists will defend the tournament by reminding us that Ireland and Wales were this year both victims of a casualty list as long as Martin Bayfield. So were France, but they prevailed because of a priceless commodity: strength in depth. The Celtic minnows lack that luxury. It is no surprise. The combined population of the three countries is nowhere near that of England's.

But the greatest problem of all is the long-term one. Now I know that we British prefer not to peer beyond tomorrow, but if rugby union is not to shrink immeasurably to a world game played by five countries at the highest level, it must address this problem: profes-sionalism, in all its untrammelled glory, is rather more free market than the Conservative Party or even the United States of America. The result has been an influx of seriously rich businessmen and entrepreneurs who have invested huge sums of money to make club rugby financially viable. There is no reason why it should be anything else, especially as the lure of money procures the services of the best players this nation has to offer (and a considerable few from outside the United Kingdom). Scotsmen, Irishmen and Welshmen are queuing to join the Keith Woods, the Allan Batemans, the Scott Quinnells, the Doddie Weirs and the Alan Taits in the English league. That may well advance their personal playing standards, but the close proximity of so many Englishmen, who, they suddenly realise, are not all despicable, arrogant shits, and the relaying of family roots must have a detrimental effect on the almost paranoid rivalry that has fuelled the history of this championship. Longer term still, if the best players of this and the next generation are lost to England, who will be the role models to convince the children of Limerick, of Melrose, of Llanelli, that this is the game to play?

The Five Nations may yet be standing near the precipice. How bitterly ironic that it would be the onset of professionalism, although raising the standards of the rugby and the lifestyle of the players, which may be condemned by history as the catalyst that destroyed this great old tradition. The shed-like gloom of crusty old Twickenham, the concrete cauldron of the Parc des Princes, the mighty open bank swirling with Murrayfield's threatening bagpipes and the cathedral of the Arms Park's North Terrace all are gone, leaving that lovely little cottage in the corner of Lansdowne Road as the last reminder of times past. If the respective Unions of the Celtic countries cannot find a way of cementing their club game beyond banning their players from representing their country if they ply their trade overseas (and it is incredibly naive, now that rugby is business as well as pleasure, to think a player would turn down security for a 30-point pasting at the hands of England), then I fear the Five Nations will not last long into the next millennium. Imagine a rugby season without all those wonderfully excessive hangovers, those noisy Dax bands and the vain Welsh promises of a renaissance – and I thought it was bad enough without a single cockerel invasion of Twickenham.

Bath FC: A Bad Business Plan

Some aspects of the transition from amateur to professional sport had a comforting familiarity. Comforting, that is, if you were a South African or a New Zealander. Even viewed through the wrong end of a British set of binoculars, it was impossible to question the iron-fisted superiority of these rugby superpowers that seemed to date back to the dinosaurs.

From 1905 onwards they slugged it out for superiority. They drew the curtain on the amateur age locked in combat in the 1995 World Cup final. Professionalism, like a good New Zealand back row, arrived early – a year early, to be precise – for them. The Super 12 series and the Tri-Nations tournament confirmed the dawn of the new age . . . and yes, a New Zealand province met a South African one in the provincial tournament's final, while New Zealand dominated the international series. The game was faster, the players were fitter and the razzmatazz razzled, but this was rugby union supremacy as we have always known it. The masters of old were the masters of new.

If the English domestic scene had the temerity to compare itself with the rarified atmosphere and history of the Blacks and the 'Boks, Bath would be the only side who could ever possibly have regarded themselves as comparable. Or at least a Russian doll miniature.

Unlike the All Blacks, Bath stumbled and groped their way through history's haze for over 100 years. In the West Country it was left to neighbours Bristol and Gloucester to illuminate the gloom. It was a city as genteel as a Jane Austen novel and one which had no sporting tradition, yet when Bath found their muscular muse, they were to engulf their English rivals with a tidal wave of trophies that smashed any opposition in the way. No other club is ever likely to match Bath's achievements; certainly no other club will ever have the opportunity to rival Bath's amateur record.

It was a century before Bath troubled the record books, but from the moment they walked on to the Barbour-coloured baize of Twickenham's turf as underdogs against Bristol in the John Player Cup final in 1984, no other club has more than sniffed the sweet smell of success. Since that day Bath have stormed HQ on ten occasions, and, aided by the spirit of Houdini, have won every time. In the amateur age, their Courage League record of six triumphs in nine years has also been investigated by the Monopolies and Mergers Commission. The elusive league and cup double, beyond the grasp of any other team, has become almost as inevitable as sexual revelations in Parliament in the dying days of Conservatism. Bath's last four captains have all won the double in their first season in charge.

Rugby league had Wigan, football still has Manchester United, and in rugby union there was Bath. All great champions, but don't for a moment think them as alike as Pinky and Perky. Similarities start and end on the pitch and in the trophy room. Or they would if such a room existed in the Bath clubhouse. Despite Rupert Murdoch's cash injections, Wigan remain beset by financial woes; Manchester United, by contrast, are probably more successful off the pitch than on it. Such is the power of their commercial wing that the ghost of Sir Matt Busby is rumoured to walk respectfully in the shadows of great bankers' and business leaders' entrepreneurial spirit. As for Bath, well, they were champions of a game that was played for the players and for the love of the game – but never for the money.

It was appropriate that amateur rugby's greatest champions were Bath. The grieving hosts of committee men from club and country will remember that Bath, the team apart, was a rugby club that epitomised and exuded amateurism. Check out the *Concise Oxford English Dictionary*. 'Amateur – One who practises a thing only as a pastime . . . hence -ish – having the faults of amateurs' works, unskilful in execution.' You think I exaggerate. Read this auditor's report to the members of the Bath Football Club.

'We planned and performed our audit so as to obtain all the information and explanations . . . to provide us with sufficient evidence to give reasonable assurance that the financial statements are free from material misstatement. [How I love the *vers libres* of an accountant's singing pen.]

'However, included in match income is £90,000 of estimated income due to the club from the Wigan versus Bath game, which is under the control of Wigan Rugby League Club. [Fair enough, but . . .] Further to this, £206,949 of match income arises from takings for home matches over which the system of control was not satisfactorily operated to provide evidence on which we could rely for the purposes of our audit. There were no other satisfactory audit procedures that we could adopt to confirm that this match income was properly recorded.' After 13 years of persistent packed houses, Bath's management could not record a gate receipt accurately. What would Martin Edwards make of that?

Find a grey-haired shuffling blazer and ask why amateurism is perceived as a reason for nostalgia. He will find it difficult to articulate the exact reasons – possibly because of 40 good years of guzzling G and Ts – but when he walks into that council-owned ground, now famous as the Recreation Ground, the very essence of the old ethos wafts like perfume or silage from the banks of the Avon, depending on your age and point of view. For over a century he had a better than evens chance of watching a match for free. Walking through Bath from the station, you catch a first glimpse of the club across the river, over the bandstands and deckchairs. Bath has an unhealthy interest in reminiscing. Stare closely and there is the Main Stand. It has the look of a sheep shed, although in winter it serves as an unofficial shelter for the homeless. Only the corner of the more recent Teachers Stand, dedicated to the corporate antithesis of the more regular Main Stand sleepers, hints at success. The floodlights are so small it is almost impossible to notice them. It is not a stadium to make the pulse race.

Through the non-existent turnstiles, across the pitch to the empty space where the quaintly nicknamed Flowerpot Stand is temporarily removed each year for the Bath Cricket Festival, the club has the feel of a team from Trumpton.

A stroll in the vice-president's lounge adds to the meandering atmosphere of the place. The memento that takes the biggest wallspace commemorates the 1954 French tour, where the club marched triumphantly across the land, beating such giants as St Claude, Givor and La Tour du Pas. What do you mean, 'Never heard of them'? Only the nearby photograph of the 1938 team, beaten 10–3 by Weston Super Mare, could explain the grandiose scale of the French recollection.

In the public bar stands the roll of honour in a place where all rugby legends should be remembered and respected. Behind the bar, as the 1996–97 season unfolded, were the names of 52 international players who had represented their country and Bath – a proud record in the club's 135-year history. But look carefully. Twenty-four Bath men received the national honour in the first 123 years of the club's history, 28 in the last 12. A staggering metamorphosis. It is scant wonder that a committee comprised largely of men with a proven, proud record of amateurism have feared and mistrusted the playing side; it is even less surprising that the players have spent a decade in frustration. While the club forged ahead with European fixtures a decade before the rest of the world even considered the overdue creation of the European Cup, the 28-man committee would spend hours arguing the merits of blow-dryers or towel rails in the toilets. One group wanted to conquer the world; the others would have settled for revenge against Weston Super Mare and comfortable toilets.

England's best team were arguably its most amateur club, and when Sir John Hall played Zeus, using a chequebook instead of lightning bolts, Bath had to face their greatest threat. The Leicester pack was one thing, but the wallets of Thatcher's acolyte entrepreneurs were quite another. In August 1995 the committee knew something was happening, but, like Bob Dylan's Mr Jones, they were not sure what it was. Ernst and Young chartered accountants were commissioned to produce a corporate plan. The report deduced that the club needed a financial backer (another breathtaking piece of thinking for several thousand pounds); the committee created a committee to find such a person; it dragged its feet cautiously. Rightly, they recognised that such a decision had profound implications, but many critics saw a lack of urgency derived from wishful thinking and from hoping that maybe it would all disappear and the old guard could retain their little bit of self-importance. For rugby union administration is overburdened with self-protecting egoists.

When Bath lost their talismanic number eight Ben Clarke to Richmond, a club that had only gained promotion to the Second Division the season earlier, the situation reached crisis point. The rumours of discontent were not rumours at all; they were all too blatantly a reality. The wildly ambitious rugby union circus plans of Ross Turnbull had convinced players that Father Christmas actually did exist. First there was the scenario in the North-east and then Richmond proved it. Loyalty was reaching breaking-point. Clubs were queuing for Bath players. Sign a Bath man and you get the secret recipe of their success; that was the philosophy. John Hall, Bath's director of rugby, was urging haste. His eyes were bloodshot, not from the golden days of his youthful boozing, but from the midnight hours spent convincing players to wait on the club. In desperate attempts to force the issue, Tony Swift, the recent Bath wing who would become non-executive chairman and later chief executive, willed the players to threaten strike action. John Hall was against it. The club had the short-term matter of a league and cup double to concentrate on, but once that had been achieved, the crisis intensified. The sums rumoured to be on offer from Richmond were 'the sort of sums which players could not refuse unless Bath could get close to matching them', according to Swift. In the wake of the double, Bath's players were being forced to decide – 'Sign, now or never' – and it was not Bath asking the question. Mike Catt was supposedly bound for Richmond, Callard for Gloucester, Ojomoh for Harlequins . . . Swift believed that 'The whole team were hours from being lost'.

Not only were Bath in danger of losing their players, but they were proving incapable of attracting others. Kyran Bracken turned down Bath for Saracens – on the surface the equivalent of preferring Björk to Beethoven. But Michael Lynagh and Philippe Sella had also been lured by Nigel Wray, the millionaire with the power over Noddy. Harlequins had signed Laurent Cabannes, Gareth Llewellyn and Laurent Benezech; even bereft Bristol had lured Robert Jones from the Valleys. Bath, the kings of England, were on the verge of dethroning themselves. (Now that is a thought in this country, isn't it?)

Under this pressure the inevitable happened, and player power, combined with panic, changed the nature of the club forever. Racing frantically against the clock, the management engineered the sale of England's finest, a club with an asset base of some transient players, a name, and zilch else. That was a battle that Hall would rate the equal of any triumph on the pitch. On 12 July 1996, Bath quite literally sold its soul to keep its players.

Weeks beforehand, rumours had drifted inexorably towards fact. Andrew Brownsword, a greetings card magnate based in Bath, was about to take over the club, which would be known as Bath Rugby plc. It was more through a sense of obligation than expectation that the dribs and drabs of journalists arrived for 'the special announcement'; we all thought that the sum was £5 million and, besides, the RFU AGM was happening later that afternoon in London.

The only doubters were the vestiges of the old committee, ensconced in the clubhouse. They talked of 'brinksmanship', of Brownsword demanding late obligations. But as these people had refused Brian Ashton an office in which to work as club coach, and as they openly admitted 'We're one side, they're another', pointing to the corporate stand where the press conference was to be held, I took it with a pinch of salt large enough to avoid cramp and bad luck for the rest of my life.

At the other end of the ground there was much activity in Box 20, where Swift, Hall and Brownsword's team were in conference. Ken Johnstone, Bath's long-time press spokesman, whispered that there was a hitch, and that press statements had been withdrawn. At 11 a.m. there was no sign of the conference starting. That in itself was no shock, Bath were always slow starters. But when Richard Mawditt, the outgoing chairman who bears a striking resemblance to the bald lawyer in *Murder One*, announced that Brownsword had just left home at 11.35, well, that seemed odd. The delay grew longer and only the early arrival of red wine calmed the tender tempers of the media.

At 11.50 a.m. Mawditt announced that the conference would start at 12 noon and promptly fell off the platform. Ankle twisted, he howled in pain; the media stifled their amusement and a black crow flew past. It was an inauspicious start to the new age.

Brownsword eventually arrived and the news broke. The £5 million deal was only £2.5 million; that was hardly a surprise. Many of the tabloid newspapers which break these stories suffer from an untreatable disease called exaggeratitis – whereupon deluded souls think everything much bigger than is really the case. Only a poor journo would ever quote an accurate figure (unless the figure was actually sensational). It was a point which Brownsword reiterated. More significant was the share stake. In possession of 75 per cent of the club, Brownsword had huge control over Bath. He also implemented his own management structure to ensure that business was managed 'in the style the investor wanted', according to Swift. He added, 'The aim is to make the business profitable, so that it can be floated and the equity within the business can be shared.' With a three-quarters stake, a profitable Bath made good sense to a businessman – but that did not necessarily equate with a great team.

Unlike at Wasps, who sold 49.9 per cent to Chris Wright of Chrysalis and kept control, Brownsword was in total command. He spoke without passion but with heavily commercial overtones: 'The club will be thoroughly organised as befits the era of professionalism, an era which, I believe, makes immense demands on every club to behave in a financially responsible and sound manner. Those who fail to do so run the grave risk of imperilling the entire future of their club, and professionalism may well see some casualties. It is not the intention of anyone at this famous club that any such scenario be allowed to ensue.' It was official: Bath was, at last, a business. It was inevitable, but it was also sad. A little magic had died – and ticket prices exploded. Bath were a bottom-line band; the accountants were at the gates.

The club's trustees knew that. They were the reason for the delayed announcement. One member of the new management structure confirmed that 'Various people at Bath had to sign an agreement to give away Bath Football Club. They were shitting themselves and wanted more reassurances.' But the sands of time had run out for Bath defectors.

Brownsword left and Swift spoke of 'stakeholders within the club'. The chartered accountant sounded like Tony Blair in a nervous phase; the phrase 'new committee, new danger' fleetingly crossed my mind. Mawditt then reiterated the 75/25 shareholding split. 'The membership will maintain 25 per cent and they will have 75 per cent.' Even the sleepiest hack caught the cold 'they' reference. Richard Mawditt, the outgoing chairman and the only man with a club tie on, called the deal 'a lifetime marriage'. I didn't point out that Britain has the highest divorce rate in Europe. And this had been the rockiest courtship of all.

The merger of sport and commerce was hailed as a triumph by a first-team squad which had remained almost irrationally loyal to the club. But, then again, the *Titanic* was considered unsinkable. There were few signs of ominous icebergs on a Bath July afternoon as the squad trained at Bath University. But beneath the surface the ripples were starting to spread.

Barely two months from commencing their defence of the league, the squad remarkably had no kit deal. Steven Hands, the new marketing director, saw the club as a powerful brand and negotiated accordingly. Russell Athletic, the major American clothing company, thought that Bath's negotiating stance had been both bullish and a little naive. In pursuit of profit, the marketing side of the club were accused by some of ignoring the prime criteria of kit, which should be one of quality. Commercial aspects should be secondary. In Bath, not everyone was convinced that this was the case.

Other problems, small on the surface, were proving disconcerting behind the scenes. Accommodation and transportation for games was one such example. From a purely commercial point of view, one hotel is the same as the next for an overnight stop. Price is the only factor. It is not for a team. Quality of food, service, comfort, location and plain and simple superstition all play fundamental roles in team preparation. John

Allen, a long-suffering first-team secretary, had years of this experience. He had already booked hotels and transport prior to the first kick of the season. Yet suddenly the club were questioning the decisions. Allen, like many others, was disappointed with both the communication and the lack of understanding. The blinkered sportsman believes only former competitors can fulfil a management role within that sport, but, equally, it is a blinkered man from the world of commerce who thinks he can translate business practices to sport without any empathy.

In a club with as much soul and community feel as Bath, such an imbalance was detected immediately. The players were largely unaware of any teething problems, but they did notice the absence of their manager, John Hall. Pre-season training started without Hall. The great man of Bath, in the manner of British horse-racing trainers, was spending a few weeks of the off-season in the Caribbean. A manager of a club such as Bath needs a healthy complexion. As amateurs, the only emotion such a holiday would have stimulated among the lads was jealousy. But as manager he was open to accusations of double standards. It was not a particularly thoughtful decision and added to an atmosphere of unease created by Hall's apparent growing reluctance to swap his suit for a tracksuit as he attempted to adjust to added responsibilities, under the eye of Ed Goodall, the chief executive. As director of rugby, Hall should have been sensitive to these criticisms from the men who mattered to him: the players and the coaching staff. But it was July, the rum was cool . . . and it was a new era for everyone.

It was indicative of a bygone age which smacked of amateurism. As such it had more symbolic importance than anything else. More pressing was the absence of a strategy concerning the medical team. Julie Bardner, who had been supervising the physiotherapists for a decade, could only force her way through Bath's door two days before pre-season training. The club lacked either the inclination or the imagination to think logically about this crucial back-up service. Management were happy to rely on volunteers supervising expensive athletes. Imagine a football team without a professional medical team . . . but here were Bath, champions of one of the country's most taxing and physical games, without any real contingency. Bardner was preparing to retire from club duty. She did not believe the club would pay sufficient amounts to compensate for the loss of her profitable private practice, and her concern was that England's leading club would be left to rely on a part-time staff who would be stretched beyond the limits. It was not just the old guard struggling to adapt to professionalism in Bath. The fact that Bardner would see the season out is something of an indictment on the club's professionalism.

Ged Roddy, a Mancunian in his mid-thirties and once undermined by the fact that the players discovered he had played soccer for Accrington Stanley, had the task of ordering and supervising players' conditioning programmes. As he watched the squad training, he offered the only sensible definition of professionalism: 'It's a state of mind, not the size of the wad in your pocket.' Not every Bath mind was particularly well tuned as the season drew near.

Several players, including Jon Sleightholme, Mike Catt, Jeremy Guscott, Graham Dawe and Eric Peters, were absent from training, limiting the innovations with which Brian Ashton, the coach, was keen to experiment. The rest of the squad met early for an optional lunch. Forwards flexed their pectorals and munched bananas in the way older players once consumed alcohol. The squad lacked the collective look of a professional team. While Simon Geoghegan was immaculate in his new Adidas gear, Phil de Glanville had a rougher look, wearing an old and ripped England training shirt. Jack Rowell once described the sartorial appearance of the team as one most closely resembling a pop group. Appearances had moved on since then, but the team still looked a mishmash. An individualistic gesture as collectivism grew around them.

This endearing reminder of the individual nature of amateurism irritated the Cash Flow King of Bath, Ed Goodall, Bath's new chief executive. When Bath faced Western Samoa in December of '96, Goodall was appalled by the sight of the Bath team warming up for the match in multi-coloured and varying splendour, while the Samoans looked the collective part in their matching tracksuits. He turned to John Allen and complained, 'Why do they look such a mess? Can't someone do something? Before the Cardiff match they looked a shambles.' Here was a man who was commercially cute, but totally oblivious to Bath's almost Bohemian individualism that had helped shape a glorious legacy. Business and sport were not mixing and the diehard supporters were unhappy. But that is further down the road. Back to the professional optimism of pre-season.

Diet and conditioning were two new facets in rugby's new world. Professionalism had thrown Roddy a whole set of problems previously unencountered. Prior to being full-time, the majority of players had their day accounted for by the tedious routines of a nine-to-five existence. They could only train infrequently and they had little time for boredom. Suddenly Roddy had to hold players back. Devoted trainers such as Jon Callard wanted to train all the hours possible. In July, Roddy was concerned that Callard was too fit. Bath could have half a dozen players peaking a week before the season began. Imagine Michael Johnson running 19.3 seconds for the 200 metres six months before the Olympics and you will understand the problems of handling committed sportsmen for whom professionalism was both a novelty and a career.

The nine-to-five habits could be hard to break. Roddy had a major task ensuring that players actually did rest between training, that all training was appropriate and that spare time did not lead to the pub, the bookies or one of many other assorted places of ill-repute and undoubted entertainment. It had trapped a generation of footballers; now it was the turn of rugby players to run the gauntlet. Roddy worried that 'If they drift in their professional life, which is rugby, they will drift on a Saturday'. Would the professional rugby player prove that ignorance is not inherent in footballers, but that inarticulacy and limited general knowledge were common to the singular breed of the necessarily narrow-minded world of professional sport? As rugby moved towards professionalism this appeared to be the developing trend . . . although don't think that this line of argument draws to some sort of conclusion that Paul Gascoigne would have been a rocket scientist had he not revealed a precocious talent for football.

Linked to that was Bath's other challenge on the playing side. To maintain the independence of mind that had marked the club's continued run of success. The team's ability to make snap decisions on the pitch had been a more decisive factor in their winning decade than just any degree of pure skill. That had been the legacy left by Jack Rowell. His difficulty in preaching the gospel of individual and instinctive decision-making in the national side underlined the reasons for Bath's success. Bath players wanted responsibility where others did not. But the relationship between players and coaches had undergone a subtle shift. As amateurs everyone was on a level playing field. Now it was a world of employers and employees. Ged Roddy enthused about the contributions made by players to training and planning, one of these players being Bath's veteran second row Nigel Redman. Oddly enough, Redman claimed otherwise. 'I'm paid to play now. It's a job, so I shut up, get on with it and go home.' (As you read this, Redman, as an assistant coach, is being paid to do precisely that.)

In a claustrophobic rugby city, an existence centred entirely upon the game was a fearful prospect, especially for the family men who needed an escape route. In year one there was no escape. As the technical session ended and Bath's new-age professionals trooped off, Roddy spoke of his own great challenges – to constantly stimulate the players, to manage their leisure time and to manage men as part of the job process. This would prove a major and insurmountable challenge. Words were not to be translated into deeds. The infrastructure would not be put in place.

Bath's professional coach, Brian Ashton, had an even more pivotal role. To keep them at the top of rugby's increasingly competitive tree, Ashton had left his career as a schoolmaster in nearby Wincanton. The target was also the conquest of Europe.

The overbearing threat of one year's failure in this small city was illustrated by the presence of the new Bath Rugby Academy. The club had signed ten of the most outstanding young talents in the country. They would live within the confines of the University and be managed by Andy Robinson, another former teacher who had thrown his hat into the professional ring – and would ironically replace Ashton. It was the equivalent of an apprentices' school. Bath have always relied on recruiting young blood because the one area where the club had once been vulnerable was the financial one. More importantly, it was the best way to build a committed squad, who believed in the collective as much as in the individual.

Robinson's charges were Bath's investment in the future, but Ashton had both eyes on the present. Five foot six and balding, he is not an imposing figure in the Jack Rowell mould, but Ashton had earned the total respect of every Bath player. Born and bred in Wigan, he carried an open mind, rather than a hole in the head, and he was tough. Ashton was brimming with ideas for the modern age, but the absence of so many key players left him little short of fuming. Ashton set high standards for others and for himself.

Bath's popular Lancastrian, once nicknamed 'Coco' because of the classic balding clown's hairstyle, is not a man to worry about image. Earthy and honest, he loves the sport, but he loathed the politics that were surrounding this season, like the smog that hangs over major cities. Whereas Hall seemed touched by the understandable excitement of a new age, Ashton's attitudes had undergone few, if any, changes. If you tried talking to Ashton about rugby politics, you were more likely to find an opposition political leader giving precise budget breakdowns before an election. That can be a major benefit. Ashton thought he possessed no real new pressures; his world revolved around the same orbit: success on the field. It was not for me to remind him that his income also depended upon success.

Ashton knew what he wanted; the problem was that he did not have the power to go out and get it. That was part of his former player, now manager, John Hall's admittedly ill-defined brief. Ashton had identified a lack of front five forwards as the Achilles' heel of the club. So what did Bath do? Sign two of Wigan's most glamorous names, Henry Paul and Jason Robinson. It may be that Ashton, as an avowed Wigan fan, literally saw stars, but undoubtedly the result of these high-profile and exorbitantly expensive signings was to stimulate even more publicity for England's amateur champions. That was imperative for teams like Bedford, who needed to attract players and make national impressions, hence the signing of such names as rugby league player Martin Offiah, but for Bath it was madness. They simply had no need to make such a splash. Success depended more on ensuring a solid platform for their extravagantly talented backline.

Ashton made this known and simmered as the request was ignored. His alleged impotence in matters of recruitment was an appalling blunder of management that would create considerable internal problems throughout the year until his departure. Rumours flew. Olivier Roumat, Robin Brooke, Steve Atherton . . . a host of lineout luminaries were suggested, but none reached the Rec. The most professional side of the amateur era were apparently falling behind the calculating efficiency of some other clubs.

The other area where Bath had once held unprecedented sway was the *esprit de corps*. There is no English phrase for this elusive quality, perhaps because it is not an English trait – but Bath had always summoned this spirit in times of crisis. The signings of rugby league superstars who were due to return to Wigan half-way through the union season indicated that this intangible force was disappearing under the weight of Brownsword's money.

Ashton started his first year as a professional coach with a team bursting with talent, but one about whom there were more unanswered questions than there had been about any Bath team of the last decade. Professionalism had been the agent of such change. That antiquated and admirable northern club Orrell were the champions' opening-day opponents. Television duly chronicled the 50-point hammering, but to those who knew Bath, doubts persisted. The style was breathtaking.

They started by throwing the ball wide; as the game developed it became wider still. For an hour Orrell held out, an Alamo of an effort. It was only Bath's superior fitness and individual skill that cracked the Lancastrians. So what, wasn't it a 50-pointer? True, but Bath played the game like visionaries, or converted Christians. There was a new style and Bath would follow it, no matter what the consequences. The style was dazzling, the philosophy flawed. Teams need the ability and flexibility to adapt their game. Bath had benefited from other teams' 'visionary one-dimensional rugby' while Rowell's pragmatists had mixed and matched their way to success. The constant battle cry of 'Evolution, not revolution' was apparently forgotten. It was impossible to doubt that Bath would win friends playing with their expansive brio, but would they win titles . . . and did Andrew Brownsword download £2.5 million for style before substance? All intriguing early-season questions.

The intrigue gathered as Bath went on a metaphorical early-season tour of a Coney Island big dipper. Mike Catt and Jerry Guscott cut Leicester's defence to shreds at Welford Road, but the superiority of the Midlands pack overwhelmed the champions. That was defeat one. Then came a stunning home defeat against Wasps. When I heard the score of 36–40 I demanded to be told just who had dumped the mescalin in my coffee. The wider Bath played, the more they exposed their defence. The theory of evolution was absent. After three weeks of the season, mighty Bath were eighth in the table.

A series of wins against weak opponents restored a credible table position before Bath took another hammer blow. This time it was in the European Cup. Bath had stated their intent before the season started: the European Cup was number one priority. Later Brian Ashton rephrased the aim as 'one of the number one priorities'. And he once a schoolmaster.

Bath travelled to Sardis Road, home of the Rhondda's heroes Pontypridd (who would become Welsh champions that season). Inspired by a man called 'Chief', Bath were humbled 19–6. The pack were mugged by the media, and Pontypridd even claimed that team spirit had been their superior weapon. The Bath pack had been questioned before, but never the spirit. Bath, four points behind Harlequins in the league and needing to beat Olivier Roumat's Dax and Treviso by heavy margins away to qualify for the knockout phases of the European Cup, were in their first crisis.

But this club had seen it all before. Nobody more often than Nigel Redman, the Bath veteran to end all veterans. Bow ties at cup finals and two-day piss-ups after victory are two of Bath's happier traditions. The crisis team talk at the training ground of Lambridge after a defeat is the dark side of their tradition. John Hall called the pack in for 'a heart to heart', à la Jack Rowell, more commonly known as a bollocking. Backs who tried to listen to the exchanges were threatened physically, but to 'Ollie', as Redman is affectionately known, it was the same old Bath. Hall criticised the forwards with an earthiness worthy of Chaucer, Redman responded in the time-honoured fashion of a Bath forward: he refused to take any of the blame. Deny, deny, deny. That has always been the policy, but, on this occasion, Redman honestly believed he had a point. 'The tight five were pissed off. We felt that the press had jumped on the bandwagon. But the team lacked balance, and that is not conducive to front-five play. Sure, we have responsibilities, but so do the rest of the team. We were the same team that had won the double, the only change was the game plan.' The pack wanted the balance right between backs and forwards – the reversion to evolution rather than revolution. Blood was let, and 'it was as honest as it could be. Bath and international positions were on the line.' Not totally honest, then, Nigel.

Redman painted a picture of timeless Bath. His adverse reaction to the rota system being employed by Ashton and Hall was classic Bath: 'Large squads can be detrimental. It's great to fall back on internationals if you have injuries, but a first-team place should be a trophy. If you employ a rota and you know when you will next play, performance in play can slip. You should play to your maximum, so you keep your place a week later.'

Redman's passion had not been doused by professionalism. He thought that Bath's famous player power had disappeared with the new contractual relationship. 'I am paid by the establishment to play to the game plan . . . my ultimate responsibility is to my wife and family.' Superficially this sounded like a different animal, but to counter this it is worth recalling that Moseley had offered him a better financial incentive than Bath and he had remained. On the need for a new stimulus, Redman is adamant. 'I've never needed it. Playing here is stimulus enough. People buy players to beat us; I'd rather stop them getting their £2,000 win bonus than pick one up myself. No, for me the beauty will always be travelling back to Bath on the A46, seeing that beautiful city in the valley and thinking, "What a bunch of c**ts we are." I also know that the beautiful city is not a rugby city like Gloucester. If the bubble bursts, a lot of that support will leave. I don't want to be responsible for ending that story. If the pig-headed 15 at no cost played the professional 15 with a massive bonus, in this place I'd fancy the pig-heads.' The newcomers had a fine man to explain Bath's glorious traditions. Classic Bath mule. Results and rumours suggested that Redman's was a fading voice, but some West Country traditions die harder. On the way back into town the team had found a new stop-off, a pub called the Beehive. No chrome-plated bars, just rough cider. Good old Zummerset Scrumpy.

Money had not quashed the spirit of all Bath's old warriors. Fired by that burning pride, Bath closed their game up and faced down formidable Dax. The European Cup dream was still alive. Bristol were then torched by a human fireball called Jason Robinson as the Wigan star performed brilliantly at full-back. The local rivals were dispatched by 76 points as Harlequins and Wasps slipped. Bath were apparently bouncing back off the ropes. For Guscott it was sheer joy. 'I take no greater joy in rugby than thumping our old rivals, Gloucester and Bristol. We stuffed Gloucester by 48 in a cup final, now 76 on Bristol.' The smile was broad, gloating Bath.

Brian Ashton was not quite as smiling. Asked if being a professional coach put extra pressure on him, he replied deadpan, 'My salary is not worth talking about.' Whispers that some second-team regulars were on more money than England's most innovative coach stressed the ridiculous inflation that had gripped the early days of professionalism in England. Ashton's life had changed, but it was hard to tell whether he thought for the better. 'I had ten weeks holiday as a schoolteacher, now I have none. I've more responsibility for producing performances *and* results. Otherwise I'm in a dilemma, because those outside the playing side think only in terms of results.' It was an oblique reference to the new management of the club. (The chief executive, Ed Goodall, was almost a cult figure due to his tight pockets. On away trips, Bath players looked in vain for their sandwiches on the bus. They were nowhere to be seen – victims of cost cutting. And free beer for ex-players? Forget it.)

Ashton was less euphoric about the Dax win than a eulogising media. He thought the performance regressive, claiming, 'We've reached a staging post whereby we've had to draw back in for a variety of reasons.' Like Redman, he wanted the team to assert the winning balance. He also had harsh words for some of his new professionals. 'Some players are more motivated by money than they ought to be. It's generally players sitting on the periphery of the first team. There are players playing for the United team week in, week out who are on fairly comfortable salaries. That could be a disincentive to a few.' Stories emanating from wide-eyed ballboys of players warming up as replacements and talking about the £450 appearance fee should they take the field hardly cheered those who questioned the depth and intensity of commitment from a few of the squad. Comfortable is a bad word at Bath. The team has always gone out of its way to make everyone uncomfortable, even during periods of huge success. It keeps the edge.

There were also early problems in Ashton's relations with John Hall. The Bath director of rugby was Ashton's junior in terms of years, coaching experience and expertise; in fact, in just about every way bar the management line. According to Ashton in late October, 'It's a relationship that is still developing. It seemed odd to me to take a job where he is my direct boss to whom I'm responsible. I am almost 17 years older. I've also been his coach and have so much more experience of rugby at all levels that I feel strange. I didn't consider how strange it would be before I took the job on. I do find it difficult at times.' The absence of front-five signings was one of the difficult times. 'We've had our good times, but we have also had some uneasy ones so far.' The signing of the Argentinian front-row forward Federico Mendez helped heal any sore spots between the two.

Ashton's greatest therapy continued to be the style of Bath's game. Statistics were secondary to feel, encouragement more important than criticism. Relaxation and confidence were the key tenets of the Ashton philosophy. He was tense himself about Europe. He called the European Cup 'the best thing to happen to the northern hemisphere game', and admitted that Bath were into the unknown. Bath, the great English rugby voyagers, had to cross Treviso on 2 November to keep their expedition afloat. Defeat would constitute a massive disappointment for Ashton, who claimed, 'To fail to even qualify for the quarter-finals would be a massive setback to the programme we put into place at the season's start.'

At Treviso the flames of hope burned due to a coruscating four-try performance from Mike Catt that booked his place in the England number ten jersey. The party that night was long and hard in the best Bath style. Mike Catt was stretchered off at 9.30 p.m., battered by the booze, while Charlie Harrison paid the price of youth and left some poor Italian street cleaner with a miserable job on Sunday morning.

It proved a false dawn. Bath returned home to face Northampton away. It was a vital game to win – and also a tough one, but the Saints were without the brilliance of Gregor Townsend. Whereas Bath once prevailed through will alone, here it deserted them as the Saints deprived them of two valuable points. This had been the week when de Glanville had been appointed England captain and Jeremy Guscott had been dropped. The distractions had undoubtedly played a part in the defeat.

That left Bath with three defeats from eight league matches. It was an unprecedented start to a title defence. The Bath crowd were restless and the match against Cardiff in the quarter-final of the European Cup became even more vital. The tournament was the one Bath had earmarked; it was the one to prove the boasts had not been idle. For once the Courage League was of secondary importance. In the Welsh capital, Bath fell, 22–19. It was the low point of a decade for Bath. No Beehive on the way back to Bath, but a more anonymous pub on the outskirts of enemy territory in Bristol. The wounds were bleeding, both deep and profuse.

Christmas approached but it was not a time of cheer for those who had an emotional involvement with the club. Nigel Redman's fears of desertion from the massed ranks of supporters were in danger of becoming a reality. Disaffection with unexpected defeats was an obvious reason, but even that could not account for the depression that pervaded the public bar on a cold Monday night in December as Bath, multi-topped and irritating to their chief executive, warmed up to face Western Samoa.

The corporate face-lift that Brownsword's millions had given the club was as amateur, if not more so, than those dreadful nights of four-hour committee meetings. The business suits had committed a cardinal corporate sin: they did not know their market. How else could they have failed to understand the subtle forces that had helped metamorphose Bath from minnows to monsters in the world of English rugby?

As an old-stager like Nigel Redman well knew, Bath's strength had been drawn from within. All those matches where Bath had squeezed home by the odd point had been the result of quixotic individual genius, allied with a burning desire not to fail. That will was stoked by the community feel of the place. Players mingled with spectators in all the bars. Jeremy Guscott might have appeared a superstar to the outside world, but in Bath he was just another bloke who could play a bit of rugby. The crowd responded to such geniality and the players responded to the crowd. It helped turn the least threatening of environments – an 8,500-capacity stadium in a genteel little city – into one of rugby's most intimidating arenas. Fly-by-nights like the multitalented Harlequins could sign all the best players, but the money would always have been down on the mules from the West. Thanks to the 'professionalism' of men more comfortable with a balance sheet than a pint of bitter, Bath seemed intent on throwing this intense and immense advantage away.

The supporters were in a mutinous mood. As they discussed their string of defeats, the immediate reasons cited were the shapelessness of performance, the inability of Catt to run the game, and so on – but then the real feelings poured out. This was the view of a Bath supporter who had followed the team for 25 years, since way before the glory days. 'There are problems here and until they are resolved, we are in trouble. There is a groundswell of opinion against the management. Tonight we are being charged £19 to watch this fucking game [Bath had made it all pay, so membership was void for the night, and had then selected a shadow side]. It is completely wrong for a club of this stature to entertain Samoa and field half a team. We also have a problem with the focus of it all. You know who I mean.' The reference was to John Hall.

That view was cruelly unfair on Hall. He had to work with people who controlled his future if he wished to stay with Bath. But it is impossible not to fault him for one single and central reason. Hall, above just about anyone, knew the secret of Bath's brilliant success. Under pressure, he allowed corporate thinking to undermine it. Jerry Guscott cried with laughter as he recounted the tale of being called into Hall's office one day. 'I thought, Christ, I might be dropped, especially when Hally said, "It's about Saturday." Then he asked me if I would refrain from smoking cigars around the club – which is what I was doing after that match. He told me that Ed Goodall thought it created a bad example.' It was akin to ordering Oscar Wilde to stop cracking clever one-liners; it was the antithesis of everything for which Bath stood. And the crowd were unimpressed. They complained about the players no longer mingling because they had allegedly been told not to drink in front of supporters. Instead they headed for the Beehive, a cider house where snooping accountants were not known to hang out. The symbiotic link between player and fan, the reason behind the awesome soul of the club, was being torn asunder by the whims and failings of a misguided new age.

Another supporter: 'We've been into this "family thing" for 20 years now, but now, the only player I've had a word with after the game has been Jeremy Guscott. Apparently they are not supposed to drink with us.' Others were too bitter for print. Some complained, 'We are just numbers on a cash-flow sheet.' The brains behind Bath may have been formidable when it came to making money from greetings cards, but in rugby terms they appeared to be in the apprentice stage. As were Bath.

We read of fixtures with the Super-12 champions Auckland, visits to the Currie Cup winners Natal. The players even released a single written by local pop star Manny Elias (formerly of Tears for Fears). It was called 'Push 'Em Back', a title that must have caused the Leicester front row to smile. It was hardly the Bath forte. Their choice of fixtures with the élite of the southern hemisphere and this single hinted at a team intent on telling the world, rather than proving, just how good they were. The real supporters did not want to see Henry Paul and Steve Ojomoh rapping, they wanted to see them winning matches. This was a strange form of professionalism. The talent was still there, but what about the heart? Five days after Western Samoa, the Harlequins visited. It was another acid test. The reformed prima donnas against the champions who seemed on the slide. It was not the last stand, but for many critics, it was getting pretty close.

And what a day it was for Bath. The press box, ready to write the Bath obituary, was a giant red face as Harlequins tore Bath to tatters in a mesmeric first-half performance. Bath were on one knee. The vultures were swooping over the Abbey . . . and then came the fightback. The heroes were the unlikely Americas combination of Federico Mendez and the captain of the United States, Dan Lyle. Maybe not quite Herculean, but good enough to recall John Hall at his West Country prime. By full-time, the talk was once more of Bath's glory and of brittle Quins. Everything was as smooth as Beau Brummell.

The clubhouse was bracing itself for its Christmas concert, courtesy of Richard Webster's girlfriend's all-female band. Bath, a club in crisis, breathed a huge sigh of relief. But not for long. In the blink of a cider session at the Beehive, John Hall found himself in a state of Christmas exuberance. Relief and joy triggered off a party that turned sour. Hall left the cider house for the trendier setting of a bar called PJ Peppers. Two days later he was making headlines, charged with assault. Following a court case in September, he was found not guilty, and to those who know the real John Hall, the allegations had been tenuous – but so was the general behaviour of Hall. As Bath manager, he could not afford the overflowing wild excesses of his youth. Certainly not in a manner that was public. In his heart, Hall knows it was irresponsible. It cannot have lightened the mood of Brian Ashton, the next member of Bath's coaching élite who would make the headlines. Ashton's headlines threw into context all the lurking concerns and fears of the supporters, senior players . . . and, yes, a couple of scribblers.

Even as the gossips of this small city raised their eyebrows and shrugged their shoulders at the mention of the name Hall, Ashton was about to steal the headlines. Days after Hall's much-chronicled alleged action, the Lancastrian gave the club another headache as he resigned from the position of head coach.

His discontent simmered back to his first day in that post. Within six weeks he believed that he and Bath were inexorably heading for a separation. On 31 December he walked away. His explanation of the long and torturous route to the broken relationship is a tale of deep irony. Andrew Brownsword's comments to the press on 12 July, the day Bath became a business, were 'The club will be thoroughly organised as befits the era of professionalism'. Brownsword had left the new board to run the business; in Ashton's belief, that had been the prime cause for the club's problems. 'The management team was not good enough. There were people in jobs who should not have been there.'

Ashton was stunned and disappointed with his perceptions of the club's management. 'It became fairly apparent that we were thinking about the short term. I can only describe it as crisis management. There was no long-term planning.' Here was one former schoolteacher most definitely not in awe of the business world into which he had jumped, almost naively, back in July. He was no longer naive as we sat in his rented home in Bruton, near the wonder world of Wincanton racecourse. Ashton had fallen on his feet with his stunning appointment as coaching adviser to Ireland, a temporary appointment that would lead to a contract to take his new adopted country through the next two World Cups, granting him the security he had foolishly thought Bath had guaranteed him. But the fact remains that the 50-year-old coach had been rocked by the startling birth pains of Bath and professionalism.

Ashton's tale epitomises the problems of rugby's brave and occasionally frightening new world. The cosiness of a Hobbit's home which once filled every corner of the English game was, like Tolkien's creation, pure fantasy. Rugby post-1995 had entered the real, unforgiving world. The genial Lancastrian had entered it with his eyes closed. 'I took the Bath job thinking it would be my last job in life. At the end of this job, I expected to retire. The decision to leave Bath was no mere whim. I had spoken long and hard with my entire family, as it would affect everyone. I am paying for my daughter to go through Bristol University and my son is at boarding school. For the major wage-earner to be out of work was pretty significant.' Ashton revealed the unseen side as master of the understatement.

Ashton as a hard nut is also a rare comment, but the voice had a serrated edge when he thought back to those unhappy last months at Bath. Rather than a former schoolmaster, he sounded more a disciple of John Harvey Jones. Before departing from the Recreation Ground, Ashton had sent a series of proposals to Tony Swift, then non-executive chairman. He outlined in them his major concerns for the club and himself. The fact that they were sent to Swift and not to Ed Goodall, then chief executive, is itself a clue to the disaffection of Ashton.

The proposals' key points suggest that Ashton resignedly believed the relationship was beyond repair, even before the club could respond. 'Primarily, I was unhappy with the management team. There was not a lot of experience in terms of man-management and rugby people, in terms of how rugby clubs are organised. [This, of course, applied to every professional club. Nobody, including Ashton, had all the answers.] Too many people had too much interest on the playing side of which they knew so little. That was a real irritation.'

Ashton's description of Bath's regular coaching meetings, where preliminary selection issues and the forthcoming week's activities were discussed, is a picture of chaos and amateurism in the most bumbling sense. 'They were almost open house. It took me some time to get in charge of that which I felt, being head coach, I should have been. Numbers would vary from five or six to two or three. That was a theme throughout all meetings at Bath. Eventually Ed Goodall insisted on being present at coaching meetings to review the weekend and plan ahead. I found this very bizarre.'

In Goodall's defence, it can be argued that his personal weakness was this lack of empathy with and understanding of the playing side of the game, so what better way to at least try and understand the rudimentaries than to sit in on these meetings? Ashton argued that he did more than just sit in. 'He was often throwing in what he thought were very serious questions, which I thought were red herrings. They were of no value to the previous weekend or what would happen the next one – which is what you would expect from someone who knows nothing, or very little, about the game.'

If John Hall had been more secure in his own threatened position as director of rugby, he may have taken a stronger hand in controlling Goodall's alleged contributions. Ashton felt he was helpless to take any sort of stand. 'Goodall expressed an interest in attending the meetings and John Hall thought it a good idea. I was answerable to both these people, so I would have been on thin ice if I had said, "I don't want him here."'

Ashton's anger at the memory is barely concealed. 'I have a reputation as being a pretty laid-back and easy guy, but I'm not the sort of bloke to tolerate a situation like that. I wouldn't go into an accounting meeting and say, "I don't think last month's figures are up to much; this is what you ought to be doing." I wouldn't even contemplate it.'

Good relations are imperative in any team, be it one dedicated to profit, sporting success or, in the case of Bath, both. The man-management skills needed to mould Ashton, the rugby man, with the business ethics were absent. Neither side seemed to have a clue as to what the other was trying to achieve. They didn't come close. 'I only met Andrew Brownsword twice. Once in Queen Square [the club business offices] and once at a drinks party at the Priory Hotel. When I arrived for my first day's work on 1 July, the atmosphere was almost apologetic . . . there was nowhere for me. I worked in six offices in four weeks. I didn't bother to unpack. I was told that I would be based at the University. The director of rugby told me it would be advisable to get up there as quickly as possible because, in his words, "You don't quite fit in here". Maybe it was just an inappropriate choice of words.' Ashton's face betrayed his innermost thoughts on the subject as he added, 'And maybe not.'

Here was a man who had been a schoolmaster for 26 years, and a man who still takes pride in the professionalism of his former occupation. While elements of the Bath board, in true corporate fashion, dismiss *any* credibility for teachers, Ashton threw the lack of professionalism back in their faces. 'From 1 July to my resignation on 31 December, I did not have a job description. I hadn't a clue what was expected from me. John even warned me on a couple of occasions that Ed Goodall wanted to know what I was doing and how I was filling my time during the week. I have never been one for doing nothing.' He positively bridled at the recollection. 'As a coach you can easily spend two or three hours a morning watching videos, and it's a damn sight easier to concentrate at home than in an office environment. But that was not what they wanted, so I actually spent some time doing nothing, when I could have been better employed being elsewhere. The work ethic of the business world is based around a nine-to-five existence. I thought, "Christ, they don't trust me." Here I am, aged 50, being thought a shirker. That was quite annoying.' It was an interesting use of the word 'quite'.

The failure of the business and the rugby world to merge may not be too surprising, but the flaws within the organisation of playing affairs was a different matter. Andrew Brownsword must have believed that the double winners from the previous season could manage themselves. Hall had been manager and Ashton coach, so why should there be a problem? Days before the departure of Hall, Tony Swift, by then chief executive, made that point. It revealed the naivety that had turned England's champion club into a crisis club. The previous season, players and management had been amateur; professionalism had thrown up a different set of problems.

Ashton was right to assume that he, as head coach, would imprint his own hand on the style of training. He was stunned to find that this was not the case. 'When I started on 1 July, I discovered that the training and organisation, in terms of which type of training would take place at which time, had already been sorted out by John and Ged [Roddy, the fitness adviser]. I had not been consulted. I had assumed it would be one of the first things we would sort out, but suddenly, it was done. It was all based at the University, which I thought wrong. [Bath University overlooks the city from a hill and the wind rarely gusts under hurricane levels – or so it seems if you try to practise individual ball skills.] It should have been based at the club. In addition, all the sessions were back to front. The heavy work was done in the morning and the technical work in the afternoon. It should have been technical work when fresh and the heavy training after that.'

Ashton's confidence had been undermined from that day on. He admits that he wondered whether he or Roddy was Hall's deputy; he also asked himself serious questions about the nature of his new job. 'Something as crucial as the organisation of where we would train and how the structure of training should work had not actually been put together by me. I had done it at home before 1 July and I still worked at school until 30 June . . . it was almost the total opposite of what I wanted.' As we spoke in early February 1997, Ashton indulged himself in a rueful smile. 'Now it is how I wanted it. It has almost all changed in the past four weeks.'

It was sad that something as cataclysmic as Ashton's departure was needed for Bath to rethink their position. Ashton retains a degree of bitterness about the whole period which is almost inconceivable in the light of his warm personality. 'Some of the fundamental changes I wanted have started to happen now. I find that quite ironic, really.' His eyes glazed for the merest split second; when they refocused, I had never seen them look so sharp. 'I am not happy and I never will be. The top English coaches must want to work at Bath [a point Clive Woodward would reiterate when he joined the club to work with Andy Robinson]. The players are bloody awkward and bloody-minded, but they have outstanding talent. I will continue to feel angry about the waste of potential.'

The waste of potential was something that the club were throwing back at Ashton. He had been involved in the grave error of rotating the squad, he had perhaps forced the pace in terms of Bath's revolutionary style – by 'revolutionary' in England I mean 1995 in New Zealand – and he had played his part in some downright poor selection decisions such as Henry Paul's out-of-position choice as wing for that crucial European Cup defeat in Cardiff. That match was being used as a weapon in the propaganda war which Bath were losing badly in the media. Ashton was unanimously declared the aggrieved party. The club did have a point, but the greater blame for Bath's various demises lay with them, not with Ashton.

The lack of a job description, good, bad or indifferent, underlined the hurried amateurism with which Bath had hurled themselves into the cauldron of professionalism. Eventually the management drew up a proposal which Ashton believes illustrated the similarity of his and Hall's roles. If the head coach thought two was a crowd, Bath confused the issue further by appointing a playing administrator. 'It was something the director of rugby should be. We had too many Indians and not enough Chiefs.'

Ashton was adamant that his lack of responsibility in the contractual side of playing affairs undermined whatever his position was supposed to be. He denies any involvement in signings, with the exception of that of Jason Robinson from Wigan. Without Ashton's input, it is difficult to understand how the club could arrive at any scale of value. If a player asked Ashton why he was being paid less than another, it was Ashton's responsibility to explain why he was less important. That, at least, was the coach's view. It can be perceived as naive. Professional sport is a hard world, and if Bath could drive a good bargain and sign a player cheaply, well, that's the nature of the beast. Swift believed Ashton lacked the hard edge of realism to be considered Bath's director of rugby; his thoughts on this subject partially underline the thoughts of the ex-winger.

What was indefensible were Ashton's protestations of an undermining ignorance. 'Dan Lyle and Brian Cusack appeared at the club from nowhere. I thought Tuigamala was coming.' Feelings of impotence surrounded his position. As coach of the team, it would have made sense for Ashton to have had the crucial input into the personnel who were the cutting edge of his vision. Of course, he did talk through positional issues with John Hall, but 'I never felt that what I was saying would be an undue influence on anything that might happen. Even though I knew Mendez was a possible recruit, I couldn't quite reconcile the priority for him rather than a second row where we had no real cover for Redman. I wonder whether we were pushed into Mendez because of the public perception of the front five after the Pontypridd game.' That is a terrible indictment; such leadership qualities may have been the trademark of John Major's Tories, but at Bath such weakness had always been reviled.

In the area of selection Ashton was even more bemused, bewildered and embittered. He had earlier called the advent of the European Cup as the single most important development in the history of the club game (barring professionalism); little did he know that the tournament marked the watershed of his days at Bath. It was the beginning of the end. Prior to the tournament, Ashton and Hall had rotated the squad. It had irritated the senior players, who believed that a Bath shirt was a privilege to be fought for rather than shared. It helped deprive the team of some competitive edge and undoubtedly contributed to the unsettled start to professionalism. Ashton played a major part in the creation of a system that was anathema to Bath's meritocratic traditions. Ashton accepts a hefty share of the responsibility for the débâcle.

But Bath's main eye was on the European Cup, the trophy that inspired their dreams which were nearing satiation with league and cup doubles. Hall and Ashton decided it was time to revert to old Bath. Ashton remembered a statement spelling out Bath's selectorial commitment to a regular full-strength team. Yet after their first win over Edinburgh, there were six or seven changes. It is with horror that he recounts the selection meeting before that first match. 'John came into the meeting and said, "We don't want this to last long, do we?"' Ashton's forehead wrinkles at the memory. 'If any selection was important it was that one. We were supposedly picking a team for the next three or four matches. We should have been ready to take three or four hours if necessary.' That appears to be a seminal point in the growing disaffection of an Ashton already distressed by what he perceived to be a new-found amateurism in the professional age.

'For selection we were supposed to meet at Lambridge for 6 p.m. That hardly ever happened. The selection team was John Hall, myself, Phil de

Glanville, Ged Roddy and John Palmer [one of Bath's most brilliant centres and the current coach of the second team]. Well, JP only attended the first meeting. He had no input after that, although some second-team players are internationals themselves. Sometimes it was John and me, once it was John alone. Phil was sometimes there, and Robbo [Andy Robinson, who would eventually take Ashton's role] – which was sensitive, as he was fighting for a place himself. Ged came to the first one and never came again . . . Sometimes it was almost a spur-of-the-moment, back-of-a-packet-of-fags approach. I thought to myself, "Christ, we are dealing like this with full-time professionals, guys whose livelihoods are dependent on us."' Not the sort of picture to sit comfortably in the National Gallery.

One telling comment Ashton also made was that he had an input into selection 'as far as backs are concerned. Mind you, the way they were playing any fool in England could have picked them.' Before the end of Bath's European dream in Cardiff, Ashton selected Henry Paul, the union novice, out of position on the wing. That mistake probably cost him the backing of Tony Swift, possibly the one man who could have arrested the rupture between Ashton and the club. Ashton's visionary ideals were a contributory factor to his own demise.

If the management were not yet aware of Ashton's disaffection, they became so during a meeting of playing management held in Lyme Regis. He attended this meeting with Swift, who chaired it, Ed Goodall, John Hall, Ged Roddy and, perhaps significantly, Andy Robinson. He was, admittedly, a forwards coach, but primarily he was contracted to the club as a player. Ashton thought the meeting should not involve the actual playing staff. He claims to have raised all the issues which have just been covered. He also realised that 'Everyone in the room realised we didn't have a job description. Pretty impressive for a business.'

It appears that Ashton returned from the Dorset sojourn steeled for departure. 'After Lyme Regis, nobody came near me to discuss my concerns.' It was that feeling of isolation and unwantedness again. 'I then put my proposals to Tony and Ed Goodall. We agreed to keep them quiet so I could continue to coach. I walked into the office first thing the next Friday morning and Andy Robinson, with Ged Roddy, said, "What the bloody hell is happening?" Phil de Glanville also found out. He was with the England camp preparing for Argentina [the captain was injured for this game]. He said he would return for an emergency meeting and obviously informed his vice-captain, Jason Leonard, so the whole England squad knew. On the eve of the Test match, Jon Sleightholme phoned me at home. I told him to concentrate on the England game and that it wasn't his problem.'

That made it untenable for Ashton to prepare Bath for the forthcoming match against London Irish and so he took the year's most heralded week's holiday. Bath did not reply in any hurry to his proposals. Ashton's mind reverted to his 'officeless' beginning at Bath. When the club management informed him that it would be sorted out some time in the new year, Ashton concluded that his services were definitely not a priority to the club. Reluctantly he handed in his resignation and Bath had lost the most innovative coach in the country.

The Lancastrian received widespread sympathy as the media were openly incredulous at Bath's willingness to lose him. The club faced a crisis of credibility within the media. It was not as one-dimensional as 800 newspaper words generally tend to make matters seem. Ashton had his faults and must share some responsibility for the nosedive on the field. But the greater problem had been that of management. If the right structure had been in place from day one, Ashton's shortcomings could have been avoided, allowing those undoubted coaching talents to illuminate the Georgian city.

The club were demonised near the back page of every national newspaper, on the terraces and within the muttering ranks of the diehards who remembered the 'good old days' of amateurism, when Rowell and his team's omnipotence on the field left them free to manage themselves however they wished.

It is a savage irony that the greatest mistake made by the Brownsword organisation was the assumption that the one area of management where new standards would not be needed was on the pitch. Bath were regarded as being as professional on the pitch as they had once been amateur off it. Brownsword was not the only person making such assumptions. Bath's non-executive chairman Tony Swift, a stalwart for over a decade, reached the same conclusion, as he openly admits. 'It did not cross my mind that the management team on the field were lacking. Maybe that was naive. Last year I only watched two games, so I was off the pace. As far as I was concerned we had won the double. What more could be done to prove a point?'

Swift has a point, but the previous season's double had been won with an amateur squad of players. Demands were very different. Neither John Hall nor Brian Ashton had a great deal of business-management skill, and that was part of the new era. As an accountant who has spent a great deal of time working on corporate planning, Swift's oversight has to be regarded as disappointingly surprising. In his defence, Andrew Brownsword had only asked Swift to become non-executive chairman at the start of his tenure in charge. His was the role of the figurehead. He was expected to work a half-day a month, attend board meetings and listen. 'I was not expected to stand there and say, "By the way, things are not right."'

But who was? The playing side within management lacked management skills, the management of the club were devoid of playing skills . . . and so Andrew Brownsword's board began life in limbo. Swift is quick to defend any early management error. 'I do not see how the Brownsword people could have expected to know that problems in team management could have arisen from a team just off a double. I do not think it was possible for them to get that close that quickly.'

Ed Goodall's understandable lack of knowledge and the equally understandable irritation he caused the playing side of management were not necessarily primarily the fault of the individuals involved, but instead a sure sign that the most fundamental element of management, the choice of key personnel, was on a par with Bristol's back play.

In hindsight, the changes within the club were so dramatic that it needed a certain type of person to comprehend and oversee them. Tony Swift was one of the few people to fit the bill. 'Clearly I am not the only person in the world with business acumen and likewise I am not the only person with some rugby knowledge, but there were not many people around Andrew Brownsword at the time who possessed a bit of both.'

Instead, Ed Goodall carried the mantle of chief executive. He could have sat in a thousand team meetings but he would still struggle to understand the rights and wrongs of managing a rugby team. To a business that must prioritise the pursuit of silverware, this was folly.

Bath's stated objective in the 1996–97 season was the European Cup. When Cardiff ended that dream, Brownsword acted belatedly. That was when Swift was asked to look at the playing side. His early-season fears were realised. 'I knew we had two problems. The style of play was crap, but I wasn't brought in to be a rugby guru. As non-executive chairman at that time I couldn't interfere; it was not my role. The use of the squad system was wrong [something both Ashton and Hall belatedly admitted], but, far more importantly, the preparation of the team was very poor. Forget the results and the style: day in and day out the preparation of our team was very, very poor. That has to come down to bad management; you cannot just blame the players.'

On 16 December, the evolution of Tony Swift from sinecure figurehead to full-time chief executive began with Andrew Brownsword asking him to work two days a week. The Ashton crisis was beginning to blow a storm as Swift shifted career from chartered accountant to full-time fire-fighter. He believed that Ashton's mind was already made up before his resignation. 'I had my suspicions that Brian had decided to leave, but I thought it important that the club be seen to try and keep him.' These are significant words that echo with resonance: 'the club be seen to *try* and keep him'. There is a suspicion that Swift's disillusionment arising from what he saw as the lack of a professional structure made him less than enthusiastic about retaining the services of an undisputed premier coach. Ashton did not feel that Swift acted decisively enough if Bath really had wanted him, and Swift's comments sustain such a theory.

Ashton's departure was painful, whatever Swift believed. The Lancastrian who was about to become an Irishman had been the schoolmaster of the Lancastrian who would soon be chief executive of Bath. 'Since Andrew asked me to help with the Brian Ashton situation the whole thing has been a fucking nightmare. I have not enjoyed it at all. I have hated every fucking minute of it. It should be an enjoyable role, but it is all shit at the moment – and there is more to come.' These words were uttered on 17 February, a matter of days after Swift had dismissed his coach and friend John Hall from the post of director of rugby.

Hall's dismissal was the inevitable result of Swift's unhappiness with the absence of tight professional management within the playing structure. In the city, Hall's exit was linked to the legal charges that were hanging over his head. But the intensity of Swift's attitude to the management indicates that the decision was predominantly a professional one.

'There was a lack of professional leadership, the absence of an understanding of what the standards actually are. We had nobody looking at the team saying that the quality of the preparation of this team was dire. Nobody raised the stakes . . . to be honest, I don't think anybody knew what to do. There was a lack of cohesion between the people working in the team [although both Hall and Ashton have refuted such assertions in print] and there was a lack of right people. For example, not having a full-time fitness coach was a crucial area in which we were weak.' It was no surprise that Ged Roddy's head was already on the way to Versailles as Bath scoured the rugby world and beyond for that full-time coach. In the end they signed New Zealand guru Jim Blair. As Pat Fox, another Kiwi fitness adviser, had delivered such an edge to Wasps (their superior fitness was a prime reason why they deprived Bath of three league points), that is probably one of the better decisions made by Bath in the last 12 months.

But the headline-making decision was the one that tore the heart from one of Bath's greatest players and loyal servants. John Hall had his career at Bath terminated the Monday after another crushing loss for England's ailing champions – this time a humiliating home cup defeat at the hands of their greatest English rivals, the Leicester Tigers.

Again the media accused Bath of acting like a panic-stricken football team; again Swift rebuffed the claim. 'It is true that the final decision was made after that defeat but it was not because of the fact that we lost. That game with Leicester was indicative of the problems we had seen before. If we had seen a team that was brilliantly prepared run on to the field and fuck up there is no way this would have happened. But the reality is that the lack of preparation of the team was becoming debilitating as far as performances on the field were concerned . . . so what do you do? I did not think there was an option. I had talked to Peter Wheeler [chief executive at Leicester] about the professional approach his guys had been taking. Anybody who thought team management no problem was wrong.'

Hall's case was not helped by an interview with Graham Simmons of Sky Television in the aftermath of the Leicester defeat. Hall diagnosed a lack of passion in the Bath team as the main fault on the day. Swift was furious. 'After Leicester it was said there was a lack of passion in the Bath team, as if that is the players' fault. It is not, though, is it?' It was, in fact, an awful lot more than merely lack of motivational skill. Bath, the tightest outfit in England, had indulged in a game of follow the leader. If Richmond, Harlequins or Newcastle signed a big name, so did Bath. The signing of the Wigan duo was a fundamental flaw in the thinking of the Bath camp. Americans and Argentinians arrived to boost the squad, but at the transparently glaring price of stretching the once-mighty team spirit to breaking-point. The unspoken bond that held Bath together had snapped in the pressure of the first year of rugby professionalism.

In the bar after the game, Bob Dwyer, the Australian in charge of Leicester, was amazed at just how 'nice' the Bath boys were in defeat. He would have been devastated if his men had reacted in such a balanced way. Steve Ojomoh stressed that Leicester won because 'They wanted it more'. If a sixteenth-century Pope had said, 'Actually, you know, that German guy called Luther is probably right in his theological beliefs,' he could not have been perceived as more heretical. Great teams lack maturity and balance where it matters: in the heart.

Hall has to take some of the blame for the radical change in the mentality of the Bath team, but Swift claims it was anything but impulsive. 'I'm not blaming anybody for doing something purposefully wrong. I'm just saying that the quality of the team management has not been good enough. You cannot say that Bath made too hasty a decision on Hall's departure.'

It may not have been hasty, but it was agonisingly painful for Swift to tell Hall. The two men had been comrades in the days when friendship and spirit counted for more than money and the size of a squad. Their respective partners were close friends in a small city. There will be few harder decisions for a rugby man ever to make. This was not a case of dropping a player; this was linked to far wider issues. Hall had just purchased a new home and was preparing for marriage in the summer; suddenly the future was shrouded in doubt. Swift had to break the news. 'I have been lucky in my personal life. I have had no deaths to deal with, but with this, it was embarrassing. I was so upset that I could hardly speak. I was alone in the room with him and I could hardly get it out. I was holding back the tears. By the time I arrived in the office I had suffered a sleepless night and was totally fucked off, but I would have felt even worse if I had not been the one to break the news.' Here was professional sport in all its fickle horror. As we spoke, Swift complimented Hall on being 'great about it afterwards, but I suspect John's getting a load of people saying, "You have been badly treated, shafted, screwed." I think his views will harden.' Rugby is not a matter of life and death, but it is a business now and, like business, it carries what can be a brutal price. The appeals of amateurism can look wonderful to those on the losing side.

Instead of replacing Hall with a new director of rugby, Bath promoted Andy Robinson to head coach and brought in Clive Woodward, the former England centre and co-coach with Robinson of the Under-21 national team, to work alongside him. Swift's rugby knowledge as chief executive was designed to remove the need for the extra step in the ladder of the playing management. He was required to take an informed overview: 'As Peter Wheeler said, you appoint people to let them get on with the job.' How ironic that Andrew Brownsword initially appointed a chief executive who the playing side felt did not know the job and a management team on playing affairs who Swift believed lacked requisite management skills.

Swift was the off-centre objective voice of reason. 'My view is to give them what they need and raise the stakes by asking, "Are we going for the best?"' On the playing side he was keen to redress the balance between loyalty and the chequebook. While admitting that Bath would sign if the right man came along, he emphasised that 'The focus has to be, in the next six to 12 months, to get the very best out of the players we have. The focus is on maximisation. If you buy a great player and you do not have the right internal structure, he won't be a great player for long.' In the professional world of Bath, John Hall and Brian Ashton probably have the right to ask the same questions on the subject of coaches and managers.

Deprived of success in the European and Pilkington Cups, Swift and company had targeted the league as the new focus. Bath were 5–1 third favourites, and Swift admitted that it was a quiet priority. 'I want us to go for it without putting everything on the line. I don't want to say to the players "It doesn't matter" because it does, but laying foundations is the most important thing.'

It was a tall order, but Swift remembered that Bath had been 'here before'. He was referring to the first year of the Courage League, back in the distant amateur days of 1988, when Bath last failed to win a trophy because of 'a failure to adapt'. The ex-wing smiled as he admitted, 'Of course, it's higher profile now, with more dosh and more at stake, but . . .' At this juncture I wondered why he had agreed to leave the relative comfort of the accountancy firm where he was a partner for the knife-edge of rugby's new era. Swift was actually retaining his place in the practice as all consultancy fees from his '70 hours a week' at the club were being ploughed into the firm.

A lot of people in Bath questioned Swift's sanity for deserting the company audit sheets for the brave new world of rugby madness. I always thought accountancy was the last refuge of dull normality. God bless Swifty, he was proving me wrong. 'In some respects you can say that Bath have been at the top of the tree for so many years that you can only lose. In other respects it doesn't feel like that because there is so much room for improvement. There is huge scope for improvement as long as there's an investor who is backing the pursuit of excellence. If that's the case, then I think it's a bloody exciting role.'

Swift was not the only former player to consider his new situation an exciting one. Andy Robinson, Bath's battle-scarred vegetarian, had been a schoolmaster at Colston's School in Bristol less than a year previously. That security had been scorned for the challenge of joining the first wave of rugby union professionals. Now, as Bath's imperial pretensions were apparently crumbling, Robinson had accepted the even-more-tenuous position of Bath coach. The poisoned chalice had already accounted for Brian Ashton and John Hall, but Robinson grasped the nettle, either fearlessly or insanely. I will let you judge that one. It was 12 months that changed his world, but Robinson shrugged off his dramatic transformation with a tranquillity that was diametrically opposed to his frenetic playing style. 'It was not that big a shock to get the job. I could see it coming. My life has been a bit like that. Suddenly something comes up and you're in the right position to take it. You can either say, "Look, I'm sorry, I need two years to develop, I'm not ready to coach the club" – or you dive in. I was keen to take the plunge.' And so Robinson, as brave in life as he was on the bottom of a ruck, plunged into the terrifying depths of the Bath coaching role. 'I hate talking about "if onlys" and Sam [Robinson's wife] was supportive throughout. There is a time to go for it, and this is the right time.' That is an incredibly courageous statement considering the Robinsons' fourth child was *en route* to the world and the West Country.

His appointment had been in the face of perceived wisdom. Bath, accused of endless insularity, had appointed a man not even retired from the playing side to replace another who had generally struggled to keep his distance from erstwhile friends. The appointment of Nigel Redman on to the coaching panel only caused more eyebrows to raise. The advantage that Robinson held over Hall, however, was experience. He had witnessed the all-too-human pitfalls at first hand. 'I understand my limitations. I know that I am still involved with the players but I know I can take a sideways step. I am also aware of the people who reckon we are too insular, especially with the appointment of Ollie [Redman] and myself. That is why Clive Woodward is so important; he is the balance.' Woodward's extra experience was another factor that Robinson recognised, and Bath will miss him now that he has left them to fill the vacancy left by Jack Rowell at Twickenham. Bath still have Robinson, however: 'I have a lot of learning to do as a coach, but I think I understand the game of rugby, the needs of Bath rugby and the way to play a winning game. That is important to Bath Rugby Club. Success is paramount.'

That success is paramount has been the unspoken truth since the days of Jack Rowell. The reality of this demand had resulted in the demise of Hall. Robinson undoubtedly faced an easier task. Bath's ambitions remained, but the majority of the club, from Swift downwards, were realistic. They did not believe the championship could be salvaged from Bath's wreck of a season. Expectations were lower and previous lessons, however painful, had been learned. Like Hall, Robinson was a rookie in terms of management skill; unlike Hall, his working environment was comfortable. John Allen, Bath's first-team secretary, the silent man behind the team, watched matters from a distance. He had seen Hall manage Bath to a double in the last days of amateurism. 'He did a bloody good job that season. He was excellent [an opinion with which Swift had concurred back in the lost summer of 1996] until he became director of rugby. Then he appeared to become totally stressed out. The club wanted an overall director, not just a players' man.' Hall's management training came too late to save him from Bath's initial folly of creating a top tier of management with no experience of playing affairs. Swift's appointment was a sign that Andrew Brownsword had belatedly recognised the problem, and this helped Robinson. 'I am learning about the management side, dealing with players and my relations with "the suits". I like my relationship with Swifty; it's developing well.' Hall never had that opportunity.

The problems that could develop with being too close to the players had also been signposted by the unfortunate Hall, Bath's unlucky pioneer of the new age. Robinson was aware of the importance of creating a distance between himself and his team off the field, but the ghosts of his playing days were still there to haunt him. 'The biggest problem I have is telling players not to concede penalties. I tell them how important this discipline really is, but too many know that I had the highest penalty count in the team.' Robinson laughs at the forced hypocrisy before musing further on the new relations with old comrades. 'It is a challenge working out what Guscott is thinking. If I was worried about someone upsetting me it would probably be Jerry, what with his profile and ability to put you down. He asks the odd question at team meetings, saying "What do you mean by so and so?", testing me in front of the boys.'

In the best tradition of the boot-room philosophy, Robinson is devoted to the passion and integrity engendered by the loyal and longer-serving players. Bath blood runs deep in the Somerset man, and he expects such pride from every team member. One of the first and most symbolic decisions made as coach was the dropping of Bath's world-class hooker, Federico Mendez, for Graham Dawe, the hugely respected Cornish man of granite. Dawe is a creature from a distant time when the laws of survival in rugby union were harsh. John Allen recalls Kevin Yates, a talented young prop forward, complaining about the treatment which his opposite number had administered throughout one particular game. Steaming in the dressing-room, Dawe took the rhetorical high road: 'What did you do about it? Fuck all, so stop whingeing and whining.' Dawe is a hard man with a hard edge. Robinson likes that. 'Dawesy added that little bit of spice that only front-rowers know about. By playing him I wanted to force Mendez to regain that spice.'

The imposing Argentine was just one of Bath's high-profile signings who Robinson believed had been shown the door to the first-team changing-room too easily. He pined for the days when a Bath shirt was a prize. Nigel Redman had made this point in the autumn. 'I wanted to instil the need to fight to make the team. Just because someone is paid a lot of money, they should not regard a place as their right. Maybe too many thought, "Hey, they wouldn't pay this sort of money to keep me in the second team." Now they know that whoever they are and whatever they are paid, if someone is performing better, they will not play. It bodes well that players know that's how it will be from next year.

'It was right to strengthen the squad, but we made it too easy for them. I was involved in the selection process before becoming coach. I didn't want to push myself, but I expected Hally to say to me, "You should play." Some players, like Dan Lyle, were given the treatment – he spent months getting shit from us all – but too many came straight in. The mistake we made was not sticking with the successful team from the previous year for the first month or so, then making changes if there were problems.' A Bath shirt is not regarded lightly by Robinson.

Only through sweat and blood did Robinson see Bath's shining heritage remaining. He had seen too much of professionalism's downside. 'I hate that "professionalism" which leads people to think, "We have lost, but we are professionals. Tomorrow is another day; we'll be back." We must reassert the fact that winning is paramount. When you play on that pitch you must hate to lose.' Robinson even sympathises with his old sparring rival Neil Back, who missed several months of the season due to an infamous shove that sent the referee of the 1996 cup final, Steve Lander, on to the turf after a controversial late penalty-try decision had deprived the Tigers of victory. 'I have sympathy with what Neil Back did to Lander; I respect it in a perverse way. Place yourself in that position, with all that pain . . .' It is through careful resurrection of team spirit and respect that Robinson believed Bath could rediscover that intangible will to win.

The coach had the perfect model for his new Bath: the old amateur one. 'I don't think that our players currently match the old lot. Those earlier teams would run on to the pitch and we believed that we would win, whatever and whoever we were against. We could always convince ourselves. I am desperate to recapture that. If we do, we will win ten games out of eleven. The mental game is the winning one. My greatest task is far more mental than technical. The players have enough technique. I want winners and the hunger to win. That is what I know. That is what I was brought up on.'

Robinson articulated his beliefs one day before Bath faced Leicester in a game that Bath started as 20–1 outsiders for the league. But Robinson's compelling competitive nature burned through. Asked if he felt that the league was beyond his team, he glowered, 'People in Bath may have said Bath cannot win the league [Phil de Glanville had conceded the point a week earlier], but I believe we will win it – and I will continue to do so until Wasps have enough points to make it impossible. I have deliberately talked about the lesser target of qualification for Europe to take the pressure off.' This was anathema to every Bath team of the Rowell era. They *only* thrived on the pressure of the last-chance saloon. But Robinson defends what for Bath was almost an admission of mental weakness. 'Best teams create their own pressure and at present we have not reacted well to it. We become too insular. We are a better team with the pressure off. Pressure, to work, must come from within, not from outsiders. In the past, we created our own pressure that frightened us and we played in fear of losing.' It was much easier then. Amateur sportsmen walked the tightrope without the safety net of a salary. There was no other possible reason to train in the cold and wet if it was not for the glory . . . sport was not a job, it was a passion. The average professional sporting team regards itself as another part of a corporate entity. Paradoxically, that belief is seriously unprofessional. Bath, under Robinson, had to rediscover that missing element if they were to defy the Wasps and Tigers who were attempting to storm the ramparts of the empire's once-impregnable walls.

Robinson had been captain for two of those years and yearned to rekindle those fires. 'We were the best not so much because of the talent, but because of the friendship. We pulled together. We felt all of England hated us, which bonded us even more [even though the club realised this 'hatred' was at times a form of mass hypnosis within the dressing-room – the sort favoured by Alex Ferguson of Manchester United]. We were single-mindedly prepared to win in adversity.'

Such martial musings had appeared more the stuff of daydreams in the first few weeks of Robinson's reign. Unconvincing wins against two of the table's strugglers, London Irish and West Hartlepool, were followed by defeat against Sale. This represented the club's nadir. Sale had rested four key players and had not fully recovered from the hangover of a famous cup semi-final victory against Harlequins. Bath were encamped on their line for a full 15 minutes without scoring or releasing the ball to Guscott and friends behind the scrum. In adversity, Bath had reverted to the worst traits of English rugby: conservatism. Clive Woodward, still treading carefully, made his first impact. 'It was so bloody awful that I had to say something. We were heading nowhere.' Robinson also spoke with Brian Ashton, who was stunned by the absence of the occasionally excessive swashbuckling style of his former charges. A decision was made. Bath would throw caution to the four, five or even six winds. If the season was to end without a trophy, the club decided it would end with a bang.

Bath travelled to Loftus Road, the new home of Wasps. The London team were league leaders and the bookmakers' favourites. Watching Bath prepare before the match I could see why. Where once Bath teams would not have acknowledged a brother or a best friend in the opposition ranks before kick-off, here they chatted as if over the garden wall. John Allen remembers how much such innate decency irritated Robinson's predecessor, John Hall, at a time when that cutting edge should be foremost. 'He was in the changing-room, looking on to the pitch, watching the Bath boys chatting with the other team, and he said, "Look at those bastards, laughing and joking" – before ordering them back in.'

The two players who were unusually quiet were Lawrence Dallaglio and Jeremy Guscott, two of the consummate professionals within the English game. But Bath seemed set to defy appearances as they stormed into a clear lead until Wasps, through a combination of will and fitness on their part and an absence of control on Bath's part, scored a last-second try, which Gareth Rees coolly converted to snatch a vital point. It maintained Wasps' championship momentum, but it almost exterminated the hopes of Bath. Within seconds of the final whistle, the television cameras closed in on Phil de Glanville, smiling with a Wasp. It told the tale of Bath's season. The nasty ogres had become fuzzy, unfocused good guys – but not winners. Robinson was unimpressed with such social niceties, but explained the strange sight in a different way. 'That was an important moment for the club. It emphasised just how awful a season it had been and how great our resignation was. We used to mock teams that were now outsmarting us. To celebrate a draw at Wasps showed the extent to which we had lost our ambition, and against Sale we had played with no ambition.'

By this stage, Tony Swift was thinking more about Europe than about the title. By that criteria, Bath had encouraged greatly with the nature of their 25–25 draw. Robinson's post-match emotions were a combination of satisfaction at that encouragement and, primarily, fury. He harangued the referee for giving Wasps a dubious penalty award which had led to the try. In front of the television cameras he called the result a loss. In his ultra-competitive mind, his numbing disappointment equated to loss. As he entered the changing-room to talk with the players, he admitted that 'the only thought going through my head was how did the referee give that penalty? That is a point lost.'

But amidst his emotional wreckage he saw a light, perhaps the brightest of the season, at the end of Bath's gloomy tunnel. 'I was in the changing-room and it was silent. What could I say? "We didn't deserve to lose, we had played well"? They didn't want to hear that. They just sat there without saying a word for 15 minutes. That was the start of something.'

Nobody else rated Bath's title hopes, but hope trickled eternal in Robinson's battling heart. On the eve of the Leicester game, unrestrained, relaxed and not selected by himself, he sipped some burgundy in Bath's most disreputable and roguish restaurant (and obviously the best), The Beaujolais. I asked him if he thought Bath would beat Leicester, the team that had already beaten them twice during this troubled time. His answer was unequivocal. 'I believe that we believe we are the best. I believe that we will produce an outstanding performance.' This was the old-fashioned Bath conviction. It was no vain boast. Leicester, in pursuit of the double which only Bath have won, were lacerated by the brilliance of Bath. The Tigers lost 47–9 as the sun shone with unseasonal strength over the Abbey. Bath believed that their winter of discontent was nearing its welcome end.

The supporters found the smile that had been missing for months. Suddenly fans asked about the result of the Wasps match with Saracens. The unthinkable was being thought; Bath were anxious to retain their title. The trickle became a spring-tide torrent of hope: 'We could yet win the league.' Wasps, in fact, beat Saracens and were left to win two out of their last three games to win the title. The odds were heavily on their side. But for Tony Swift, consigned to Europe, it was consolation to

Tony Hallett, then secretary of the RFU and a former Navy man.
There would be no plain sailing

Brittle by name, but not by nature . . .

A familiar Scott Gibbs charge; an unfamiliar Welsh win in Edinburgh

Back to normal: the Irish celebrate another dead-end Welsh renaissance

Olivier Merle, the French team and every wine grower in France erupt in joy
at Twickenham

Tim Stimpson scores for England as Wales's Farewell to Arms ends on a flat note
for the Welsh

Jack Rowell, England coach and bon viveur, wonders whether that French comeback cooked his goose

Andy Robinson, former Bath player and current coach. Out of the frying pan . . .

. . . and into the fire, as he replaces John Hall,
a pioneer victim of the new professional age

All smiles for Tony Swift in his playing days. As chief executive at Bath, there were to be a few tears as well

A prophet without honour in his own land, but Guinness on tap in the Emerald Isle for Brian Ashton

An English rose with a Chianti nose: Lawrence Dallaglio of Wasps,
England and the Lions

consider another of Robinson's remarks from the day before: 'I am so excited by next season. I want it to happen straight away.' Smiling, he reminded me of the inaugural year of the Courage League. That had been a decade previously. It was the last year in which Bath had failed to win a trophy. The prophets had predicted the end; the next year Bath won the first double. Robinson persisted in title dreaming; others were happy to drink their cider, ready to believe that this swallow of a performance was ready to make the 1997–98 season a sweltering summer of success.

The players believed that the club had turned a corner. A title might not have been around it, but a place in Europe awaited them. Orrell, sadly relegated, were 40-point victims before Sale, resting almost their entire first 15, were defeated by a Bath team eager for revenge following the defeat at Heywood Road. The margin of 84–7 hinted that Bath were on course to rediscover the elixir of success that had been carelessly lobbed from the cupboard earlier in the season.

The irrational obstinacy that had been Bath's trademark in the glory years of amateurism was rekindled in the worn but animated face of Andy Robinson. Even as Bath were avenging their defeat at Heywood Road, Robinson was suffering terrible pangs of pain. The 84 points were to no avail. News arrived that Wasps had won at Northampton. The title that Robinson believed Bath could somehow save had slipped from their grasp. The champions were dethroned. The European Cup, the Pilkington Cup and the Courage League had all eluded Bath. They had paid a heavy price for those long winter months of mismanagement and misdirection.

Yet, while Robinson grieved the loss of the league title, the atmosphere elsewhere was far from overcast. Bath turned their eyes beyond this depressing season to the new challenge of regaining their crowns. In the depths of January the odds were on a total collapse. The fairy-tale or nightmare, depending on the colour of your shirt, appeared at an end. Hall's departure, laden with the symbolism of a bygone age, hinted at the end of Bath's era. In fact, by the time Bath faced Gloucester on a soft sunlit evening the day before the general election, the club glowed in the warm comfort that the denizens of Millbank must have been quietly feeling. Hall, Ashton and Bath's invincibility had been cruel victims, but Bath had finally found that elusive feelgood factor. Thank the forces of evolution that John Major did not.

Gloucester arrived in an unusually contented mood. Unlike Bath, they had achieved their objective – the slightly less ambitious one of survival – and one day earlier had received life-saving financial backing from Tom Walkinshaw, the owner of the Arrows Formula One racing team and boss of Damon, as well as Richard, Hill. Their season was over, but Bath were already gazing towards the autumn. The writing was writ larger than the graffiti on the walls as you enter Paddington by train.

Within two minutes, Andy Nicol (perhaps Bath's most underestimated player and one whose injuries had played a part in their free-fall season) had crossed a less-than-impregnable Gloucester line. It was to be a revelatory and joyous display of new-age rugby. Bath, with their 15 professionals, were playing on a different dimension from a Gloucester team laden with men who still arose at 6 a.m. for work. This was a hell of a lopsided playing field. Bath, who in the recent past had found it impossible to score three tries in a season against Gloucester, notched a trio in 12 minutes. It was psychedelic stuff, and the crowd, embittered throughout the year, loved every second. Sports fans are fickle; quick to disparage, they are even faster to forgive. The Bath fanzine, *Ere*, had been a focal point of discontent throughout the winter, but the last edition of the season was more *Coronation Street* than *Eastenders*. The reason? Bath's annihilation of their great rivals Leicester.

If the Tigers had usurped Bath, it is likely that the mood of comfortable acceptance of a trophy-less season emanating around the ground would have been different. Wasps were seen as mere guardians of the crown. The arrogance of the '80s and early '90s had resurfaced. Jeremy Guscott, rested after a magnificent season for Bath, watched the demolition of Gloucester from the press box. His smile told the tale of a team who had barely survived their tribulations but who, battered by confusion, ineptitude and inconsistency, had somehow done so, and now the players were breathing clean air. 'We were really down for a week or two after the Hally episode. Then we lost to Sale and thought, "Christ, this isn't our style." That was a turning-point.' The style with which Bath were blasting opponents aside bore intense similarities with the formula laid down by Brian Ashton. The difference was consistency of selection, an understanding of a concept with which the pack had been uncomfortable in the autumn, and, fancy as the suggestion may seem, an outbreak of a feelgood factor that was the exact opposite of the earliest days.

Guscott was infected with it. 'We can stuff the rest next season. When we play at pace, no one can live with us. The confidence is back, and we'll have a really good year.' New horizons. But even as he spoke, the deficiencies of this failed season unfolded once more on the pitch.

Gloucester scored a try, coasting through a Bath defence that had leaked too often. More symbolically, Federico Mendez, the Argentinian front-row forward, made an elementary handling error which the merciless travelling group of 'Shedheads' from Gloucester seized upon. The chant of 'What a waste of money' burst into life from the terrace. That is no indictment of Mendez, but a reminder of the fatal flaws that deprived Bath of so much spirit in the early part of the season. In the rush to match Harlequins, Newcastle, Richmond and Wasps, Bath had purchased the rugby league pair of Henry Paul and Jason Robinson and the Argentinian duo of German Llanes and Mendez. All are high-quality rugby players, but none understood the special ethos that separated Bath from other clubs. The misguided policy within the transfer market was a watershed in the club's mismanagement problems. But Bath had learned from their mistakes. This team played with a combination of flair and pride. It did, indeed, look ominous for the rest of the First Division.

On the touchline, Andy Robinson exchanged angry words with Richard Hill. West Country pride was alive and, for large parts of a combustible match, quite literally kicking. Within a few feet of the finger-pointing former colleagues sat the Bath physiotherapist, Julie Bardner. Tears were not far from her eyes as she managed the physiotherapist team for the last time in 12 years. These tears were not for the present. They belonged in the past. Her emotions were derived from the nostalgic recollections of the amateur days. The eternal truths about professional sport had confronted her and she had not enjoyed what she saw. 'The players are driven by money. It is no longer the same. The sense of fun and the sheer *joie de vivre* has disappeared.' That is the inevitable outcome of professionalism. These guys no longer looked as if they played for fun. Mike Catt was substituted near the end of a match that Bath had played at a blistering pace. Lean as a greyhound, he hardly puffed. You have to be fit for serious business. Robinson paced the touchline, urging his former playing colleagues forward. Every try was an orgasmic moment, every knock-on a personal slight.

Bath were playing at a different pace from any other team in England. Their failing was their inability to think at the same rate until the quest for trophies was a pipe dream for all bar Robinson. But the club were back on track. The first year of professionalism has changed Bath forever. The club will never hold the romance that enraptured me and so many others throughout my playing career at the Recreation Ground. Success will never be quite so sweet as Bath Rugby Club, a body of imperfect human proportions that in the past had a superhuman will to succeed, is replaced by a sense of corporatism that will value the magic spirit for the sake of winning. This is a different universe from the one where we worshipped that spirit for its own intrinsic worth. I wonder what the 1938 Bath team, beaten 10–3 by Weston Super Mare, would make of this new age?

Lawrence Dallaglio: A New Model Player

Off the field, it was the year of revolution, not evolution, to borrow from Jack Rowell's little box of phrases. Internecine strife between clubs, Celts and Saxons, and even members of that once most respectable of institutions the RFU tore, like a ravished crow, at the game's very soul.

Traditionalists and commercialists battled in the boardroom as journalists scratched their heads and wondered what the hell was happening. The civilised refinement of this rough-house sport disappeared into the mists of time, presumably sharing space with Welsh rugby glory. At least those of us earning incomes attempting to unravel the ever-changing puzzle could take consolation. Money makes headlines and rugby opinion was in demand. It was a profitable time to claim some understanding of the politics behind the scenes. It was also bloody frustrating, but we could spend our profits on booze – after all, that's part of the deal.

The players, so often the forgotten men in the press, were not so fortunate. Like hacks, beer was once a welcome and integral element of the sporting life. But with professional contracts had to come a change in lifestyle. Bemused and sober, the first generation of professional rugby players stumbled into the sport's new age.

Their metamorphosis was less chronicled than the tales of greed and cash. We have all churned through the hackneyed 'day in the life of a professional' piece, where players exaggerate the downsides and downplay the perks – but that has always been the case. The reality for the élite was something very much more radical.

Rugby superstars were a rare breed in the amateur days. Wales had them in the '70s, New Zealand and South Africa are full of them now, but in England, where rugby remains in the realm of Middle England, it is the Alan Shearers and the Paul Gascoignes who hog the headlines. Rugby has been too refined for the screeching shouting of tabloid fantasists. Will Carling was the exception, not the rule. He was extremely well managed by John Holmes, the man behind the images of Gary Lineker and David Gower, and the England captaincy proved a launch pad to national fame. Even Carling could not match the column inches of Gazza, until his trousers were, so to say, pulled down in public. But it was the late Princess of Wales who was the real *cause célèbre*; rugby and Carling were unwittingly driven to media megastardom. If the mother of the future king had fraternised with a dustman, feature editors would no doubt have taken an interest in our refuse workforce.

Carling was England's first rugby superstar, but with professionalism came the increased footlight coverage. Agents swarmed around a commodity that was priceless in its middle-class decency. Money was thrown at players: contracts, boot and kit deals, nude *Cosmopolitan* shoots. The world was suddenly their oyster, but for those who overreached themselves, the traps that had caught so many footballing stars awaited. Not so much oysters as giant clams.

Superstardom can carry a price. The bleary eyes, bleached nostrils and financial ruin of so many tells a cautionary tale. In the first year of professional rugby, new victims stood poised on the sacrificial altar of fame. As with Christ in the wilderness, the Devil stretched out his hand and offered temptations the likes of which a century of rugby players had never dreamed. As all devotees of the decadent are well aware, one of Satan's most successful temptation spots for sportsmen is London. 'Look at those bright lights burning in the casinos, the all-night clubs, the gorgeous girls, that wonderful food. What a party time.'

But Satan's bored. Footballers are a-dime-a-dozen conquests. Oh, for one of those 'nice rugby union chaps'. The time was right. And if the horned one could have chosen one man to lay his talons on, it would have been Lawrence Dallaglio, captain of Wasps and, as the season drew near, the punters' favourite to inherit the mantle of the England captaincy from Will Carling.

Dallaglio had the perfect CV for a sporting derailment. At 24 he has found success with ease. He was a World Sevens winner with England, a tourist to South Africa at the tender age of 22 and capped against those opponents a year later at Twickenham, aged a precocious 23. The comet was transformed into one of the brightest stars on English rugby fields.

Talent alone is not enough for the Devil; image is equally important. Dallaglio fits the bill. Tall, chiselled and with the requisite Latin allure that is rooted in his Italian blood, he can stand alongside Jeremy Guscott on the pantheon of rugby heart-throbs. Better still, the man started the season domiciled in Chelsea, that hedonists' heaven which puritans call hell, and, yes, he has a reputation as a party animal. On tour in South Africa, the not-so-callow youth breezed into the battle-hardened playboy club, a group that was dedicated to lifestyle above and beyond the call of duty. *In vino veritas*, and the truth is that Dallaglio loves a good time.

Fate was apparently conspiring to drive Dallaglio into the arms of the Devil. Wasps were once an unglamorous outfit based in the cracked-pavement suburb of Sudbury in north-west London. Hidden behind kebab houses, used-car garages and pizza parlours, it was no place for a sporting icon. Then Chris Wright, the owner of Chrysalis records, bought Wasps together with QPR and created Loftus Road plc. Okay, so Shepherd's Bush is not quite Chelsea, but Dallaglio was moving west, back towards the bright lights. Mighty Leicester approached Dallaglio, only to be told that the place and the individual were 'socially incompatible, no matter what the money'.

And to cap it all, Dallaglio had the time of the modern professional rugby player (plenty) and the money to burn (even more). A regular Wasps training day consisted on a Monday of a couple of hours conditioning in the morning for the 18 full professionals within the club. On a Tuesday, the excitement of a team drill or fitness session in the morning was followed by a break until the amateurs arrived for a seven o'clock session.

That is a lot of time to kill. Dallaglio was not concerned with the dual danger of boredom and novel amounts of cash that had changed the life of the former Kingston student. 'You have to keep yourself busy from the time you wake up until the end of training.' (It was pre-season, so the compulsory talk of rest and recovery was not quite ingrained in the rugby vocabulary.) As Dallaglio was in the process of buying a two-bedroomed flat in Notting Hill, the early weeks offered too few hours in the day. He was eager to complete the move to find the time for the ubiquitous 'odd round of golf'.

That may be a sporting cliché, but Dallaglio's attitude to the virtue of gambling reveals the more original side. 'I won't be spending too much time in the bookies and the pubs, like other professional sportsmen. I do my betting over the phone. There's nothing wrong with that and nobody knows what I'm losing.' The twinkle in the eye is evidence that we are not in the sad and painful realms of addiction in which poor Paul

Merson stumbled. Dallaglio has too much perspective and too much sense. There is a time, a place and a balance. It's an art form most sportsmen never quite manage to understand, but the 24-year-old Wasp had a clear vision. 'Generally, away from rugby I have fun. There is a need for distance when you're away from the game. When you return, it's not for a laugh and a joke, but for work. Just watch the best; they are focused, clinical and concentrated. Someone's paying a lot. They won't pay for long if they don't get results. You don't get results by pissing around in training.' That work ethic would carry Wasps to great things in this first professional season.

Mature as Cheddar. So too in the celebrity stakes. Any rugby player who could stretch a jockstrap started the new season under the wing of an agent. Dallaglio was signed up with a company called James Grant. Fellow rugby players Phil de Glanville, Andy Gomarsall and Alex King were also in these ranks, along with such esteemed celebrities as Zoë Ball and Anthea Turner.

Turner's husband, the former Radio 1 DJ Peter Powell, controls the operation and, in best populist tradition, these people are seriously nice. Their relationship with Dallaglio would prove as crucial to his development as a player as his ability to tackle. A partnership geared towards the short-term gain can flog a player on the altar of the supermarket opening. Both Ashley Woolfe, his own personal agent, and Dallaglio himself claimed a healthy wariness of the unbalanced approach to money. To their credit, the agents appeared more interested in the long-term development of their man; otherwise, they would probably have lost him. Dallaglio was worryingly awash with good sense. 'You must not lose track of the fact that you are paid to be a rugby player. Don't overbook yourself and make life too full to the detriment of your rugby. The spin-offs are all results of what you do on the field. There are dangers from agents who want to maximise you, and it's absolutely critical that you remain enough of an individual to be able to say "no".'

Cynics mutter that the player who is concerned enough to find an agent has his mind on things other than rugby, and that Dallaglio's 'you are paid to be a rugby player' could be construed as lip service. It is a view with which I would have concurred as recently as three years ago. But not now. Agents are responsible for an awful lot more than raising both profiles and pounds. Dallaglio has no doubts. 'They deal with a lot of unnecessary calls that rugby would not have seen a few years ago when the exposure was next to nothing. I am looked after in totality. You can't realise how good they are until you become so high-profile that they deal with lots of problems.'

One of the problems is the thorny issue of remuneration, especially if the person who wants a piece of a player's time is a lukewarm friend. Dallaglio has obviously had early experiences of the problem. 'Yeah, they say *how* much and then call you a bastard.' Dallaglio did not begrudge one single per cent of the 15 taken by James Grant for rendered services.

Pure common sense off the field, those faculties would be equally tested in his capacity as club captain. He knew that 'Captaincy is not something you learn overnight. I try and lead by example, and if I am playing well I expect the same from the people around me.' The Wasps challenge was intensified by the presence of a host of big-name recruits. It could not have been easy for a relatively inexperienced player to captain the likes of Tuigamala and Gareth Rees. But mention that and the man will bridle. 'Age is a complete irrelevance. So what if there are players much more experienced here? That's a help, not a hindrance. They have a lot to do before they impress me, and I've probably as much to do before I impress them.'

That maturity again. Dallaglio has always seemed to mix with older people, and that has left a confident mark on the man. He also has the horrific memory of the death of his sister, Francesca, aboard the *Marchioness* in that tragic Thames riverboat disaster. Rugby is easy to put in perspective alongside bitter tragedy.

And so the man who was widely tipped as Carling's successor led Wasps on to the field for their first match of the season against Sale. All the confident pre-season talk was inconsequential as Sale forged ahead. Wasps' director of rugby Nigel Melville was furious. 'We started so badly. We just waited for it to happen; it didn't, and we then tried to force our way out of the mess.' That sounds like a minor indictment of Dallaglio's on-field leadership. Melville was critical of his tactical naivety at the lineout. 'He called lineouts for the sake of them, rather than varying them.' Such inflexibility has been the bane of the English game, but, as Melville quickly pointed out, 'He will improve because he is willing to learn and to listen.'

Tactical issues were left in the air at Sale, but Dallaglio's exemplary leadership qualities were not. Melville again: 'He's extremely well motivated, and the greater the challenge, the better he is. He's okay against average teams, but the better the opposition, the more he plays.' As Sale improved, so too did Dallaglio, and Andy Gomarsall sealed a fine comeback with a last-second try under the posts. Dallaglio had his winning start, but he was unhappy. 'Look at the tackle count; I was in front of the rest.' From him, this is a positive statement, not a gauche display of arrogance. His men did not follow his example and he was not happy.

But the Wasps were buzzing, as was the name of Dallaglio. The EPRUC crisis was at its peak as the clubs withdrew players from the England squad. Whatever his hopes of captaincy were, Dallaglio was at the forefront of the players' views. 'I can say strong things, but the truth hurts.' Pick up a paper and the thoughts of Dallaglio were being aired. Like Carling, he had signed up to ghost a Sunday newspaper column; this one was with *The Sunday Express*. He was in dialogue with other captains, including Jason Leonard of Harlequins and Phil de Glanville. One of them had the imprint of a future England captain. Dallaglio made no excessive claims about how much he wanted that post, but his accessible profile hinted strongly.

There was one Dallaglio who travelled to watch Chelsea scrape a fortunate draw with Arsenal at Highbury, the one who was happy to chat late into the night in a Soho Chinese restaurant; there was the other who was working on the right image. Professionalism was about much more than 80 minutes. Dallaglio appeared at ease, but vague signs of immaturity were still evident. Graham Simmons, Sky Television's rugby reporter *par excellence*, noticed a nervous tendency to rock from foot to foot during an interview as if hiding some guilty secret, while the sentences flowed with all the ease and affectation of a meaningless soundbite. Dallaglio as a politician? Nah, the guy is far too decent.

Yet as the international season drew near and the announcement of Jack Rowell's new captain became ever more imminent, Dallaglio did change his stance. Suddenly the EPRUC man was stating that neither EPRUC nor the RFU should try and force the players to take sides. Fair enough, but a month earlier Dallaglio had been vociferous in his defence of EPRUC, the leading players' employers – as if somebody was advising, 'Hey, Lawrence, now is definitely not the time to rock the boat. That captaincy is worth, well, an awful lot of prestige and assorted goodies.' Image, image and more image.

Profitable is the life of an England captain. But Carling's private problems were a reminder of the pitfalls and problems of the high profile. Dallaglio was so concerned with tabloid publicity that the pregnancy of his girlfriend, Alice, was a matter of near state secrecy, for fear of tabloid involvement. Dallaglio and Alice were an elated couple, but the lurking worry about media intrusion prevented them sharing the information with even close friends.

The shadows of media attention gathered on the horizon, but Dallaglio's good start to the season continued to improve. Saracens were humbled in the much-hyped first Sunday match at Loftus Road, then came a titanic victory at Bath, before over 11,000 witnessed Wasps become the first team ever to defeat Bath and Leicester in successive league matches. A routine away win at Orrell, the early-season doormats, had Wasps sharing top spot with London rivals Harlequins. Lawrence Dallaglio and the Chris Wright roadshow were on the move.

They were flying, but then again, so was Icarus. He flew too near the sun; the wings of the Wasps were clipped in rugby union's red-hot-bed of earthy fanaticism, Gloucester. The proud West Countrymen were two points from the bottom of the table and immersed in talk of relegation.

Dallaglio was reminded of an old adage in that grey and grizzly English rugby city: pride comes before a fall. Dallaglio himself could have warned the younger element of the Wasps what to expect. Gloucester had ejected Wasps from the Pilkington Cup the previous season and, as Dallaglio readily admits, 'Good teams don't get away with playing badly at Kingsholm'. Bath, Leicester, you name them; all have fallen at Kingsholm in recent times.

Wasps were downed on a Sunday and Lawrence Dallaglio's year dipped into its lowest period. His character was to be severely tested. Six weeks later, locked into the Chelsea Ram (makes him sound rather like a cosmopolitan sheep shagger, don't you think? – and no, he is not!), he wondered whether the England captaincy had slipped from his grasp that October. As the media became more obsessed with the issue of Carling's successor, Rowell delayed his announcement. Officially the idea was to prevent his leader from becoming embroiled in the English civil war of the suits and blazers. Dallaglio had other ideas. 'I wondered whether he was shrewdly buying more time for himself, giving himself extra time to mull over the decision.'

We will never know the truth, but if the amiable half-Italian was right, his captaincy hopes rollercoasted to the bottom of the slope as Wasps slumped from the sublime to the ridiculous. Dallaglio has an impressively rounded perspective for a 24-year-old, but maturity is no replacement for experience. With experience, Dallaglio might just have prevented the slide. That was the view of the media; it was not necessarily that of Richard Hill, Gloucester's director of rugby. 'I could not believe that, after we had beaten them in the cup last year, the management left out Tuigamala and Sheasby. They had dismissed us and were looking to Europe. Had they been playing Bath or Leicester they would have selected them both.' To Hill, it was less Dallaglio, more the management that had engendered a fatal complacency. To his credit, the Wasps captain shouldered his burden of responsibility. 'Over the previous few weeks we had beaten Bath and Leicester. A bit of complacency had crept into the team, perhaps including myself.'

Dallaglio should probably absolve himself of Wasps' psychological blunders off the field, but it was a bad day on it. 'I set myself high standards and didn't achieve them. There was a lot of panic on the field. Expectations were high and we struggled when we found ourselves points behind after 20 minutes. Cool heads were missing.' Unfortunately, Dallaglio's was one of the most prominent heads. Hill recalls, 'Dallaglio became very frustrated and lost it himself, arguing persistently with the referee.' Watching from the stands was Jack Rowell.

Then came the European Cup, and still Wasps' complacency plagued them. It was a real Achilles' heel. The bookmakers fancied Wasps, but after two matches the dream was over, and the disappointment was intense. 'I felt the English clubs were better than the best of the Welsh. To a certain extent we have been forced to eat our words.' It was a late drop goal by Jonathan Davies of Cardiff which forced the literary feast upon the Wasps.

The nadir came a week later in Limerick, when Wasps were handed the famous Munster treatment and a 40-point beating. It was a defining moment for the Wasps skipper, and one that forced him to draw upon his Latin background. His words could have been uttered in a Sicilian bar: 'We had a lack of respect for them, as we had for Cardiff . . . when an Irish team puts 40 points on you it's a shambles, a disgrace. It's the lowest moment in my club career.' These are the sort of words you could imagine Pacino uttering to de Niro in some gangster movie.

Dallaglio, stung by adversity that even a winning Sunday at Limerick races could not dispel, had been taught a lesson. His memories of the preparation and match with Toulouse a week later are not even couched in northern European terminology. This was pure Italian. 'I told the boys that we had lost respect for each other. We'd lost respect for other members of the team and that was the reason we were playing so badly.' Toulouse did not heed his advice. 'They didn't show us any respect and everyone knows a wounded animal is most dangerous.' For a while I couldn't remember whether I was sharing a rioja with Dallaglio or a character from *The Godfather*.

Lessons were learned, but it was too late for Dallaglio and his faltering hopes of becoming the new England captain. Jack Rowell reverted to the bosom of Bath and, ironically, chose Dallaglio's stablemate at James Grant, Phil de Glanville. If Rowell was delaying the decision to allow himself more time to choose the right man, it was hard on Dallaglio. He was the front runner and it was he, more than any other player, who had to face the media music. He was home and hosed, according to most of the critics.

There is no doubt that Dallaglio suffered from the weight of expectation. 'I was not subjected to anything in a nasty way, but there was a lot of tension. There is no doubt that it was having an effect on my game and the way I was playing at Wasps. It was bloody unsettling. Every time I went anywhere, either professionally or socially, people would say, "So, you're the next England captain." It became almost debilitating and I thought, "God, announce it and get it out the way." I told myself that once it was over I could revert to refocusing my targets.'

Talk from Dallaglio of needing to refocus comes as a shock. He is a man who emanates road sense in his life. But the headlines had impaired his normally sound vision. 'It [the captaincy issue] was throwing me slightly. It was always hanging over my shoulder. I didn't read all the headlines, but I was aware that it was a persistent issue.' Considering that rumours were indicating a financial difference of £250,000 between being named as England captain and not, it is easy to sympathise with any loss of equilibrium.

But those who believed money to be the only issue were wildly erratic in their conjectures. Dallaglio wanted the job because he genuinely believed in his ability to succeed. As it is with all top sportsmen, money is a glorious accessory, a wonderful thankyou, but never the driving force.

He admits to a sense of disappointment, but will always maintain that it was far less than anyone imagined. We all read daily headlines, but Dallaglio was not writing them. Indeed, he quickly became sick of them. 'I did get fed up. I found it remarkable that one position in sport could generate so much hype and publicity. Football is the national sport, yet when Shearer was named England captain hardly anyone noticed the fact. There were no fanfares. A lot of it is linked to Carling – who he was and the fact he had been captain for so long. Not just what he did in rugby, but also what happened in his personal life. He created a monster, really.'

It is a pity that people believe everything they read. Instead of saying 'Well done, Lawrence, you're in the team to face Italy', locals of the Chelsea Ram were almost embarrassed to make eye contact and utter 'Bad luck about the captaincy'. As the rioja rolled down our throats, the utterances of another failed contender in the bid to replace Carling (for obvious reasons we will call this jovial fellow Mr Nobody) came back to Dallaglio: 'Never mind, Lawrence, at least we can still shag royalty if we want.' With that, the topic of conversation changed to Wasps' away match in Milan. Dallaglio drooled about the Italian love of wine, food and passion for life. Big Lol had survived his trial by newspaper.

The media's growing interest in rugby union has not been received with such phlegmatic good sense by all the parties involved in the playing of the game. Even as experienced and intelligent a man as Jack Rowell had taken two years before he realised that nothing can be achieved by railing against the columns that can be spiked. The England manager's wife, Sue, must read every daily and Sunday from cover to cover. Rowell has persistently claimed that he does not read the papers, but woe betide a hack who has raised his hackles.

The Wasps back-row forward is almost diametrically opposed in his relations with the Fourth Estate. 'No, I don't ignore the papers or the television. I've obviously had a swift rise since the 1993 World Cup Sevens and, because of the way my life was outside rugby [a reference to the tragic death of his sister], there was a honeymoon period which lasted a long time. Then there was our version of the presidential campaign for the England captaincy. Even though I did not earn the vote my profile had been hugely raised. I watched it grow, thinking, "Phorr, that's fine by me."'

There is little exceptional in these sentiments; we all love a high and popular profile. It is Dallaglio's reaction in adversity that sets him apart. 'Everyone knows when they have played well or badly. In this country the problem is that they only read the papers when they've done well. You have to accept criticism if you are prepared to accept the praise and all that goes with it; you have to take the rough with the smooth. After all, it's the press who have raised your profile in the first place. So I guess they are entitled to write what they want.' Dallaglio accepted that he had received easy treatment at this stage, but he was pretty adamant that any future private attack would not change his balanced opinions. 'If someone was to make a personal attack on me, I don't think I would send a horse's head round to their bed [very Cosa Nostra]. It has not happened yet so I cannot say for certain how I'd react, but I like to think that I'll be positive and turn it to my advantage by using it as a stimulation.'

Dallaglio and England's autumn campaign of international rugby was considered by many as more a case of simulation than stimulation. The British sporting public are in thrall to the tradition of the Five Nations tournament. That explains the nigh-on-incomprehensible persistent full houses for matches which traditionally mirror the eternal grey winter skies under which they are generally played. But when the opponents are newer rugby nations, Twickenham wears its Empire hat, expecting Britannia to put the foreigners to the sword with a dash of nineteenth-century dominance. Italy are amongst the foremost countries in this group of rugby nations. When the land of Dallaglio's father travelled to Twickenham, the pressure was on England to win and to win in style.

It can place an added personal pressure on a player, as Dallaglio admitted. 'Friends and colleagues who aren't educated in rugby matters expect you to win by 50 points.' He went on to recite a litany of fine Italian performances to prove the inaccuracy of such opinions. He touched on the deep difference between the autumn matches and the Five Nations. 'The Five Nations is about historical associations that have nothing to do with the game. It becomes more like a war. You know that whole thing about the Calcutta Cup. It evokes something that is missing when you play Argentina and Italy in friendly matches.'

It was fascinating to hear Dallaglio slip in the word 'friendly'. Professional or not, the players, like the supporters, remain infected by the old Five Nations fever. 'I'd certainly be lying if I said that the squad were not more pumped up for the New Zealand Barbarians game than the Italy game. The crowd, too; the atmosphere is so different from a home nations match. The crowd is under capacity, the West Car Park is not the same. In fact, I think it's a dying breed. There is a different crowd turning up now.' (Ignorant, as opposed to knowledgeable rugby Yahoos, I suppose.)

The match itself against Lawrence Dallaglio's spiritual home was satisfactory. No more and no less, but it had been a significant emotional matter for England's flanker. 'It would be crazy for me to deny that I was looking forward to Italy more than just any other international game. It's a special relationship for me . . . I'd like to think my Italian background influences me. I do not regard myself as fully British, it is as simple as that. I'm 100 per cent English as a rugby player, but through my parents I've been exposed to other things.' One is left with no doubt that

Dallaglio is rather prouder of his Continental parentage than, say, Michael Portillo.

He was not so proud of England's last autumn performance, a stuttering morass of mediocrity which left Twickenham trembling in righteous disaffection. A bunch of 'Argies' had nearly conquered Albion – the shame! Dallaglio had shared an indifferent afternoon with his colleagues. England's selectors compile the 'Good' and 'Bad' versions of each international performance. The Argentina match had the good version as the 20-minute warm-up, and the horror story as a one-hour main feature. It made grim viewing for rugby's professionals.

Before that humiliating viewing, the players had the silent ordeal of the post-match dressing-room. When a side has underachieved, even the jokers in the front row put a merciful end to the wisecracks. Some players will sit in a sunken posture for the best part of an hour, but that is not for England's finest Italian. 'I don't rewind the tape of the game in my head immediately. I was more disappointed after that game for the team than the way I played. I'm not one of those people who thinks, "I didn't have a bad game, so that's okay." That has nothing to do with the team at all.'

The newspapers dripped with vitriol. English supporters left Twickenham cursing 'exorbitant' ticket prices. This was the moment when men who had been amateurs just 12 months earlier would discover whether professionalism, with all its baggage of expectation, would bring extra pressure. Dallaglio's reaction was pretty close to 'what extra pressure?'. The best sportsmen exist in a state of perpetual pressure, imposed by themselves. That is the pressure that can cause the very best to doubt themselves, but the soundbites of newspapers, television and the host of well-meaning and, sometimes, not so well-intentioned individuals are barely acknowledged. Dallaglio was dismissive of external pressure. 'I am confident of my ability to go out and play well, even more so now that I'm picked in the right place [he had been selected for the Scotland Test in his favourite position of blind-side flanker]. I am happy to justify that I work hard enough to earn every penny of what I do. The whole professional ethos is not really an issue. I just want to play well.'

The Scotland Test would represent a definitive moment in Dallaglio's international career. As we supped a good barolo (of course) in his flat off Ladbroke Grove a week prior to the start of England's Five Nations campaign, he elaborated on the personal significance of this game. It would be his ninth cap, but only the first 14 minutes as a replacement against South Africa in the autumn of 1995 had been in his regular blind-side slot. Dallaglio hinted strongly that the subsequent selections at open side had always irked him, if only slightly. On his debut he recalled that 'I felt that I had made enough of an impression to be worthy of inclusion for the next game, but I came in at the expense of Robbo [Bath's former open side, Andy Robinson]. In that way it was unfortunate. I came in at six and was shunted sideways to seven. I was quizzical, but you play where you are picked, and when you're 22, you don't argue and say, "Hang on, leave me in the 'A' team. I do not want to play unless it's at blind side."'

And so Dallaglio became a reluctant convert to the open side. It had been an easy ride the previous season. Dallaglio was the flavour of the nation and a convert to an unfamiliar position. He recognised that few were keen to ask too many searching technical questions. 'In the short term it was relatively easy; no one asked or expected too much of me in that position. But as I played there regularly people started to ask the questions and say "He's not a seven". In my heart of hearts I have not been truly comfortable in the position.'

It was a massive hindrance to Dallaglio and Rowell that Wasps ignored the handshake between coach and player when the latter agreed to play consistently at open side for his club. This was the tough face of professionalism. Wasps were not trying to stifle his aspirations at international level, but nor would Dallaglio's wishes come before their needs – and Wasps' needs dictated that their captain should revert to number six. 'They admitted it might compromise my England position, but they told me that, in the long term, I'm good enough to play for England in any back-row position. They said, "Even if you have to take one step back to go two steps forward, it may be no bad thing." But it did not make it easy for the England management.'

It was a tribute to Dallaglio's potential that Rowell ignored what had become a trough in form for Dallaglio and selected him in his favoured role. If confidence justified faith, Rowell would have been able to relax seven long days before his ordeal commenced. Dallaglio would lean forward and speak with frank, Mediterranean passion about the reasons why he was itching to pull on the number six shirt. 'A seven is first to the breakdown and because people do not stay on their feet long in this country, everyone has a tendency to go to the floor very quickly. For a guy my size [an imposing six foot three], getting down there becomes difficult, and when I do get the ball all I do is move it on. As England are not very adept at winning third- and fourth-phase ball, I am not getting back into the game. All I am doing is travelling from breakdown to breakdown. I was not enjoying it, which becomes a real problem.'

Enjoyment and comfort are prerequisite for sporting success at the level where the air is thin. What Dallaglio lacked at open side, he possessed in abundance at six – confidence. 'I try at seven, but at six I think I'm the best player on the pitch and capable of dominating the game.' Those are two different people. 'When I'm comfortable I feel I'm the best, and that is a hell of a difference from thinking "I must try and improve".'

Against this view is the school of thought which intimated that because Dallaglio had finally been chosen in his preferred position, he was now under a greater burden of expectation. But confidence makes mincemeat of such theories. 'As a six I'm often second to the breakdown. This makes it a lot easier for me to see what's going on, time my run and do what I do best – taking people on and running into space. I don't feel pressure now I'm playing in the position that best suits me. If anything I'm absolutely ecstatic and looking forward to playing there. I can give it my best shot without any problem. I do honestly believe that.' Others may have doubted Dallaglio's all-round rugby ability as a result of his adventures at seven, but the Wasps captain had no doubts in the only mind that really matters to a sportsman (apart, of course, from the dreaded selectors): his own. 'I know full well that I'm up to it.'

And up for it, because Dallaglio, like nearly every other British international, had his mind set on events months away and thousands of miles from the claustrophobia of the Five Nations. The hunt for a place on the Lions trip to South Africa was about to start for real. Dallaglio's undisguised excitement a week before the Five Nations started for England was a reminder that not all traditions have been overthrown by money. He willingly acknowledged that the Lions were already on his mind, and not isolated at the rear, either. 'No, they are at the front of my mind. Obviously I am not playing against Scotland *for* the Lions, but I am already thinking about what being a Lion would be like. I am certainly taking note when I hear Fran Cotton saying that he wants big, fast, mobile forwards. If we can get a 15–20-point win against the Scots that's a statement against Scottish players, so we can help each other get on the tour. If we win the Grand Slam in style, Ian McGeechan and Fran Cotton will find it hard to leave Englishmen out.'

England achieved even more than a 15–20-point victory against Scotland. The rat-a-tat rhythm of the last 20 minutes helped the team storm beyond their best ever score against the Auld Enemy. However, if nothing else, our politicians have proved beyond doubt that statistics can lie. In this instance England were flattered beyond recognition. The record books will tell a tale of crumbling records, but they will not reflect on a poor 60 minutes and an even worse set of opponents. Few players imposed themselves for the duration of the match, but Dallaglio, wherever the trip to South Africa was locked in his mind, lived up to his promise; he was one of the best players on the pitch and he did enjoy himself.

Dallaglio seemed oblivious to the pressure that the shoddy performance against Argentina had placed England under. But he did believe that 'Post-Argentina the team did suffer a little bit from a lack of confidence. It was crucial that we got off to a good start.' Those who do not know Dallaglio have found it inconceivable that he suffered no personal pressure. Throughout the media, he had been widely quoted as saying he wanted the chance to prove himself in his favoured position at six. It reminded me of the time England finally selected me to face Scotland in 1993. Jack Rowell, then coach of Bath, turned to me and said, 'Now you're in a fix; you'll have to go out and play as well as you keep telling everyone you can.' Dallaglio readily admits that 'I had been making all the noises saying I should be at six, as that's where I play best. There was a feeling that I had said what I thought, now it was time to cement that base and do what I want. I had to make sure all the talk was backed up by a good performance.'

He had not arrived at the team camp at Marlow on the Monday before the Scotland game in good spirits. When observers envy the apparently glamorous lifestyle of sports stars, it can be worth a second thought. Dallaglio, a proud captain of Wasps, was less than a week from an international that had profound implications for England's season and his self-confessed South African aspirations. An Olympic athlete would be in peak condition, but such stars are fortunate to serve only one master: themselves. Rugby players, especially in the age of pay for play, serve two masters at the zenith of the game: club and country. Lawrence was in poor shape. 'Marlow on Monday is generally a recovery session, but the previous Saturday we had lost to Saracens, which had been one of our worst performances. I had been kicked to pieces and arrived in quite a bad way. I remember thinking, "I am completely shattered and could do with doing nothing for a couple of days."' Instead he had to lift his massive frame for the biggest game of the season so far. He also had to divorce himself from the mental anguish of defeat against Saracens. If you want to survive in rugby's harsh world, the mental edge is as vital, if not more so, than the physical one. 'I was very disappointed to lose, but I had to shut that out of my mind. You cannot afford to carry any emotional baggage from club level to the England squad. You have to place those disappointments in the past and switch into the next battle.' It was this mental hardness which enabled Dallaglio to rise from the disappointment of losing the battle for the England captaincy when most critics had thought him home and hosed.

The Wasps skipper brooded over the defeat for 24 hours – he admits to having lost sleep after the few Wasps defeats throughout the season – then came to terms with it. His club had played badly but 'That's a problem to be addressed with the team, not with anyone else'. And so he moved into Marlow, battered in body and mind, but crusading for Club England (a new form of corporatism that is geared towards the creation of a club identity and, presumably, a collectivist spirit).

Willing as he was to place the body on the line, the Italian is no lover of the English charms that Marlow has to offer. 'I do not think that there is much to do, to be honest. It is all a bit twee for my liking [Dallaglio, let us not forget, is a Chelsea supporter]. There is a sign in Marlow which proclaims "Britain's tidiest town – 1992" or something; I am not too impressed by that. Yes, we are playing serious and professional rugby, but there's nothing wrong with having a bit of fun. I don't mean going out and drinking 20 pints [although Temperance Society devotees should avoid this particular London Italian], but recreational stuff, like paintballing or whatever. I like to find out about others off the field. That does wonders to unify the team through the creation of light-hearted banter, and I think that has been overlooked this year. The whole experience of playing for England should not be just on the pitch; it should be collective, and you should grow as a team. I don't think Marlow really allows us to do that as well as other places might.'

One of those 'other places' is the Petersham Hotel, set high above the Thames on the edge of Richmond. There is something odd about a rugby team staying here. It permeates refined civilisation, something that is rarely coupled with a rugby team. Dallaglio loves it. He cites the fact that it is almost within touching distance of Twickenham, the fact that Richmond is very much a rugby town, its efficiency and proficiency, and, most of all, the fact that 'It's the hub of where everything is going on in west London'. All roads do lead to the England camp and that suits Dallaglio. He is not, by nature, a creature of solitude.

Another advantage about the excellence of the hotel service is the freedom to prepare mentally, leaving the hotel staff and camp aides to sort out the mundane worries. Come match morning the players have a focus as clear as cut glass. The Five Nations is fuelled by the loathing of the underdog Celt for the English. That is the general perception. As a half-Italian, it would be no surprise if the Wasp dismissed such parochial historical connotations with the same contempt as Brian Ashton. But Dallaglio subscribes to the old theory with a vengeance, differing in only one important way. 'As an Englishman preparing to play against Scotland, motivation is not difficult at all. We are always criticised for not hating them as much as they hate us, which is how they raise their game. I disagree with that. I mean, there is so much antagonism, and so much history gone under the bridge which just cannot be wiped away. The same things are told in team meetings again and again: remember 1990, and all that stuff.' Dallaglio has something of Chronos to his character. On rugby matters he is as English as Wedgwood clay, but move away from the sport and he becomes the archetypal cosmopolitan. This is less the result of some elaborate play acting and more the way he builds himself, almost without thinking, for Test matches. Such single-mindedness answers rugby's great question: 'How is it that the big guy over there is such a good bloke in a bar, but such a psycho on the field?' It is all in the head.

That mentality made it possible for him to play against Wasps team-mate Andy Reed without a glimmer of *bonhomie*. 'It makes no difference playing against him; he's Scottish, quite plain and simple. When you are back at the club you are pleased for your mates if they are picked for another country, but in terms of translating any friendship, that respect issue goes out the window. If you do not close off the matter of personalities on the other side, they will get into your psyche. If you do not expect to dominate, I think they will get an edge on you.' This is the stuff of gladiators.

In the changing-room prior to the match, Dallaglio sensed a tension that explained the poor first hour. 'Everyone talks about the style that England are developing and how we are playing 15-man rugby, but that type of game comes from playing with confidence, and the confidence was not there on the first whistle. I think that was clear for everyone to see. But I did not think for one moment that we could lose. On my own performance, finally playing at six was something I had so wanted to do for ages. I was so happy. I felt free of the shackles I had felt when I played open side, to be honest.'

Relieved with England's win and quietly delighted with his own form, Dallaglio headed for the grand dinner at the Park Lane Hilton, where the music is from a distant generation, as horn-blowers play ear-splitting halloos. You almost expect a fox to rush through the ballroom, with Prince Charles and chums in pursuit and Tony Banks after them. Fitness levels, commitment and media pressure on players may have changed dramatically in the space of 12 months, but the professional rugby player hates this dinner every ounce as much as his amateur predecessor did. 'I don't think any of the players want to be there any more; I don't think any of them enjoy it.' Dallaglio had one pleasurable task, however. 'I was on the back-row table, which was nice, because it was Richard Hill's first cap, so it was good to welcome him into international rugby in the well-versed tradition.' Dallaglio chuckled. The man who sounded like a member of the Salvation Army when discussing life in the relatively tranquil town of Marlow was back in London. Bright lights, big win, much booze. Good man.

More a man of the Cross Arms than the cross, Dallaglio thrived on the unique party atmosphere that is Dublin when Ireland and England crossed swords at Lansdowne Road. Once again he produced an immaculate performance that cemented his position somewhere in the bubble of an aircraft that would be bound for South Africa in May. He knew that this had been a good afternoon. 'I finally felt free to offer my contribution to the team game a lot more than when I had played seven. Not only is that immensely satisfying for me, but when, say, Jon Sleightholme is on the end of a try I have helped create, then it is satisfying for the entire team. Even more than in the Scotland game I was able to take the ball forward and draw defenders. I felt so much more comfortable.'

'Comfort' is a word that crops up regularly in the Dallaglio vernacular. On the subject of playing at Lansdowne Road, his debut visit to the stadium, he made these points. 'You do not have the little comforts that you experience in your own changing-rooms, your own special little space in which to carry out your own routines.' A clear picture is emerging: Dallaglio is a sportsman who has to feel comfortable and at ease in his environments. The art of mental adjustment is the greatest weapon in his armoury. His initial action before the Irish match was to walk on to the pitch to 'get a feel for the new environment and make myself comfortable. I had a good look around the ground and realised that, for an international ground, it is not that intimidating. In fact, it appeared quite small. I remember thinking, "God, one stand seems to be a wooden frame that has just been modified."' Having mentally steered himself into a comfortable position, Dallaglio was then able to take the psychological upper hand with the Irish. 'I thought to myself that a stadium is as intimidating as its team – and the results that Ireland had posted pre-Christmas [the embarrassing defeats against Italy and Western Samoa] had intimidated nobody.'

His pre-match musings were spot on. Deprived of their traditional dual allies, the wind and the rain, Ireland were flattened and Dallaglio could drift contentedly off into the darkness of Dublin. In the wake of the Scotland victory, Dallaglio indicated that his had been the fatherly role in the initiation of the new cap, a process that demands a frenzy of alcohol abuse. Richard Hill had been the 'protected' debutant at Twickenham; on this occasion it was the chirpy Leicester Liverpudlian Austin Healey. Perhaps Dallaglio fills the *Godfather* mantle with disturbing ease. 'After dinner, having taken care of Austin Healey [read total ambiguity into that remark!] and made sure he was okay, I hit the town with the "Usual Suspects" [yet another criminal analogy]: Jerry [Guscott], Ben [Clarke] and Jason Leonard.' These are the hard-core social animals within the England team, the ones that the mothers-in-law would love, but only after some serious 'get-to-know' time. 'I kind of lost my bearings in Dublin. I think we went to Annabel's, had a few swift ones in Leeson Street ['a few' is any number between four and eight] and then drifted back to the team hotel. I think we arrived back at one or twoish.' The 'ish' lacked any conviction and was said with a wide grin. When a rugby player with thirsty habits adds an 'ish', it is best to add around three to four hours. Dallaglio later admitted that this was not the wildest of estimations. Professionalism has not dented the natural instincts of every rugby player on this planet; rugby will be a lesser sport if it ever succeeds in doing so.

And so to Twickenham a fortnight later, as the usual suspects scrapped out the rights to the championship. France and England were both unbeaten. Victory would take either side to the brink of the Grand Slam and a decent Dallaglio performance would finalise that plane seat to South Africa. Twickenham, if it ever can be, was in a state of heat. The battering of the Celts is a traditional ritual, but France is a different matter. Our European neighbours have held the upper hand with England on too many occasions. The nation has a culture and a history of success to challenge England's, many of its citizens are even as arrogant, and, damn it all, France performed far more successfully than we did in the last Olympic games. They represent a threat to the innate sense of superiority that a certain sort of Englishman carries around like an intimate private belonging. Beating France provides the sort of lift that wins elections for Conservative governments (*Allez les bleus*). Real emotion swirled around this giant and, generally, unemotional stadium. The passion was almost tangible. England's one man of Latin descent sensed it as he waited for battle. The Five Nations was to be decided this afternoon, and Dallaglio can still relive the occasion.

'In the changing-room I already knew that they would be the side kicking off, so I was thinking about where they would line up, to be on my guard . . . but then you remember you still have to go through the anthems. But that is the technical stuff that goes through the mind. I was enjoying the atmosphere, playing at home, in front of friends in the biggest match. I wanted to soak it all up just before kick-off.' Many players actually hate the tension of the match itself, the pleasure coming like a second wave in the aftermath and the contemplation. Not Dallaglio. 'No, I love it. There was a huge buzz as I ran out to face the French. I could not help but think about it there and then. As a pack we were in a huddle, trying to keep each other focused and stay strong mentally. It went through my mind that we were about to receive a kick-off that needed sorting.'

Those fortunate enough to have played any sport, but especially such a gladiatorial one as rugby union, before crowds in excess of 70,000 will understand the power of emotion as the moments leading to kick-off drift by in slow motion. It can kill the weak with nerves; it can inspire the strong. 'I love it when they play "Land of Hope and Glory", much more than the anthem. It's much more stirring. It's a war song, and you need war songs to get the blood boiling – because rugby *is* a war. Think of the haka. It really gets you buzzing. I was thinking La Marseillaise was quite a good tune too.' While the anthem may lift the opposing national supporters, for Dallaglio the definitive frisson was still to come. 'The wall of sound that builds up five seconds before kick-off is like no other sound I have ever heard [it has been known to drown out Concorde as it flies overhead]. The crowd make that noise seem something solid. For me that is the best moment of the entire week. The game is about to start, it raises the hairs on the back of your neck, it is an awesome sound: let the battle commence.' The noise reached its momentous crescendo as the teams kicked off, and at the first contact Dallaglio mixed relief with elation as the body received and gave the long-awaited initial blow.

As France prepared for the first lineout one minute into the game, the preparation of the past week flooded Dallaglio's brain. 'We knew exactly where it was going, which is why I was ready to bring them down immediately. We had studied the French video and realised how limited their options were.' Despite England being forewarned, France unleashed a fluid attack that ended deep in the English twenty-two. As Dallaglio retreated he thought, 'If that is how they are starting, it is going to be one hell of an open game.'

England had the put-in to a scrum in a dangerous and defensive position. 'As a forward the first scrum, whether it is on our line or theirs, is hugely important. It's a battle for the psychological edge.' This particular scrum resulted in a penalty for France which the immaculate Christophe Lamaison kicked to take them into a three-point lead. Dallaglio did not worry, and his mind moved forward to the England restart. 'Okay, let's get into them and get some momentum back into the game.' From the kick, England pressurised France into a knock-on and the sides packed down for the second brutal confrontation. Dallaglio did not join his fellow forwards. Instead, swapping positions with Tony Underwood, he became the Englishman designated to breach the mythical but all-important gain line. 'We called a "Lomu" at this juncture,' said Dallaglio, the name of the move hinting at its abrasive nature. Dallaglio waited, a bull ready to pulverise the matador. He stormed forward, his job to draw defenders. 'A Lomu is not a breakthrough move, so I concentrated on recycling the ball.'

Four minutes into the game, Grayson was awarded the penalty. 'I was thinking, 3–3 now, a job well done. I don't think about the kick. I concentrate on the fact that if he gets it, the restart is from the half-way line; if he misses, where am I for their twenty-two restart, and where is my opposite number?' Grayson kicked the penalty. 'That is a good start. We have both sortied into enemy territory and have both left with three points.'

The flanker's next involvement came after seven minutes as he followed Carling and de Glanville in pursuit of a kick. 'The Frenchman had already caught it, so I piled in to try and earn a scrum.' England were ambitious and confidence flooded the previously nervous team. 'We realised that there were huge holes in the French defence. We had all had a touch, we were settled down and we were able to feel lifted. There is no second wind at this stage; I was still pumped up.'

The match was nine minutes old and France dropped out from their twenty-two. The ball headed towards the Wasps captain. 'I had my eye on the ball, when there was an overcall from Martin Johnson. When you get a call from the Lord of the Lineout you leave it for him.'

England's pressure resulted in a penalty, which Grayson thumped imperiously through the uprights. England were in front and the

Twickenham faithful, in best fashion, burst into a pre-emptive version of 'Swing Low'. Dallaglio could hear the noise. 'There are 75,000 people watching, so you hear everything, but at this stage you don't need a crowd to lift you. You're up, in the lead and on a high.'

The lift was slightly deflated when the referee penalised Dallaglio for offside from a scrum. He was in front of Andy Gomarsall when the scrum-half chipped into the blind-side box. 'I was irritated with myself for being careless, but the main feeling was frustration at the decision itself: it was bollocks.'

His initial tackle 13 minutes into the game brought him face to face with the imposing frame of French captain Abdel Benazzi. 'I was not head on to him. I came from the side, so as I tackled, I thought, "Pull him down and stay underneath him." I knew instinctively that we could then create a turnover.' A myriad of decisions are being made by the split second. Benazzi is a giant of the world game, but ask Dallaglio if he feels the presence, the bulk, of an opponent, and the return look is unusually quizzical. His concentration was fixed on the larger event as England carried the battle to France. Tony Underwood stuttered and a half-chance went west, but England were in control. Nigel Starmer Smith worked hard to sound impartial; Dallaglio worked hard without any real opportunities to make a significant impact. His chance would come. France conceded a penalty, and as the pack headed towards the lineout Dallaglio communicated the precise location of the throw to Richard Hill, helping him to understand the nature of the attack.

England won the lineout but the high ball was too long. Pressure was not being translated into points. England's pack drove another lineout and France conceded another penalty. '"Yes, we have them up front," I thought. The pack oozed confidence, but Grayson missed a sitter. I remember an unwanted thought entering my head: "This may come back to haunt us later." I suppose that it's easy in hindsight.

'At 30 minutes I knew we should have been a try in front, but we all realised that if we cut out mistakes, the game was ours. There was no doubt about that. Mind you, I believe that you have to be that positive for the whole game, even if it is injury time and you are losing.' That is the power of the winning mindset. It can and must defy logic at the highest levels of achievement, especially within sport.

France weathered the strong English breeze and clawed their way back into the English danger zone, but Dallaglio 'did not feel under any pressure. They were going nowhere with the ball in hand, and then Lamaison dropped a goal. I thought that we should have been 12–3 up and instead it was 9–6. When that drop goal soared through the posts my thoughts were, "Fucking hell, that's another three points; they've got six now and they have only been in our half twice.'"

Dallaglio surged forward into attack, taking a ball from Paul Grayson. 'Your mind tells you to stay on your feet, drive forward and lay it back.' Not all English forwards adopt that attitude, and in an angry aside Dallaglio pleads, 'Tell me if I'm wrong, but I believe that although there are players who take the ball in and you know when and how it will come back, there are others who fall too easily, who don't control the ball . . . I was thinking to myself that this will come back. You have a responsibility, if you take a ball into a certain situation, to ensure that the ball comes back. Some people think about this too late; by then it's either too slow or it's lost.' That is the primary difference between southern and northern hemisphere forwards. It is not about physical strength, but about mental agility.

That charge of Dallaglio's was stopped; his next was to prove irresistible. One minute before half-time, he was to score a try that sent Nigel Starmer Smith into alto and Twickenham into orbit. Dallaglio recalls it, hiding any trace of relish. 'The French were offside, about 45 metres out, but Jim Fleming played a good advantage. Shawsie carried it on and drove it forward, then Rowntree came in and drove it round the side. It was a bad ball for Gommars, but he fed Phil, who headed left down a big blind side. I was coming from his right and deep.' The French had men defending wide and Dallaglio spotted the options immediately. 'Phil was going to have to turn inside. He was tackled, but fortunately he made it available and I hit the gap at speed. He just checked before Merle came in to tackle him. Once I took the pass I was always going to score because I had the angle. The only man coming across was the scrum-half.

'The pass was slightly to my side, but the gap was a big one with Sadourny and Benazzi either side of me. Coming from depth, I was aware that the pace with which I hit the ball would carry me through the gap and I realised it was a matter of pinning my ears back. I could feel Tony [Underwood] wide outside me, but all I could see was the tryline. The closer I got, the more aware I became of Carbonneau [the scrum-half] coming across from my right-hand side. I knew I had loads of room into which to run to my left, but I was confident that I would make the line. I felt him try to thump the ball out of my hand as I hurled myself across the line; he had two pops at me, but I have big hands and am comfortable with the ball in my right hand. I did actually switch the ball through my hands earlier in the run.' But the supreme moment of personal joy was not quite the elevated moment of which so many armchair sports fans dream. 'I was so focused, I didn't hear any noise. When I touched it down there was a moment's realisation that I had scored. I realised that *we* had scored on the stroke of half-time and I knew that made a big difference to the scoreline . . . I thought that all that pressure had finally given us a cushion, and that was pleasing.'

Dallaglio was hardly euphoric in the description, nor in the reaction. 'A lot of people jump up in the air, smiling and laughing when they score a try, but it's the team's job to score a try. If I do, that's fine, but my reaction is controlled. It's "I've scored a try but we haven't won the game yet".' As Starmer Smith eulogised about his 'great pace for a man of six foot four', and as Bill Beaumont said 'Like a good sprinter, he knew what to do', he celebrated by plucking out his gumshield and picking deep into the recesses of his left nostril. 'I did feel good and proud, but most important was the confidence within the team. We knew at half-time that we had a cushion, and we felt confident – but we knew we still had work to do.'

Despite his genuine protestations of modesty, Dallaglio admits that at half-time 'I felt in good shape, I had just scored a try, and I was on top of the world'. This is an apparent contradiction of all that he has recalled only moments earlier, but in reality it is another example of Dallaglio's ability to submerge genuine feelings for the sake of the greater cause. Again it illustrates that mental strength.

Shirt torn, Dallaglio swapped jerseys and prepared for the restart. He was disappointed with the decision to kick the ball ten metres. 'There had to be some doubts in their minds over whether they could win the game, so we should just drill it down there, let them shit themselves and run it out again.' These opinions are a mixture of the moment's thoughts and hindsight. The frustrated captain does not lurk far beneath the exterior. But Dallaglio concentrated on the job in hand. Underwood hit a tackle situation, and Dallaglio secured rapid second-phase ball before 130 stone of furious Frenchmen descended on his prostrate body. He arose to see England further from the French line than they had been when he won the ball. 'Things like that are disappointing, but I think to myself, "Be constructive, forget about it." If I get on Grayson's back and ask why we aren't here or there, it doesn't achieve anything.' This is another example of natural feelings being checked.

There were seemingly few reasons for England to think negative thoughts. Grayson dropped a goal and five minutes into the second half England were easing into a 17–6 lead. A back-row move went wrong, but 'If you don't try things you will never improve'. As we watched the game, benefiting from hindsight and another Italian red wine, he became increasingly animated at the errors made. 'If we had secured that ball and switched back to the open . . . if we had done that I have no doubt that we would have scored. I am on the other wing, waiting for the ball to come back.' Another chance wasted and France were throwing their trump card, substituting Meiron for a fresh Richard Castel. Dallaglio was so involved in the match that he didn't notice the change. The minutes marched on and Grayson kicked another penalty to make it 20–6. There was no time to consider victory as England began missing kicks to touch. Within seconds Grayson missed a second touch and Dallaglio recalls what sounds remarkably like the first note of concern, even if he will not recognise it. 'We were trying to defend and becoming disorganised as we offered them broken-field chances.'

Fifty-three minutes had elapsed and France were a distant 14 points adrift, but Dallaglio remembers the nagging doubts. 'We were under the cosh and we knew it. There was a lineout five metres from our line and I thought, "Let's keep them out; this is an important time for them not to score. If they score they will get an edge here."' England held at the lineout but one minute later it was a scrum that threatened their beleaguered thin white line. The pressure was mounting. 'There was a lot of weight coming on from the French pack; it was time to get the hit spot on and lock out the scrum.' This was a hot moment in the match. Dallaglio's mind raced through his tasks: scrummaging, awareness of the opposition attacking his channel and filling in gaps that may appear if they run it. It was a moment to absorb French pressure. The French tried a secondary shove; Dallaglio expected a period of attrition and stood firm.

England conceded two penalties, France chose another scrum. 'Everyone knew the noise from the crowd signified a key moment of the match. It was as important as any try or penalty. Stopping scores is just as important as scoring.' Merle, the hero of the French effort, attacked the line; Dallaglio tackled high, but firm; the siege continued. Martin Johnson, the 'Lord of the Lineout', soared high, but the clearance kick was short. France had been within try-scoring distance for nine long and wearing minutes. Rowntree lost a contact lens, Leonard acted the Shakespearian part and England gasped deep breaths. From an ensuing scrum the French bore in, backchatted and were marched back a demoralising ten metres. The crowd's roar told the tale. England had survived the siege and had the lineout throw a distant 35 metres from their bloodied but unbowed tryline.

Dallaglio was lifted. 'They had thrown everything at us and failed to score. We believed that we had the edge. They came out of their best period of play short-changed. I really thought they were doubting themselves, especially when Benazzi left the field injured.' But Dallaglio's relief was short-lived. He described the next lineout, one hour into the battle, as the key moment of the game. 'The ball was called short to Martin and I was certain he would take it, so I took a step forward. It clipped his hand and I was helpless as it deflected beyond my reach. Had I been a step back, I would have cleaned the ball at the back of the lineout; instead Magne picked it up as I was preparing to drive the forward momentum. This left the tail of the lineout with three Frenchmen against one Englishman. I should have just held my line a bit . . . If we had won that lineout and driven them upfield, I reckon they would have broken and we would have beaten them by a further ten points. I really do.'

Alas for England, France, inspired again by Lamaison, scored a try from that lineout. England thought that the storm had been weathered and suddenly the men in white were hit by a bolt of blue lightning. 'I was bloody annoyed. It was soft. We should have won the lineout, but we were flat-footed. It was a carbon copy of the Welsh game.' Dallaglio's competitive nature is as evident watching the match four days after the event in his living-room. The voice rises steadily, in tandem with his disgust at the French comeback.

The score was now 20–13. 'We are a try ahead, no need to panic. Okay, they have a score, but it's not the end of the world. Let's get back into the game . . .' He was no longer in the room with me. 'I think the team panicked now. We hadn't touched the ball for 12 minutes, so we kicked short when we should have gone long.' He now addressed the television directly, as if he could change the shape of things past via the wonders of video.

There was no tiredness in his frame, but there was frustration in his mind as the half-backs started to panic. 'I was not thinking about defeat – that had not entered my mind – but I was aware that we were losing shape.' On the screen in front of us, the mask of moderation crumpled in the 67th minute. 'What's that?' he howled. 'That's shit. That's a lineout and a scrum where we have just fucking thrown possession away.' It was at this point that the tension began to grow on the field.

Lamaison scored the try to bring France within two points. 'Right, we have a game on our hands. He is not going to miss the kick, so it will be 20–20. There's ten minutes left, so let's get upfield and start to reassert control.' Dallaglio still claims not to have considered defeat, but admits, 'I would not say I was totally calm. We were flapping a bit.' As England flapped, France and Merle grew. Tim Rodber conceded a stupid penalty and the visitors kicked England deep into their own half. 'Swing Low' had disappeared along with England's sang-froid.

Five minutes from time France were back on England's line. Dallaglio prepared for the French catch and drive. 'My job was to get their drive down.' He succeeded, but France recycled the ball and the Gallic momentum resulted with a shrill killing blast of the whistle from Jim Fleming. England had been penalised, and the man accused? Lawrence Dallaglio. 'It was never a penalty. Fleming told me that I "flopped down on it" – no way. When I heard the whistle blow I expected to get up and find them penalised for holding on to the ball. I had turned Sadourny our way in the tackle, and I can't believe the referee gave the penalty against us. I didn't look at the clock because I knew we had time left to win.'

It was not to be. 'Collectively we were devastated that we had let ourselves down on the pitch. We didn't even walk in as a team. It was a very painful lesson to learn. France couldn't even believe it themselves.' The video was turned off as the restaurant beckoned. In an effort to comfort Dallaglio I reminded him that it is 1999 that matters. 'Oh, yeah,' was the retort. Winners are not good short-term losers. Dallaglio wore his bravest face as he explained that his heavily pregnant girlfriend, Alice, was 'half French anyway, so I knew she wouldn't be too disappointed. I couldn't really stay miserable for long, could I?' It was ironic that Alice, too pregnant to watch the game live, had invited friends to the flat to watch it. Half of them were French. Dallaglio had to hide his disappointment, although he grimaced with theatrical pain when his partner said, 'He is very good at losing.' That is one thing at which Dallaglio is clearly not very good, but we knew exactly what Alice was implying.

Dallaglio's calm under fire had been proved beyond reasonable doubt on the field of play, but these heroics paled into insignificance beside his ability to control his nervous tension off the field, when the pressure was really on the man. The Wasps captain was recovering from a virus that had forced his withdrawal from the England team to play Wales; his illness, perhaps not coincidentally, ran parallel to the anticipated birth of his child. As Alice started her labour pains, Lawrence, with a remarkable display of self-delusion, for the sake of keeping the calm, rolled up his sleeves for action.

Dallaglio was not about to test his powers of midwifery, but he was determined that his girlfriend should eat. He convinced himself that the early signs of labour were of little significance in order to keep her from hospital until the latest possible time. Unique is the man who can react to the growing evidence that he is about to become a father by rushing into the kitchen to cook broccoli soup. Alice protested that this was no time for broccoli soup, while Dallaglio searched for the right herbs to mix with the veal escalope that was to follow. It was a classic example of his ability to try and change the reality that stared him in the face. Eventually Ella Francesca was born, a strapping baby weighing more than nine pounds. She will probably have a lifelong aversion to broccoli soup.

This tale has the ring of Apocrypha, but, believe me, it is the truth. It is totally Dallaglio. Keep your composure and self-belief no matter what is happening all around. In the same manner, Dallaglio could play with a broken bone in his hand by telling himself, 'It is only a small bone.' It is a granite mentality that has served Wasps magnificently.

In the wake of an 18–12 defeat at Welford Road which left the Wasps dependent on Leicester losing to win the title, Dallaglio was hard-edged and unsmiling. Yet there was not even a second's hesitation in his reaction. 'We can still win the league . . . our game plan was brilliant . . . the referee cost us the points [bad refereeing is a constant theme with Dallaglio] . . . we cannot wait to face Bath on Sunday.' Evidence and experts were unanimous – the title would be claimed by the Tigers. Dallaglio did not even countenance the possibility of failure.

That fierce determination moulds the man before a match. As Bath and Wasps players exchanged pleasantries before another crucial Courage League game, Dallaglio, stone-faced, barely raised an eyebrow in recognition of friend and foe. Here was total professional commitment. As the minutes ticked into extra time, Bath led by seven points. Defeat would probably have cost Wasps the title, but the self-belief which losers would call delusion, and which Dallaglio had played such an integral part in installing in his team, surged into glorious light. An Alex King try and a memorable Gareth Rees conversion forced a draw when defeat seemed inevitable. His reaction? 'That is a point that they could not afford to drop, but it has not affected our title chances.' This was positivity in the extreme. As for the draw, well, the referee and touch judges had cost Wasps the outright victory with some bad decisions – 'perhaps a TV eye was needed'. Never mind the controversial penalty awarded to Wasps from which they salvaged the draw. That is

Fran Cotton, the man and the myth. His legend was to grow greater still in South Africa

The brains behind the brawn: the successful coaching combination of
Jim Telfer and Ian McGeechan

The most mobile brick wall in the world: Lions back-row heroes from the first two Tests,
Lawrence Dallaglio, Tim Rodber and Richard Hill

The romance of rugby: 'Ollie' Redman, from the Bath scrap heap to the Lions captaincy

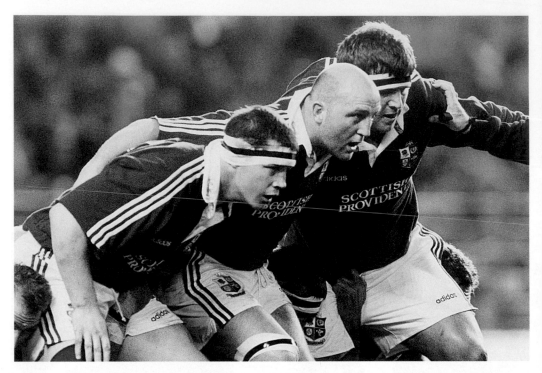

We shall not be moved: the Celtic crew of Paul Wallace, Keith Wood and Tom Smith

Matt Dawson *en route* to South Africa's tryline and a place in British rugby history

'Everybody back home will be on their knees, hoping and praying that he can find one more kick.' Miles Harrison nearly loses his cool; Neil Jenkins does not

'Bentos', beloved hero of the Barmy Army and proud Lion

Much as the Barmy Army love him, Pieter Rossouw is less keen on
an intimate get-together

Who else?!

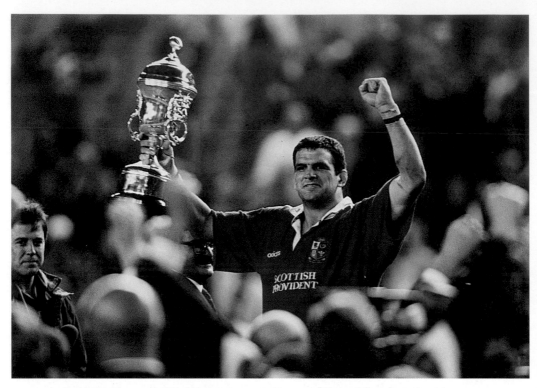

Move over Willie John, the '70s are over. It's time for Martin Johnson
and the new age to take over

'A very special group of men'

the blinkered determination of a born winner. Chris Wright, the boss of Chrysalis and the man behind the Wasps, had a fine first lieutenant to maximise his returns from rugby union.

His commitment to the club was the mark of the new and true professional. Rugby union is no longer dominated by the gung-ho nationalist mentality. Those players who would drop everything to play for their country either suffer from a terminal dose of blind patriotism or have an appalling working relationship with their employers. For that is what a rugby club has now become: an employer. Dallaglio was near the height of his playing powers and he had contracts with the England squad, the British Lions (for whom selection had been a formality because of his unyielding excellence in the Five Nations) and Wasps, but there was no question of problems with his priorities. 'There are genuine overlaps and different priorities, but Wasps are my main income and main contract.' (Dallaglio's agents had negotiated shares as well as a salary from Loftus Road plc. The amounts are unknown. I have no interest in whether the 24-year-old is rich or very rich, but the fact that he checks Queens Park Rangers' results – the football side of the plc – as hurriedly as those of his beloved Chelsea indicates that the shares are not insignificant.)

His professional attitude to the contractual affairs are matched by a more traditional sense of pride in the men with whom he works daily. This is the more familiar realm for rugby union diehards. Critics argued that Wasps were 'lucky' to be challenging for the title. They were definitely less fashionable than either Bath or Leicester, but Dallaglio bridled at the suggestion that their proximity to the top was in any way fortunate. 'We have set the pace from the start of the season.' Disagree at your peril.

Not a single Wasp has ever doubted Dallaglio's commitment to the club, but for the only man selected for the British Lions, the only regular in the England team and the one man in the club with an image that attracted recognition outside the limited confines of the sport, there are pitfalls in being captain. The vast majority of the squad were bystanders during the Five Nations. Dallaglio was forcibly absent at crucial times of the season, such as during the direct aftermath of the Pilkington Cup defeat against north London rivals Saracens. Jealousy and envy are as much a part of rugby union as they are in any other walk of life. To tread the highwire of club captain and international star, Dallaglio has forcibly set himself the most stratospheric standards. He is acutely aware of his position and its inherent vulnerability. 'I know that I am the standard-bearer, the beacon of everyone else's ambitions at Wasps, but I felt totally alien when I returned from international duty. I hadn't seen the guys for ages and initially that made life difficult. We had to regroup and get to know each other again.'

He may only be 24, but he has a maturity that has been his greatest ally in the quest for leadership skills. 'It was imperative not to lose the respect and momentum that we had created. As captain you must help yourself by the way you behave, perform and train. As captain I must set an example for the rest of the team. So when I returned from the England set-up, I didn't sit out club sessions on the physio's bench. I was out on that field. I wanted to know what had been happening. I phoned up Nigel Melville to find out who had been sharp or otherwise. Of course, this placed extra pressure on myself, but that's something I have to live with.'

The burden placed upon himself paid great dividends. To Alex King, Dallaglio was 'inspirational, full stop'. To Kenny Logan, a loquacious Scot signed in the new year, he was 'the best captain I have played under. When he speaks, you listen. He won't talk for the sake of it, but when he does, you listen. He should be the captain of England but, as a Scot, I'm glad that he is not.' Dallaglio had consigned to ancient history the dark days of the early season when the combination of playing open side and the media attention on the England captaincy had affected his focus. Those who questioned his leadership credentials only had to watch him play and talk to his colleagues. There had been doubters within the Wasps camp in the autumn. Gareth Rees, a mature and seminal figure in Wasps' season, recalled Dallaglio's abrupt departure after defeat at Gloucester and his unwillingness to share the process of decision-making. During the autumn, the strong character had not been a strong captain in Rees's eyes, but an hour after Dallaglio had lifted the Courage League trophy after victory at Northampton, his story was a different one. 'Yeah, Lawrence has matured a hell of a lot as a captain. He now has the confidence to ask for others' opinions, which he hadn't earlier in the year.' At the start of the season Dallaglio had spoken about senior players, like Rees, earning his respect and vice versa. By the end of the long winter Dallaglio's words rang resonant and true.

The change from amateurism to professionalism had been a significant bonus for a team drawn from all parts of London. In the amateur days they found it impossible to mix on a social level as easily as the provincial teams could. That change helped Dallaglio and the Wasps. 'As full-time professionals we can spend more time together.

Players don't have to rush off to business meetings, and that extra time helps with the bonding that eventually leads to spirit and success.'

But even a consummate professional can find the new world a bit of a drudgery at times. 'We are all finding our feet still. At times it is hard to find the motivation to do the same old things, like lifting weights on Monday mornings [the joys of amateurism!], but you have to force yourself along, and think, "We're in this together."' Dallaglio's relatively tender years possibly made the transition from old amateur to new professional easier than it was for others. He admits, 'It is a lot easier to educate players at 21, 22 or 23 than 31, 32 or 33.' Dallaglio, at 24, is probably at the optimum age for the professional rugby player.

Maturity merged with youthful zest as the final weeks of the league unfolded. Dallaglio's confidence in his Wasps team was justified as exhaustion finally ground Leicester to a halt. Consecutive defeats at the hands of Gloucester, Bath and London Irish left the destiny of the title once more in the hands of Lawrence Dallaglio's team. The run-in brought Wasps face to face with Sale, Northampton and Harlequins. Two wins were required to guarantee the title. The Wasps captain had faced a battering season, but the excitement of tangible success had rigorously recharged the batteries. 'I enjoy the pressure of chasing the league title. It is what we have worked for all season, and now we are on the verge of fulfilling our ambition. It is an exciting feeling. I don't think we will lose; that is my mentality.'

He stressed the fine shape of body and mind – another transparent benefit of professionalism. 'Mentally, I feel much stronger than I ever have. The games are coming so thick and fast, it's like being on the road, like touring with your team . . . we definitely could not have sustained this as amateurs. [With only three remaining league matches, Dallaglio had played in every game bar one for his club.] Physically I feel good. I could not have coped last season, though. I have carried knocks, but medical attention sustains me. After a Sunday match I can wake up aching at 9 a.m. and be on the physio's couch by 9.30. In the amateur days you might have been forced to wait for treatment until 6 p.m. That could be too late; the damage might have been done.'

Yet, even with every possible professional advantage, this year had been a long, hard and, at times, rough ride. Forget the traumas of the England captaincy in the autumn, and the pressures to succeed as an international and a club captain at the same time. Dallaglio had also metamorphosed from single man to father. Quite literally, his entire world had changed in the course of one rugby season. Paradoxically, the preparation for the Five Nations was a massive assistance. 'In the week before the Five Nations you have five or six days to rest and recuperate. To someone living in London, that is brilliant. You can be cotton-wooled in the team hotel, so the pace of life slows down. Yes, I miss Alice, but it was important to recharge the batteries. It was a bloody relief to be hidden from the media and the outside world.'

As he speaks, the real Dallaglio is stripped bare. Like the rest of the human race, tiredness, irritation and pressure reaches him. 'At the time of Ella's birth, I felt under a lot of pressure. She was expected during that purple patch of the season, in the middle of the Five Nations when everyone wants a piece of you. I felt that I was being torn in 15 different directions. Fortunately my game was going well, and that made life easier.'

Ella was due on the greatest day of the year – Cheltenham Gold Cup Thursday. It would have been an appropriate day for a Dallaglio child to be born – the man enjoys a punt – but Dallaglio was holed up in Cardiff, preparing for the last match of the Five Nations. It required all his powers of concentration and positive thinking to convince himself that he could play the game *and* witness the birth of his child. 'Alice and the baby were on my mind, but Alice and I had spoken about it. We were confident that if anything happened I would be able to leave immediately. For some reason I thought that everything would work out. I wanted to have my cake and eat it. Maybe I received my come-uppance when I was ill [he was forced to withdraw with illness on the morning of the match] – perhaps all the stress and worry contributed to my illness – but I had so much faith and belief that I would play outstandingly against Wales and finish the Five Nations with a bang and still be alongside Alice for the birth . . .' Here was the quintessential Dallaglio. Battered and exhausted, but mentally strong enough to take on the reality that surrounded and threatened to envelop him. In the end the body cracked, but not for long.

In the week preceding the Test match with Wales, Ella was born, doubtless with an inherent dislike of broccoli soup. Dallaglio's tension fell away. A father, a British Lion and a man in pursuit of the title. He was ready for the last challenge. Sale were comprehensively beaten as Dallaglio led his troops around Loftus Road in best football fashion. The thoroughly professional Wasp knew that one more victory at Franklin's Gardens against Northampton would secure the club's title ambitions. Wasps were edgy throughout and Northampton played the more positive rugby, but there was no breach in the determined defence of the

Wasps. Dallaglio was ubiquitous, a black flash smashing opponents into the turf. The jaw jutted defiantly as the home side failed to turn territory into points. Gareth Hughes blew the whistle at 3.50 p.m. and Wasps were champions of England. Dallaglio had proved himself to the rugby world, as a player and as a captain.

He had every reason to feel a deep sense of personal satisfaction as he lifted the Courage League trophy. Individually, he had been one of the best forwards in the Five Nations Championship, he had guaranteed himself a cherished place with the British Lions on the plane to South Africa and he had matured into the outstanding captain in English rugby. When Phil de Glanville was appointed the captain of England, Dallaglio had stated – jokingly, but with undoubted edge – that this would be the only thing Bath would win during the season. His leadership turned this aside into a thumpingly concrete reality. Wasps had won the title by six points, a record margin matched only once by Bath.

He could have been excused for sitting back and preparing himself for the next momentous challenge in his year, that of winning a place in the Lions Test side and a monumental collision with the South African blind side, Ruben Kruger. He had openly admitted, even before the Five Nations had commenced, just how much he longed for that moment when schoolboy dreams could be fulfilled. No matter how certain the rest of the world may be, no player can hide the sigh of relief or the rush of ecstasy when Ceefax prints the name in the squad for the once-in-four-years challenge. At the start of the season, Nigel Melville had said that the greater the challenge, the better Dallaglio responded. It was almost time to prove it under the Southern Cross.

Lions like Northampton captain Tim Rodber and team-mate Paul Grayson were in no hurry to return to action. Cotton-wool profits were at an all-time high. In Bath, the veteran Lion, Jeremy Guscott, chose not to risk himself, with Bath's blessing, once their European place had been guaranteed. All minds were focusing south. There was one inspiring exception. Wasps, champions with one match remaining, were free to lose. Dallaglio did not see it that way. The champions' last engagement was at the home of their oldest rivals, the Harlequins. The cosmopolitan conglomerate were one of the three teams to have beaten Wasps in the league, and the only one to have won at Loftus Road. Melville did not need to ask Dallaglio if he wanted to play (and risk an injury that could ruin his countless years of hard work and daydreaming). 'Lawrence couldn't be stopped from playing. He hates the "Harley Queens", as he calls them, and he wanted to be there with the trophy and really rub it in.' That was leadership of the highest calibre. His decision to lead Wasps from the front at the last, as he had from the first, was a defining moment of new-age professionalism. Dallaglio had served his club first and foremost. Level-headed, he understood the new order more clearly than any other player in England. Club and contract before glory.

His integrity received its fair reward. Wasps were duly inspired and crushed their London rivals by 20 points and more. Dallaglio rubbed the new order of supremacy into the Harlequins. Now he could concentrate on final farewells to his fledgling family and the British Lions tour of South Africa.

The Professional Lions: On the Road...

Will Carling returned from the Lions' tour of New Zealand and virtually pronounced the death knell for the British Lions. And that was before the sport became totally professional. Cassandras crawled from the woodwork. The only people who did not seem to subscribe to the 'Lions as history' view were the players. Sir John Hall may have stated that five Newcastle Lions represented a concern and a threat to the club's First Division objectives, but Messrs Tait, Underwood, Weir, Bentley and Stimpson were desperate to jump on the Virgin Airways flight bound for Jan Smuts Airport and the great rugby adventure that is the British and Irish Lions' tour of South Africa. Although it was once the heart of darkness, the 47-strong party now headed to what has always been the heart of rugby.

The British Isles teams are the stuff of rugby legend. In New Zealand, fanatics speak reverentially of 1971; in South Africa the year is 1974, the moment when the southern hemisphere stronghold of the game was indisputably shattered. In the process the posturing macho manhood of every red-blooded South African was deflated and humiliated. Foursquare among that party was one Fran Cotton, the prop forward who never stepped backwards. In South Africa the 1997 Lions manager was regarded as 50 per cent man, 50 per cent myth. A more subtle influence on the 1974 team was an impish centre by the name of McGeechan. In 1997 he would return to South Africa as coach for a third successive Lions series. Northampton may pay the mortgage but the heart belongs to that famous red shirt. McGeechan was to be the crusader leading the Lions in pursuit of the holy grail: a series victory in South Africa and a place on the high table alongside Gareth, Merv the Swerve, Slatts, Benny, J.J. and, of course, Willie John from '74.

There is no better place to reach for the rugby heights than South Africa. In White South Africa, rugby plays a starring role in their Calvinistic heaven. The South African Airways flight offered over 250 pages on the state of the game. The crumpled copy of the *Evening Standard* pictured Dennis Wise, Mark Hughes and Gianfranco Zola alongside a last lingering soccer headline. We were now in rugby country.

South Africans are proud people. They have not always had much to be proud about, but the Rainbow nation, in the shadow of the great man Mandela, were smiling. As our aeroplane circled over the Indian Ocean near Durban, the pilot informed the trapped audience that this South African plane was 'at the very top of the food chain'. God knows what that was supposed to mean, but it was somehow bound in with the notion of South African pride. The crime rate was down, the ships in the bay were a 'sign of a thriving economy'. Their stern God seemed to have discovered the art of cracking a smile. It was indeed good to be back in the land of rugby, violence, social turmoil and real excitement. South Africa has it all.

However, there was one jarring note. To a South African it was more a monsoon than a cloud on the horizon. There was a whole lot of pessimism surrounding the state of Springbok rugby. From a nation of supremacists this represented a hint of hope for the Lions. Rodney Hartmann, a South African journalist, wrote in *The Sunday Times* (Johannesburg, not London), 'I get angry when I read, as I did this week, how a pride of Lions will be hunted down and inhumanely destroyed by a herd of fleet-footed Springboks [weird things can happen, even with mother nature] . . . methinks it is based on flimsy grounds.' What prose. So maybe the wordsmith is a liberal, but, no, he continues in deep pessimism, writing of the 'very real destruction that has been exacted on our provincial teams in Super 12'.

Rugby union is a harsh game. Violence simmers near the surface and war analogies are regular journalistic occurrences. As the tour approached, the martial hype amplified to a crescendo. Fran Cotton, the symbol of Bulldog Britain, the man who would not step back, uttered confrontational pledges in Britain. The man selected to lead the Lions, Martin Johnson, was a latter-day Willie John McBride. The Leicester and England lock is a brooding presence. The forehead bulges over the eyes in a menacing, almost simian manner. Here was the personification of aggression. A statement of intent. In the first press conference on enemy soil, Johnson dismissed the question 'Do you think the Lions can possibly win the series?' with a stern 'If I didn't think we could win the Test series, I would stay home and go on holiday'.

Despite endless hours of graft ahead (ahem!), that 'look, the sea' holiday feel lifted my tired spirits as we landed at Durban, a town which 'swarms with blacks at Christmas' to quote one of the many superficial white converts to the Rainbow nation. Racism held a mighty grip on the dirty soul of the nation. The conversion was inspiring, but it was hardly Pauline in its speed. It is a country that has discovered its integrity, but the complete emasculation of the spirit is still way in the future.

Such matters did not cross the minds of the 1997 Lions, 'the first professional British and Irish Lions', as Cotton told us to the point of nausea. Professionalism may be good for the wallet and the quality of the product, but the endless focus on the one burning issue – the sport – can make your average British Lion a lot less exciting. They were here for the rugby; the good old days of beer were long gone. The 47-man squad, including dieticians, masseurs, doctors and probably a secret psychologist, were based in a seaside resort called Umhlanga, upstream from Durban, in a hotel called the Beverly Hills. It possesses a sort of *Dynasty*-style glitzy opulence. It could be located anywhere in the world, or at least anywhere with a wonderful winter climate and stunning views of the Indian Ocean. It is the sort of place that an uninquiring player appreciates.

I was more impressed with lunch at Langoustine's. Kingklip for 42 rand. We toasted sterling over rand with a decent Simonsig Pinotage until rugby reared its all-enveloping head. The owner, catching the foreign British tone, bemoaned the state of Springbok rugby. 'Ach, man [the 'ach' is a real spittoon of a guttural snarl], our chances are no better than fifty-fifty.' Inevitably he mentioned 1974; inevitably we drank another bottle of red.

Those South African supporters who feared another humiliation based their reasoning purely on perceived inadequacies within the Springbok camp. The 1997 Lions may have been called the first professional Lions, but nobody considered the possibility of them matching up to those legends of yesteryear. Yet there were substantial advantages in other areas from the very first day. The word 'professional' was almost a mantra. Yes, they were paid, but what else did this new-age concept actually mean? What difference did it make to the players? According to Jeremy Guscott, the veteran of three tours, the answer was very little in a direct sense. 'There is not really that much change in the playing sense. Everyone is pretty serious on a Lions tour [at least, they are in the early winning stages]; the attitude is always professional in a playing sense. The real difference is the input of the management.'

On too many tours the players are managed by 'the old-school regime', to quote Guscott again. Many of the pranks that have too often ended in excess and debilitating performances are the result of free-spirited adults being treated without respect. Mindless, unyielding authority is a real turn-off to an imaginative rugby player. Under Fran Cotton, this mistake was avoided. Guscott, one of the great rugby nonconformists, approved. 'Deep down, most good rugby players are free spirited, but on this tour the management have asked us to set down our own discipline procedures. It's our responsibility to uphold them, otherwise we let ourselves and each other down.' Before the tour a management company had worked at close quarters in the team base at Weybridge, and corporate jargon was lurking around every corner, but unlike the early days at Bath, the expertise was being sensibly applied. One of the great tour traditions is the existence of the dirt-trackers, the second-team squad who provide the laughs and the beer. They can also destroy the collective will. That happened in New Zealand when the tour was almost derailed by a demotivated section of the party. Ian McGeechan had been coach and admitted that he had learned valuable lessons from that trip.

And so when Tim Rodber, captain for the day against Mpumalanga, was asked about the ability of the tour dirt-trackers, it was with total commitment that he retorted, 'There are no dirt-trackers on this tour. Thirty-five guys are here with the same objective: to win the series against the Springboks. This is a professional tour. The players are professional. They handle themselves in a professional manner from the moment they get out of bed to the moment they go to bed.' But then again so did the vast majority of the '93 Lions in the early days. The difference in South Africa, as Guscott had perceived, was the extra management professionalism. In previous tours, management consisted of three or four men responsible for a multitude of areas. This tour was packed with specialists. Even Bob Burrows, the tour media liaison officer, had an assistant. McGeechan headed the coaching team, with fellow Scot Jim Telfer as the forwards' coach. Andy Keast, a former Natal coach, was the technical specialist, compiling videos of opponents and detailed analyses of the Lions. Dave Alred, the world's best kicking coach, controlled that important area of the game.

Medical back-up was provided by Dr James Robson, the Scotland team doctor, Mark Davies, the Welsh physiotherapist, and Richard Wegrzyk (pronounced Vendrick), the England masseur. Add David McLean as a fitness and nutrition specialist and the Lions management weighed in at 11. But that ignores the great tradition that is the baggage master, the wisecracking northerner Stanley Bagshawe. A deadly dozen to plot the Springboks' downfall.

The most obvious alteration wrought on Fran's first professional Lions was the extra dimensions that could be added to a training session – a good or bad aspect, depending on your love of running around. This tour party appeared enthusiastic. They had to be. Two-and-a-half-hour training sessions can drag if boredom sets in. Even the stretching exercises lasted 35 minutes during their first serious workout in Durban. Profoundly dull stuff. In the early dawn of a tour this is tolerable. New relationships are being formed, the wisecracks are original. The sun is shining.

On previous tours the warm-up was the prerogative of the physiotherapist. On this tour Mark Davies concentrated on his priority: sorting out the knocks. In the first session alone, Scott Gibbs limped off with a thigh strain, John Bentley with a bruised toe and Allan Bateman with thigh problems. The former Wales back-row forward would earn his keep.

As he worked early overtime, the able-bodied few worked with another addition to the professional ranks: the kicking coach. Dave Alred concocted a variety of drills, chips, tubes, spot, line follow through, sweet spots – the new language of the professional age. As the Lions management wanted the maverick talent of Townsend to be employed at fly-half, Alred's task of tightening his lax kicking game would be vital.

The kicking drills over, the session gathered in its grizzly momentum. The players donned their Predator body armour and, to borrow the song title, got physical. Grown men raced around the paddock like Ninja Mutant Turtles, but if it took the knocks out of the constant collisions, who cared about high fashion? Indeed, Jeremy Guscott looked positively radiant in his red body armour.

The session was very long. That is one of the numerous pitfalls of bringing together players from four separate teams. Time is no ally of a British Lions squad. From a scratch training session to the first Test in Cape Town, the Lions had five weeks and a mere eight matches to gather shape enough to beat the world champions. The temptation to train, train and train again can prove almost irresistible. Dave McLean would need to monitor fitness and sharpness. Too much stamina can lead to insufficient acceleration. It would be a fine balance needed in order to walk the highwire successfully.

One man famed for the intensity of his training methods is the former headmaster from the Scottish Borders, the legendary hard man of forward coaching, Jim Telfer. Above the babel of British voices could be heard the booming Borders voice: 'Tighten up, tighten up . . .' Heaven help the forward with a high and bent back. After his first Telfer session, Lawrence Dallaglio grinned. 'He loves his drills, doesn't he?' To smile after that grilling was a real statement of professionalism.

But a player never feels as fit as when he first pulls on his Lions shirt. Back at the Lions base in Umhlanga, Fran Cotton welcomed the media 'into the Lions' den'. There was a boy-scout excitement, no matter how worldly wise, no matter how prominent the famous chin. The chin would have to face seven weeks of continuous probings from a media tuned into the new age and suitably ready to apply the populist slant. The days of 900-word match analyses were as redundant as the Friday-night piss-up on the eve of the Saturday match.

Instead the press-conference room in the team hotel assumed an air of general disinterest whenever McGeechan enthusiastically explained the theory behind what would prove to be radically chic rugby from the backwoods boys of Britain. That was something of nothing to many of the media men gathered. The journey is not important, only the end result. That is a prime reason for Jack Rowell's tendency to check the progress of his England for the sake of short-term advance.

There is a general preconception that the journalists who cover the sport know little other than how to work a laptop. It was a view to which I enthusiastically subscribed as a player. The reality is diametrically opposed to this, be it in the press box prior to the game or, and it must be stated that this occurs with gleeful regularity, the various bars and hotels in which profits soar to record levels. These men have a genuine passion for the sport. Just as training can be unbearable if a player is disinterested, so a seven-week tour can demoralise a nine-to-fiver. The British media are, for all our faults, an enthusiastic and relatively hard-working bunch.

The problems in the press conferences do not stem from the front-line media, but from the newsdesks in London, Cardiff or Edinburgh. It is this august group of gentlemen who decide on what is good, bad and interesting for public consumption. To read one tabloid, it is fair to assume that the correspondent is a man with limited vocabulary and even less rugby knowledge. It is a light year from the truth. Passionate about Wagner, Conrad and rugby, he can, and frequently does, entertain his colleagues with witty, erudite rugby opinion – but you would never guess from the final copy. But that is not his fault. Sports journalists receive scant praise, but generally the first year of professional British rugby was fortunate to be covered by men with reasonable integrity. If a personal scandal, irrelevant to the sport itself, was leaked to the British press, 95 per cent would cover it up. The other 5 per cent would be ostracised.

But that did not stop the endless pursuit of the headline in press conferences. Do media barons dictate the public thirst for knowledge, or are we granted the information we deserve? Better not to consider the answer. If you reach the same conclusion as me, the whole concept of democracy is undermined. How else do you explain nearly two decades of substantial minorities electing an ever-shrinking minority of the self-interested? Whoa, steady on the politics, Stuart. Anyway, the general public wanted, or were deemed to want, headlines.

Headlines frequently ride sidecar with inanity, and so the first press conference started in the manner in which conferences would continue. The daft question that has to be asked, the roll of the eyes from the Lions management and the refutation. Tim Rodber had been selected to play against Eastern Province, a name laden with bad memories. In 1994 he had been dismissed, playing for England against the same team, for what must be said was a pretty impressive combination of punches. Did the management consider leaving him out because of 1994? Of course not. In that case, had the Northampton man specifically requested that he should play, some sort of cowboy riding back into a bad town to avenge former wrongs? Of course not. I did not see the headlines in that particular paper, but the odds were on 'Lions send Rodber back to scene of past nightmare. England star ready for the challenge.' Then came what would become a persistent early-tour favourite, during the cold-war lead-up to the first Test. Martin Johnson had been rested for the opening match, and rumours of groin, shoulder and God knows what other injuries whispered their way around the various South African bars. Was he injured? If he was, the Lions management were hardly likely to admit the fact before a lineout had been thrown in anger. Even more preposterous, was he being rested in order to avoid an early confrontation with the immense South African lock Kobus Wiese? First rolling eyes of the tour.

But the Lions, funded by the sponsorship of Scottish Provident who for obvious reasons saw the media circus as a blessing rather than a curse, opened their hands in an early show of generosity. In the depths of the Durban winter, when the wind rages along the coast bringing Antarctic chills that send the temperature plummeting as low as 65 degrees, the press relaxed with the players outside the Beverly Hills Hotel in Umhlanga. Fortunately the duffle-coats were not *de rigueur*; this winter's day was a moderate 81 degrees. A giant barbeque (or braai, as South Africans call their outdoor cooking) made a warm day hot, as both sides wondered whether the press and Lions would ever be so close again. It would depend upon performance. It was not difficult to differentiate between the separate camps. One group was a blurred mass of Scottish Provident and Adidas logos, the other was an eclectic mix of jeans and jackets. One group sipped orange and lemonade, the other chardonnays and cabernet sauvignons. Jeremy Guscott looked enviously towards the jeans and jackets. Glory, riches, fame? But there are sacrifices too for the professional sportsman.

Some sacrifices are worth making. As the Lions basked in the sunshine, Scott Quinnell lapped up his very existence as a sportsman. The son of Derek Quinnell and the nephew of the great Barry John, he had stunned an entire nation when he turned his back on Wales for the siren call of rugby league. The professionalisation of the sport reclaimed him for financial reasons, but it was the Lions who rekindled the romance of the game for him. 'As a boy I dreamed of playing for Wales, but being a Lion was a long way from my thoughts, because to be a Lion is to be a part of a very special, élite band of players.' Fran Cotton was already calling this squad a special group of men, but the general mood of the British media was one of unstinting cynicism.

The selection included five men from Northampton, who had finished eighth in the Courage League, and five from Second Division runners-up Newcastle. It was not firm ground for optimism. Nobody dreamed of the impact some of these men would make on the entire tour. Or maybe Ian McGeechan and Fran Cotton did. The bold selections would backfire on both men, should the controversial selections of Matt Dawson, Nick Beal, Paul Grayson and John Bentley fail. Not one of these players inspired the confidence of the British public as the Lions prepared for their first match.

Question marks about players swirled in abundance around the team hotel, but few dared to question the unswerving commitment of Jim Telfer, the forwards' coach. The silver-haired hard man from the Borders is a rugby legend. On Scotland's recent tour of New Zealand, players would have to sneak into the breakfast room in the middle of the night to enjoy the forbidden fruit of sausage, bacon and egg. The squad arrived back in Britain looking like a group who had returned from a vampire convention. There had been no escape from the team room and the video machine. Telfer, as much as McGeechan, has helped Scotland to continually perform above expectation. Here was a man obsessed with the pursuit of achievement. His objective, as Rodber stated on behalf of a midweek team, was to bring South Africa to their knees. The bare statistic of just one solitary triumph throughout this long and bloody century was a stark reminder of the challenge facing a Lions team who prepared for their tour opener as 5–1 outsiders for the series.

The opponents were an Eastern Province Invitation XV. The Lions were clear favourites to win as the macho men of South African rugby had fallen on barren times. To boost their squad, Gauteng and South Africa stalwarts Hennie le Roux and the charismatic giant Kobus Wiese were drafted into the squad. That probably benefited the Lions, who are always vulnerable against a settled side in the early stages of a tour as the players become accustomed to the different habits of men they have never played alongside before. To counter this danger, the Lions selectors would select tried and trusted units where possible.

That unit was supposed to be the English back row of Lawrence Dallaglio, Richard Hill and Tim Rodber for the tour opener, but Rodber's dose of influenza destroyed that plan and allowed Scott Quinnell a chance to live the dream that, as a boy, he had not dared to dream. The half-back link of Robert Howley and Gregor Townsend had 'Test combination' stamped all over it. The strength of this middle five was the area where the Lions believed the game would be won.

The balance between victory and development was a key theme of the tour. Pyrrhic victories would spell disaster for the British and Irish squad, but the feeling persisted that the insecurity of the northern hemisphere in the backyard of the world champions would make any defeat one of profound psychological importance. The seven weeks were about three matches, but in order to arrive at Cape Town in a mood to compete, the Lions needed every possible ounce of confidence.

Jim Telfer understood the fine line on which the Lions would have to walk. 'Winning is very important because it builds confidence, but it is not the end of the world if we do not win.' But with the Springboks, battered by the Kiwis in the Super 12, at a rare low ebb, it would be psychologically disastrous to hand the initiative back to the host nation. Ian McGeechan would later admit that Carel du Plessis's decision to withdraw the Springbok players from the Lions' provincial fixtures was a massive boost, allowing his side vital extra weeks to build their game and their confidence.

The Lions left the luxury of Beverly Hills for Port Elizabeth, a town that rates pretty low on the South African entertainment stakes. It has seen better days. Arriving on Friday afternoon, the 1997 Lions made quite an impression with *The Herald*, the local newspaper. We painfully read of their heartlessness, how children waited for their autographs in vain at the airport. 'Even the press could only manage a grunt as a quote.' Even the media . . . heartless Lions! Port Elizabeth is a friendless town. Who can blame the Lions for being uptight when the objective local press urged its boys on with the message 'Down a Lion and we'll be happy'? (Lion Lager happens to be one of the most popular brands in South Africa.)

Johan Kluyts, the Eastern Province coach, sounded all the right notes. 'I know I have the personnel to beat the Lions.' And so said every South African coach who would face the 1997 Lions. If that was typical South African arrogance, the decent side was represented by Kobus Wiese. A World-Cup-winning lock, he said all the right things, emphasising the magical appeal of this occasional touring team. 'We play Australia and New Zealand every year, so this is the big one for us now. The opportunity to play against the Lions comes once in your career if you're lucky, and I want to be there for the Test series.'

Even before the first kick in the first match of the tour, it was the Test series, four weeks away from Port Elizabeth, to which eyes peered over the horizon. Each provincial challenge would be a battle for development and confidence, but the war would not start for real until 21 June in Cape Town. To emphasise the fact, Carel du Plessis, the new Springbok coach, arrived in person to watch the Lions' tour opener. His appointment was one of the most controversial in the history of Springbok rugby. A visionary winger in the '80s, his entire coaching pedigree was a mere six weeks with a Second Division club team in Western Province. It had stunned the South African media. Du Plessis's retort to the common question of 'How can a man with so limited experience coach a national team like the Springboks?' was 'To coach an international team, you don't need technical skill, you need vision'. It was a brave call. Du Plessis, also watching the Springbok stars in the spotlight, Hennie le Roux and Kobus Wiese, admitted that he was 'interested in the patterns that emerge'. He additionally highlighted the presence of Neil Jenkins at full-back. He was not complimentary. In the light of South Africa's failure to attack this area of Lions defence in the Test arena, one wonders what diverted his mind from what proved a correct assessment.

But back to Port Elizabeth, its once-thriving port that has fallen on hard times and the train that stands high above the open bank on the popular side of Telkom Park, the stadium rugby people will always know as Boet Erasmus. That name is synonymous with some of rugby's most violent scenes: the Tim Rodber incident and, most famously of all, the legendary cry of '99' from Willie John McBride's 1974 Lions. This is not the place of Brian Wilson's 'Good Vibrations'. It was a bitter disappointment for fight fans to see the sun rise over the Indian Ocean. Like the freakishly warm weather before England versus Ireland, the sun seemed like a harbinger for something other than the traditional expectations. The dark heart of South African rugby seemed more Southern California. Weird.

At least normality was restored with South Africa's typical disregard for the visiting Lions. They might not have rated their own teams, but they sure as hell thought even less of McGeechan's men. Stan Terreblanche of *The Herald* was adamant: 'There is no doubt that most South Africans, especially the rugby critics, tend possibly to underestimate the standards of British rugby.' Obviously the Irish were not even worthy of consideration.

The only Irishman to take the field at Boet Erasmus was Keith Wood. The garrulous Munster man had suffered a career of constant setbacks due to injury. This tour was his thrust for rugby greatness. He prowled the pitch beforehand, a nervous man in a nervous team. These players had waited a playing lifetime and two weeks of near-hysterical anticipation for this tour.

Ian McGeechan strolled around the ground with his arms draped around Gregor Townsend and Robert Howley. The two worked on their passing and struggled, yet this relationship was perceived as crucial to the Test hopes of the Lions. That was the reason for their selection in the first outing. They needed as much time together as possible. The minutes ticked by painfully until the magical moment arrived and Jason Leonard, in the absence of Martin Johnson, charged on to the field. The Tannoy rather surprisingly asked the crowd to give the Lions the 'welcome of welcomes to the friendly city'. On previous evidence this was normally eight pairs of large rugby boots, being used as part of a facial clog dance. But at least Elandre van der Bergh, the infamous Jon Callard stamper, had left for pastures new in

Mpumalanga. The Lions would eventually meet the man – but that can wait.

The professional age is upon us, but there remains an intangible thrill when a British and Irish Lions tour kicks off. It reminds me of the roar that echoes around the Cotswolds when the announcer at Cheltenham bellows 'And thair orf' at the start of the first race of the Cheltenham Festival. Eastern Province, with big Kobus, Hennie and assorted guests, entered into the spirit of the tour.

Despite the warm sun, many of the home side appeared frozen and the Lions raced into an early lead. As in New Zealand in 1993, the initial name on the scoreboard was that of the elegant Jeremy Guscott. He glided lazily on to a pinpoint-precision miss-pass from Gregor Town-send, leaving the home defence looking as if they had just encountered Medusa. A welcome defence indeed. Guscott was in glorious form. His omission from the England team was a blessing to McGeechan, as his prime strike player arrived fresh and eager.

The chief creator was the enigmatic Gregor Townsend. A series of bewildering switches of direction, changes of angle and sleight of hands instigated four of the five tries as the Lions won with a curate's egg of a performance, 39–11. The half-back partnership of Howley and Town-send looked a sharp unit, but for all his trickery, the maverick fly-half had not fulfilled the job description set by McGeechan. 'Gregor must manage a game well. We all know that he is an exciting individual, but he must work hard on his options and how he brings others into play.' He could also have added kicking. Before the players left Britain, Joel Stransky had singled out the Scot as a potential weakness because of his deficient punting. The standard of his restarts in this match was appalling, the punting from hand even worse and the strategy so subtle that not one person, Lions management included, could work out what was happening. At one stage in the second half, Eastern Province even took the lead because of Townsend's inability to control the game and with it territory.

Another problem which du Plessis had indicated beforehand was the form of Neil Jenkins at full-back. His lack of pace bordered on the dramatic as the coloured winger, Deon Kayser, rounded him for a fine home score to set the old steam train hooting in celebration. Worse still, Jenkins kicked as badly from hand as the slicing Townsend. Dave Alred, the kicking specialist, was quick to state that he should be judged on the first Test and not one day earlier. It was another indication that all roads led to Cape Town on 21 June.

The South Africans were none too impressed with the Lions pack either. The Eastern Province hooker and captain Jaco Kirsten told the first post-match press conference that 'We [South Africa] can take them up front. I am impressed with the ball-handling skills of the forwards, but they are not hard.' Still, one compliment from a South African was not a bad start from the Lions. The atmosphere was subdued as Fran Cotton, Ian McGeechan, Doddie Weir, Scott Quinnell, Will Greenwood and Jeremy Guscott faced the media for the first time. The performance had been inconclusive. There had been moments of brilliance and many more of mediocrity, but it was a first game. The conference was noticeable only for its blandness and the first post-match sighting of the ubiquitous Scottish Provident cap. Guscott gave nothing away as he told the world that 'The players expressed satisfaction in the changing-room afterwards'. It was maybe a 'So, what do you think, Doddie?' 'Oh, quite satisfactory, Howlers old bean.' Come on, Jerry!

Fran Cotton gave even less away. Did the Lions achieve their goal? 'You always want to win your first game' but 'We didn't control the ball as well as we would have liked', although on the positive side 'There is a hell of a lot of talent in the three-quarters'. Thanks for pointing out the obvious. The one obvious statement made by Cotton that is frequently forgotten is that the Lions are a disparate bunch when they leave Britain, and it does take time to blend. He was right to use the word 'only' to describe the first match of the tour. This was the first step from base camp; nothing of real substance could be gleaned. The only real note of interest during the conference was the disquieting look on Cotton's face when one of the South African journalists asked how the Lions would shape up against the Super-12 teams. Most people thought that the rarified air at this level would prove too much for the developing Lions of 1997.

That was in the future. The immediate hurdle to overcome was a Saturday night in Port Elizabeth. The presence of the touring Lions added some spice, but the rhythm of this city by the sea is decidedly redneck. There were no tears as we packed our bags and headed south to East London for the Lions' next match, against Border. There were also far fewer hangovers in 1997 than there had been after the 1993 opener. This team had their eyes refocused by one word: 'professionalism'. It is a profound pity that the loaders for South African Airways had lower standards. The entire wardrobe of one S. Barnes made the journey to Johannesburg as I travelled along the coast. The exceedingly kind offer of the Scottish Provident clothing wardrobe was dismissed – not my kind of fashion, and I was neither contracted nor paid to wear it. What thoughts must have raced through the mind of the sartorially elegant Jerry Guscott.

Less sartorially elegant, but no less a character, was the surprise selection of the tour, John Bentley, the Newcastle winger who had returned to union after a nine-year spell in league. He had so impressed the England selectors during his sojourn in the Second Division that he had failed even to make the bench for the 'A' team. He was Cotton's hunch, a man with more than rugby in his favour. Bentley is an immensely gregarious character, the sort of larger-than-life personality needed to cut through the insipidness of total professionalism.

He was one of 14 Lions starting for the first time in the match against Border after a tantalising two-and-a-half-week wait. But for Bentley it felt longer still. Selected for the opener, he had withdrawn with a toe injury. Rather like with Achilles, the body armour did not cover every inch of flesh. Not that Bentley had failed to make a contribution. His big-hearted, positive approach to life had won him a dubious accolade from his manager. 'John Bentley will make an extremely big contribution on the Entertainment Committee. He is one of the reasons why this squad has come together so quickly and so well.' Damnation with faint praise if ever I heard it. Like Donal Lenihan in 1989, Bentley was acknowledged as one of the good guys. The big Irish lock played a significant part in the series triumph in Australia as midweek captain and general joker, but the Cork man would rather have been remembered in the way Wade Dooley and Paul Ackford were – as Test players.

Great teams are generally a collection of determined individuals, and none was more determined than Bentley, who had no intention of filling the role of clown prince on tour. Eyes glinting, two days before the Border game he spoke firmly. 'I have sworn to myself that I will never lose sight of why I am here. I am here to do a job and that is to make the Test team and do my rugby justice. I am not here as a good-time guy, always on the lash, keeping up morale. That is a vital ingredient of the tour and there is plenty of place for humour, but I will not lose sight of why I am here.'

The 30-year-old sitting in the foyer of the team hotel in the quiet town of East London had metamorphosed from the England tourist to Australia of 1988 – his only major union tour before he turned professional. His infectious good spirits had been a godsend as the team meandered towards the wrong side of mediocrity. Heavy nights in

Sydney and Brisbane were the order of that time. 'I had a fantastic time. I would never swap it. I grew up on that tour. I went away a boy and returned a man.'

He showed enough ability to lure the rugby league coaches, and so Bentley left the fields of union, presumably for ever. Bentley of Sale became Bentley of Leeds and the metamorphosis began. The final crystallisation was the British Lion Bentley, and he was ready to reveal his hand of aces. 'I am definitely a better player now, and the main reason is that I am older and wiser. I have been described as a cavalier, someone who will do the unorthodox, when occasionally maybe it has not been suitable.' Maturity was one aspect that was lacking from the pre-league Bentley. Just as important, however, was the mental edge that league had added to his game. 'The professional approach that I have endured over the last nine years stands me in great mental stead for what is in store here in South Africa. At Newcastle I was surprised to find that lads with 30 or 40 caps still lacked the professional edge.' Rob Andrew confirmed how significant a role model he had been in Newcastle. Cotton had selected him partly for those reasons.

Yet for all the straight-talking tough-guy stuff, Bentley too was infected with Lions fever. It glowed from within. 'I always thought that one day I would return to union, be it as A.N. Other for Cleckheaton Thirds or whatever. But never in a million years did I expect to make the Lions tour party. If someone had suggested that, I would have said, "On your bike, you're taking the mick."'

Now Bentley was 48 hours from an amazing return to the biggest time of all for a British or Irish player. The wait had been longer than Bentley would have liked because of the frustration of his Achilles-like toe. 'That was a massive disappointment. If you look back at my career, you will see I have missed very few games through injury. To get injured in training before my biggest match of all was depressingly ironic.' Even in painful adversity, the Cotton version of a true professional tourist shone brightly. 'I suppose I could have played at a push, but I was right neither physically nor mentally. There are lads in the stand who are fully fit, so it would have been pretty selfish of me to play.' Neither Bentley nor the Lions of '97 could be accused of selfishness.

Bentley was one of six rugby league prodigals to make the trip. The others were Scott Quinnell and David Young in the pack, along with Scott Gibbs, Allan Bateman (or Batman, as the entire squad called him) and Alan Tait. Four of these six would have a major bearing on the tour. They were widely perceived as offering a hard edge, but their innate professionalism would prove far more significant. Paul Grayson admitted that 'It has been good fun training with the rugby league boys in the centre. Their influence and advice has been really helpful.' In rugby union, it has long been considered 'rather bad form to make a noise at training'. The racket that is heard on a soccer pitch was regarded as a little comical and a lot common. The league boys changed union perceptions in the same way as LSD did for a generation in the '60s. The training field reverberated to the Celtic twangs of Bateman and Gibbs, together with the incessant encouragement from Bentley on the wing. Defence and spirit were weapons of colossal force that the Lions would use to devastating effect.

That was the fascinating part of professionalism. Less interesting was the debilitating effect it apparently had on the mind. It would not be too great an injustice to say that East London in the rain – and did it rain – is the sort of place where a fertile imagination is a much-needed ally. Apart from a bar called O'Hagans, which stands out above the breaking waves of the Indian Ocean, there is little to see or do, and if you are watching your diet, even that is not much of a venue. East London does not have much confidence in itself. The advertisement for O'Hagans described it as 'rumoured to have the best views in South Africa'. What conviction from the advertising people. In truth, I like watching big breakers, but that can become monotonous after a few hours. But it was more fun than some of the Lions seemed to be having as players sauntered aimlessly from their rooms to the team room and the dining-room. Tony Underwood passed the time playing table tennis with Alan Tait, while Lawrence Dallaglio fine-tuned his brain over a game of darts with Martin Johnson, Matt Dawson and Paul Grayson. The team room was already littered with laundered kit which nobody would want to claim in six weeks' time. The Scottish Provident fashion show has a limited appeal.

Fran Cotton's first professional Lions were a contrast with their opponents, Border. Only seven of this side were fully professional. A policeman and a shop-owner had to miss their last session before the big match because of work commitments. Their coach was a Kiwi called Ian Snook. He had been coach of Bedford when they had broken all records for the size of their defeats. Watching their lightweight team practise, it was hard not to think that Snook would bring more of the same magic to Border. Only Russell Bennett, a full-back with a future that was soon to become an international present, looked a threat. Gavin Rich, a South African journalist who writes enough column inches a day to make

Pliny the Elder seem a slacker, described how Western Province had demolished them 'on a bad day, by 60 points'. Sporting Index made the Lions favourites to win by 25–28 points. At twenty pounds a point I bought. This match looked a banker. I had watched Border, done all my research. I could scent the sweet smell of a successful punt.

The clouds were unleashing remorseless storms and the pessimism of the weather was matched by the gloom of the front-page headline in *The Daily Dispatch* – 'Fear of Muddy Field for Big Day'. And there was I thinking South Africa had some other problems.

In the Lions' last serious workout, the tension building into the 'second first game on tour', as McGeechan put it, was palpable. Telfer introduced a diabolical full-scale forward practice that resulted in a head-butting scene between Barry Williams and Mark Regan. That was a story for the tabloids to grasp. It is an aspect of a competitive team that frequently occurs in a healthy squad. As an ex-player I understood that; but even as I cast my mind back to those days, I realised how strange is the warrior psyche of a rugby man.

Jeremy Davidson apart, the session was good for little bar the ferocity and the quality of Tim Stimpson's goal-kicking. If that aspect of his game held up, it was universally assumed that Stimpson would play full-back in the Test matches. Neil Jenkins's nervous opening display only reinforced these suppositions. But my eyes were on the man who would kick for goal against Border, Paul Grayson. His selection, along with that of his half-back partner Matt Dawson, had stunned me. McGeechan spoke of a playing style that had appeared anathema throughout Grayson's career. He had also not played for three months. Shortly before the flight, Grayson had tweaked the injured hamstring and thought, 'My God, I might not get on the plane.' That is what a Lions trip does to a player's mind. But Grayson was here and vying with his mercurial clubmate, Gregor Townsend, for a Test spot. It was an obvious enough question for the media to ask: 'How are you and Gregor getting on?' Grayson may be a bit of a grinder as a player, but as a man he is good, sharp company: 'I'm up on the darts, he's up on the table tennis.' Not quite what we hacks expected, but a good, witty soundbite. That's another line or two done . . . Grayson sounded a more serious note on the partnership with Austin Healey. 'We have played together for about ten minutes against Ireland and that is about it.'

McGeechan summed up the Border fixture by saying that 'The side that plays tomorrow will want to go out and make a statement to those in the stand: "Beat that."' Asked about the importance of kicking – a topic that would shape the next day's match and the Test series – he replied, matter of fact, 'All good sides kick well at whatever level.'

The Lions, despite the presence of the normally metronomic Paul Grayson, kicked abominably and scraped home to a desperately poor victory. The rest of the world were treated to the classic cliché of the small team rising above themselves because of the inspirational nature of the fixture. This frequently happens, but it did not at the Basil Kenyon Stadium in sleepy East London. The Lions plummeted to stygian depths. The other excuse was the 'second first game' theory as expounded by Ian McGeechan. As the red pen was being drawn through the Lions tour, the Scot almost pleaded that 'The second game is always dangerous. The excitement of the opening tour match is gone, but for these guys, with all their nerves, it is still a first game.'

All of that was true, but so was the blunt fact that Border were infinitely worse than Eastern Province – and they were hardly brilliant. If the South African Rugby Football Union had loaded the odds against the Lions by asking them to face three Super-12 opponents in the space of seven days, this start was the counterpoint. It should have been almost too easy, but, as in Port Elizabeth, the Lions were in danger of losing. This time victory was not secured until the dying moments. The weather hindered the Lions. McGeechan had his team thinking in terms of 15-man rugby, but the storm that blew off the Indian Ocean produced the sort of conditions in which only Noah would thrive. As the rain lashed down, McGeechan emerged from the dressing-room saying, 'We will have to be tighter, but we must still play football.' The emphasis was on the latter part of the sentence. That became apparent within a minute of the kick-off, as the first of countless exquisitely timed passes from Allan Bateman released who else but John Bentley for a try in the corner. 'Bentos' had scored a try with his first touch as a Lion. His chest swelled within the famous red shirt.

I awaited a deluge of points to match the conditions, but instead the Lions collapsed upon themselves. In basic terms, the match became a struggle because Paul Grayson could not adapt to treacherous kicking conditions. Two penalties from in front of the posts were missed and Border suddenly looked at themselves and thought, 'We are in with a shout.' When Grayson again turned villain and gifted Classen with a simple try, what should have been a formality became a tense affair, as I watched £480 of my shrewd gambling funds wash away.

But the kicking problems were secondary. Watching the game in the Sky studio in London was Jonathan Davies. His verdict was that 'The

Lions were naive throughout the game'. That was the problem. It was paradoxical that the Lions fly-half was primarily a kicker and yet, when conditions demanded that the ball be kicked deep to allow the opposition to make mistakes, he ran the ball from close to his own line, placing his own side under pressure. It was a day when errors and not brilliance would be the deciding factor.

If the Lions could not adapt to conditions, the thought of playing 15-man rugby was impossible. In the aftermath, rumours suggested that Grayson's groin had suffered a relapse with his first kick. If that was the case, he should not have played on. It was in stark contrast to the selfless attitude of Bentley. Either way it was a terrible day for Grayson, especially as the groin strain would terminate his tour. That was cruel on the Saint, but lucky for the Lions management, who must have realised after a few minutes that the decision to bring Grayson in front of Catt had been a mistake.

The other injury worry was a major concern: an ankle ligament problem for Scott Gibbs. Dr James Robson flew with Gibbs, ahead of the rest of the squad, to Cape Town to proceed with emergency treatment. It was left to Gibbs's former rugby league colleague, John Bentley, to wear the brave face and try to place the match and the conditions in some context. 'They were not ideal conditions for you fellas to work in, or for us to play rugby in.' The Most Valuable Player of the day was wooing the press with the same skill as that with which he would charm the Barmy Army when the big battalions arrived nearer the Test matches. More importantly, he stressed that the Lions had indeed failed to adapt to conditions and that the game was five metres slower. If anything positive was to be taken from the poor performance it was the fact that the Lions were determined to play at pace and with the ball in hand. Better to go down running than kicking.

The press conference was also noteworthy for another hooker/captain attacking the Lions pack. This time it was the jumbo-thighed Rhuan van Zyl. 'They scored two debatable tries and were not very strong up front. They won't be able to match our forwards.' The Lions had played two and won two, but the respect being shown by the South Africans was diminishing by the game.

This did not bother the Lions management. If anything it was exactly what McGeechan and Telfer wanted. Both men admitted later that night that the Border game had been a massive disappointment, as Sky Television hosted a dinner for the Lions in 'what is rumoured to have the finest views in South Africa'. The waves were good. It was acutely

153

impressive, but also depressing, to see the Lions tucking into their pasta and orange juice with such relish, but the management showed no such inhibitions. Big Fran Cotton blazed a trail of red wine bottles, which was not a shock, but the utter relaxation of Ian McGeechan was something for which I was not prepared.

McGeechan has an unsurpassed passion for the game. Rugby union is for him what women were for Casanova. He talks strategy, philosophy and technicality in streams of words with barely a gap for breath. In 1993 his intensity was almost frightening. It was obviously similar in 1997, but the winning smile that had been so rare previously changed the entire nature of this singular Lions coach. In both 1989 and 1993 he had achieved reasonable results. He had won a series in Australia and had beaten the All Blacks in Wellington. In South Africa he finally admitted that, to a certain extent, these triumphs had been Pyrrhic. They had been based around the raw power and precision of the English control freaks, Ackford, Dooley, Winterbottom, Richards and Andrew. If anything, both series had contributed to the growing gulf between hemispheres, as we in the north deluded ourselves about the size of the gap in playing standards. The Ian McGeechan of South Africa 1997 was not about to step backwards. 'Whatever happens, I will not turn away from this vision.' The vision was the same one accepted as the norm in New Zealand. Win, lose or draw, the Lions coach was not about to compromise his beliefs. He was intent not merely on beating South Africa, but on lifting the game in Britain and Ireland. He could look at himself in the mirror, knowing that fear of failure would not drive his '97 party back to dreaded conservatism.

The hawkish, darting eyes were a thing of the past, as he cracked jokes about Barry Williams developing an English accent and mused whether the nature of the tour and the timing of the games at altitude was a bad management decision on the Lions' part, or good management by the South Africans. The Lions coach was the same dedicated man, but he was a lot more relaxed. This would have a beneficial effect on the entire camp; when the boss is comfortable, so are the workers.

Yet however calm the demeanour of McGeechan, the lack of intelligence that permeated throughout the Border match added unnecessary extra pressure to the Lions' first serious challenge in Cape Town. Fragile northern hemisphere confidence could have survived defeat against Western Province as a one-off performance, but a loss straight after the East London fiasco would have endangered the crucial morale of the entire party. The significance of the match in Cape Town was illustrated by the selection of the team. Seven English forwards were in the pack, while the Howley-Townsend-Guscott combination remained in place.

The match was also to feature the delayed debut of Martin Johnson, the Lions captain, about whom rumours of injury grew daily. If the whispering campaign irritated him, he refused to reveal it. Here was a first-hand example of a professional at work – give the media nothing. From all corners of the press room in the less-than-memorable Holiday Inn Garden Court, Cape Town, the press attempted to goad Johnson into headline-making anger. The subject was the persistent South African taunt that the Lions were nothing more than pussy cats up front. Johnson neither knew nor cared about such comments, but what about the fact that the South African media were so underwhelmed? 'We won't be worried if the press are unimpressed.' It was not inspiring, but it was intelligent captaincy from a man many thought would fail to cope with the off-field aspect of captaining the Lions.

Wheeled in alongside him was Ieuan Evans. Here was an unfortunate fellow. At 33 and with three Lions tours to his credit, Evans was the senior statesman of the tour. While other players shot pool, or stretched on their beds in a catatonic stupor, poor Ieuan had to smile at the British and Irish media. Jeremy Guscott is only one year younger and also a triple Lion, but with professionalism his features have become more youthful. By the time Evans's tour was curtailed by injury, the amiable West Walian was totally irritated by Bob Burrows's persistent smiling introduction of him as 'the tour veteran'. Evans was experiencing the less glamorous side of professional rugby.

He too would face a Western Province side that had not played in Super 12, but were enjoying a renaissance. Players of the calibre of Fritz van Heerden, Percy Montgomery, Justin Swart and the irascible rogue James Small offered a touch of the exotic for the first time on tour. Arriving three hours before the game, you could feel that the tour was moving up a gear and starting to enter a vital phase with the first Test, also at Newlands, only three weeks away.

The script read that the English-based pack would overpower an allegedly heartless Province eight and deliver the ball on a plate for the half-backs to stamp their imprint. The reality was not far from being the exact opposite; the rugby world of Britain and Ireland turned upside down. The Lions were to win 38–21, but the plot unravelled with a twist that was almost Hitchcockian in its surprise. The Lions gained command with an early try that was all class. Townsend made a break, Howley scooped up the second-phase ball and, with peripheral vision, spotted Guscott wide out, and the Bath centre drew his marker and timed a perfect pass for that man Bentley. The woes of wet Wednesday were about to be forgotten – or so the travelling British thought.

What then happened will possibly be remembered as one of the turning-points of the tour. The English pack not only struggled to play the 15-man rugby required by the Lions coaches, they were also systematically destroyed in the scrum. The Western Province front row of Gary Pagel, the 34-year-old Keith Andrews and Andrew Patterson were a veritable Cape Canaveral from which the English props were launched into orbit. In 80 minutes, Jason Leonard moved from Test certainty to the next British astronaut. The destruction of the English juggernaut pack might have proved the conclusive evidence that our old-world values were of little or no use in South Africa. Enduring power is less potent than dynamic power. If Telfer and McGeechan had any reservations about the dynamic 15-man style before the Western Province match, the last lingering doubts had now been blown into space.

The Lions had arrived in South Africa expecting to compete in the tight but struggle behind the scrum. This day was a total role reversal. The pack were flattened (with the exception of the all-English back row of Richard Hill, Tim Rodber and Lawrence Dallaglio), but Guscott, Tait and Evans all tormented their opponents. John Bentley entertained the British contingent with an 80-minute running battle with James Small from which Bentley emerged with a points victory. But it was the efforts of two men in particular that won the day: those of the half-backs. Townsend varied his play beautifully, striking the ball well out of hand to the delight of Dave Alred, but even his performance paled beside that of Robert Howley behind a real Italian tank division of a pack. One break which resulted in an Evans try will long be remembered by all those present at Newlands.

Robert Howley was emerging as the single most influential player within the Lions squad. If the pack could find the power and technique to compete with the Springboks, a feeling the size of an acorn was growing that the pre-match medley of the Lions – comprising a lurid tune from each of the four nations – could become a stunning song of success. Howley was in effusive mood at the press conference. 'It was important here at Cape Town to put this tour on the map. This is where the tour starts.' We had heard that statement before the opener; we would hear it for a third time on the eve of the first Test. In reality, this was the start of the second phase of the cold war.

If Howley and the backs were buoyant, captain Johnson and his English legion had far less reason for cheer. The Lions skipper thought it a great game of rugby, one of 'far higher standard than anything played in the Five Nations'. On the sensitive subject of scrummaging, Johnson diplomatically admitted that 'They had us under pressure. They scrummaged as a team while we are still scrummaging as individuals.' Such an excuse often rings true in the early stages of a Lions tour, but when seven of the pack had combined to blast the Celtic countries in the Five Nations, it sounds a little lame.

The scrummaging weakness of the Lions was in danger of developing into a more general problem. This was the fittest squad to leave Britain, but David McLean, the fitness adviser, was aware that too much more endurance and the sharpness that was illuminating the Lions in the loose could suffer. But psychologically the Lions forwards were at least able to find themselves some lengthy straws. The weakness was in an area of traditional British strength. They would not have to enter a new dimension to correct their problems; it was 'something that at least we *know* we can improve', as Dallaglio said. It could also be the case that, in their concentration on an aspect of play unfamiliar to most of them, 15-man rugby, the forwards were not concentrating on their basics. A lack of mental edge would soon be addressed by Jim Telfer as the big Scot prepared for the fortnight of his rugby-coaching career.

Before Telfer 'gave the forwards the beasting of their lives' in the awestruck words of Ieuan Evans, there was the small matter of departure from Cape Town to the more hostile high veldt. To some of us within the media, this was a sad moment, but for the Lions it really made little difference. After the match the team dined at a restaurant near the team hotel and had an early night, so as to be fresh for training in the morning. As Table Mountain's famous cable car was closed for repairs, the squad did nothing but think, sleep and dream rugby. The flight from Cape Town to Johannesburg is a two-hour journey. As I tucked into an above-average Klein Constantia red to accompany my beef, I caught sight of Martin Johnson, sitting in front of me, turning down his meal. Wrong food, wrong drink, wrong time. I pulled out my notebook and scribbled, 'Hope the Lions win the series, otherwise a lot of young men will return home without any memories thinking what a waste of two months.' Professionalism can be a gamble with happiness at a time of life when it is most treasured. That makes professional sportsmen either more special or more stupid than we think.

The least happy of Lions was Paul Grayson. A man considered extremely lucky to have been selected had switched to the unlucky camp. His tour was officially over, accompanied by a babble of press boys whispering, 'If Howley was injured the management would give him longer.' It is impossible not to feel sympathy. The boy-scout atmosphere remained intact, with a 100 per cent record and a healthy battle for places being fought across most positions. It was a bad time to be the first long face on tour. Grayson would depart quietly on the Monday morning, but before he did so, Guscott and Jason Leonard sneaked him out of the team hotel to a nearby dive called Oscars, where the beer eased the sorrow until the early hours of the morning. That is the decent side of Guscott which he would rather few people knew.

As Grayson left and Mike Catt made a belated return to South Africa, all eyes narrowed their gaze towards the mean grey figure of Jim Telfer. Richard Hill, Tim Stimpson and Lawrence Dallaglio sat out the session on the tackle bags, a sure sign of belated trust between management and players and a further indication of the professional management within this squad which so impressed even an old rebel like Guscott.

The three-quarters, the golden boys like Guscott and Evans, are the names that grab most rugby headlines, but Jim Telfer and the pack selected for the game against Mpumalanga, a team with a ferocious reputation, were about to change all that as well as the balance of the impending Test series. The pack selected to face Mpumalanga had 'midweek' written all over it. Tim Rodber had arrived as the third-choice number eight, Neil Back and Rob Wainwright were clear cover for Lawrence Dallaglio and Richard Hill, as were Jeremy Davidson and Doddie Weir for the English second-row combination. In the front row Keith Wood had a fighting chance, as did the silent man of the tour, Tom Smith. While he is a brilliant handler and pure dynamite in attack and defence, old stagers like Geoff Cooke still thought him too small for the ultimate test of the Springbok front row. Paul Wallace was such a rank outsider that he had only toured due to the late withdrawal of fellow Irishman Peter Clohessy.

As they bent down for the first scrum, Telfer encouraged, not without a hint of threat, 'It's our ball, get closer to the scrum, and remember, locks, keep your legs up. Come on Doddie.' Weir straightened his back before Telfer found an available stick with which to beat him. The photographers milled around this macho dream, but the pack were way beyond posturing; it was them against the world. Tim Rodber, so often the gentleman, hissed at his colleagues after one scrum, 'Let's stop fucking around and hit this machine.'

Telfer became quiet as the players accepted their share of responsibility. Keith Wood, a man who would perform like some latter-day Cuchulain from a Yeats poem in the weeks to come, assumed command for the front row. 'Crouch now and thump into this machine.' It rocked backwards and hurtled into space; even the rank outsider Wallace had the scent of blood. 'This time we're going through the machine.' Coming from Wood's crouch position, the machine shuddered with the impact, but held. Telfer interjected, stepping up the pace and the intensity. 'Run round the posts and get a head of steam up.' In deference to his previous calling as a headmaster, I will leave some of the local colour of his language from the sentence.

From intense to infernal with Telfer whipping them on. Keith Wood, all Celtic charm and wit, was transformed into a demon. In fury he rounded on his mates, demanding, 'When have you ever hit a scrum without any aggression?' Pointing at his head to illustrate a mental puffiness, he exhorted his pack, 'This is fucking shit, now come on!' There was the image of Naka Drotské, the South African hooker, etched in blood deep within his imagination. 'To get these c**ts, you've got to be low from the start, and it's fucking aggression that works in scrummaging.'

Telfer, their avenging angel, grasped control again. 'Just another five seconds' – as Rodber's backside threatened to burst through the straining shorts as every single muscle worked at 110 per cent overdrive. The machine made a hissing sound as it beat a retreat. Rob Wainwright, another army officer, added his encouragement. 'Come on, boys, Bruce Lee style, through this machine.' The tempo raised again as a controlled menace arose from the scrum, given life as a chant of 1,2; 1,2; 1,2. Telfer, as animated as any forward, joined the chorus of determination, cajoling all the time, yelling, 'Tom [Smith], you are not at the seaside now' before the final cry of 'You have new hearts, you have new bodies'. He was convincing them that they had one more scrum in them, enough mental hardness to overcome exhaustion, but he was also laying the foundations for a special group of men who would use this new-found strength of body and mind to become British and Irish sporting heroes.

The lungs burned in the Pretorian altitude, but Telfer was certain that the benefit would be reaped from this grilling. 'It is the hardest I have worked the forwards on the machine. We did 42 scrums in 46 minutes, and they know exactly what they have done. It is money in the bank. Once they get there, they know they can go to that level again.' He had also talked about the technicalities of the scrum, but this was heart-and-soul, fire-and-brimstone coaching of the highest order. The media, a few of whom were stung by the vitriol of the Telfer tongue on the training field, wondered about the stream of invective. 'It is all meant to obtain a response. No player has ever said, "Don't ever say that to me again."' He then added, with comic timing, 'If they did, I don't know what I would do. Probably consult my lawyer.'

Telfer was the management version of Bentley, playing us all like a violin. But the honesty of Telfer's beliefs burned with real passion. 'There are only two types of rugby players, the honest ones and the others. That scrummaging session was about character as much as technique. You have to be mentally hard in the modern game, as you are almost always mentally fatigued. Any Lion looking for altitude as a reason to hide from pain and suffering should think again . . . I think you have to suffer 20 minutes of agony and just get on with it.' Tim Rodber, in the press conference the day before the game, offered no possible excuse. 'I enjoy the air. It is clean, and the lads are having fun.' Yeah, well the Marquis de Sade enjoyed strange habits too.

Telfer's session did the trick, as the Lions tormented the Mpumalanga Pumas as if they were domestic tabbies with a performance of sublime attacking quality and superior scrummaging. This was the 15-a-side game to which Ian McGeechan aspired, galvanised by the enervating footballing skills of the all-Celt front row of Tom Smith, Keith Wood and Paul Wallace. Jeremy Davidson also played a great game in the tight. But the two players who were the catalysts for the scintillating display were Neil Back and Allan Bateman, two commensurate footballers being allowed the freedom to express their gifts. Their linking in the midfield lacerated the opposition defence as the Lions flowed across for ten tries. Rob Wainwright scored a hat-trick within 18 minutes and Ieuan Evans, veteran or not, crossed for two. At 33 his lungs burned at full-time, not because of the altitude, but because 'There were so many braais burning all over the place. The smoke filled your lungs.' There are not too many barbies for Ieuan to worry about in Bath.

The competition for places was white hot. As Tim Rodber said, 'We knew after last Saturday we had to play well.' The pressure was now firmly on the Saturday crew. Tobie Oosthuizen, the granite captain of

Mpumalanga, was fulsome in his praise. 'They are not here for a holiday; we were beaten by a supreme team.' Ian McGeechan would probably have been forced to Witbank Hospital to have his broad smile surgically removed had it not been for the controversy that left one of the best British performances of recent times as a byline. On the day Mike Catt joined the Lions, a savage kick by Marius Bosman ended the tour of Doddie Weir, Bentley's deputy on the Entertainment Committee and one of the most popular men on tour. He was also playing the rugby of his life.

Reporters at the press conference were only interested in the violence. At last there was a headline story for the various sports editors. Ieuan Evans's telling statement that 'This side is learning more rapidly than the other sides I played in' and fellow winger Tony Underwood's view that 'We're getting out of the comfort zone . . . the kind of rugby we are playing demands a lot from ourselves' were of immense significance. Instead the only subject was poor Doddie. 'Fran, will you consider refusing to play Mpumalanga in the future?' Cotton tried – 'Look, you are taking all of this out of proportion' – but the headline-writers had their story.

Weir returned home, with cameras clicking and gruesome replays playing in the slowest motion. Sensation was everywhere, even with the news of Weir's replacement. It was a stunned press audience who were told that Nigel Redman would be joining the squad from Argentina, where he was travelling with England. Here was another story. Rumours abounded about Jack Rowell refusing to allow Catt to leave before England's second Test; rumours flew that he asked Redman not to leave. So this constituted a rift. Few acknowledged that Rowell and Cotton were working on different agendas. Rowell's was to develop a side to win a World Cup, Cotton's to win a Test series in South Africa. Even if Rowell was reluctant to release Catt and Redman before the second Test, it is understandable. But that is an irrelevance to an audience fed sensation and conflict. Maybe that is how we like it.

Redman's arrival was a story in its own right. The 32-year-old Bath veteran had been appointed an assistant coach at Bath. Andy Robinson had even asked him to consider retirement. He missed the end of the season because of an operation and was amazed to find himself a late call-up for Argentina. He then gained another cap before the biggest surprise of his career. 'Jack called me over and said, "Ollie, it's about the Lions." I thought he was asking for my advice and I said, "Jack, who do they want?" He said, "It's you," and I said, "I can't believe it," before he grinned and said, "Neither can I."' So Nigel Redman, one of the unsung heroes of modern English times, finally arrived at the place where the choirs sing your praises loudest – with the British and Irish Lions. Another magical story.

His presence raised the Bath presence to three, but only one of them had been there from the start. He, of course, was the West Country's most famous son and scoundrel, Jeremy Guscott. He was making his third Lions tour and in pursuit of Mike Gibson's centre record of eight Lions caps, and it is difficult to reconcile the laconic West Countryman with the increased demands of a professional tour. The image screams 'no', but the reality is different from the perception. In Bath, Guscott is regarded as the ultimate professional; the Lions management were equally impressed with his attitude. It is not easy for Guscott to conform with the new age as already described with relish by Tim Rodber.

Such conformism is anathema to the man, but sufficient motivation was enough to keep his candle burning. In the Lions tour of Australia in 1989, Guscott glided into rugby fame and has remained near the back page ever since. Yet for all the international caps and Lions tours, he remained in danger of being remembered as the player who could have been so much more. England, with their rigid running lines to suit the more prosaic gifts of Will Carling, too often left the man withering on the vine, be it on the pitch or on the bench.

Guscott realised that South Africa possibly offered him the great chance to become the centre of attention and not just 'one' of the best. As Tony Underwood had stated, the Lions were playing outside the comfort zone and demanding a lot from themselves. That suited Guscott. Bath, flawed at times, had performed with a wealth of ambition, helping Guscott produce his finest domestic season for a decade. 'I have played my rugby wide and cut angles; that's what I do best.'

Wearing the four letters J–A–C–K on his gumshield, Guscott proved not to be the easiest of tourists. He and Bentley had more than the odd altercation, but if the Lions were to draw the best from Guscott, it would be on the centre's terms. 'I have no more points to prove, other than to myself. This is really about me enjoying my rugby. I can only do that getting the ball.' The Lions were supplying Guscott's habit so well that the small matter of two sublime seven-point passes against Western Province did not lead to a rating of anything other than 'quiet' from the British press. Guscott had set early tour standards that demanded a perpetual firework display.

Ian McGeechan's new *laissez-faire* attitude was best illustrated by the subtle way in which Guscott was handled. Fran Cotton hit the nail firmly on the head when he said that Guscott needs to be pampered, to feel special. On the day of the first Test in Cape Town, David McLean said that Jeremy Guscott had been 'sent off tour' ten days earlier, allowing him to remain refreshed and focused. As Guscott was one of the first players to express early signs of mental fatigue with a small subject called 'rugby', it is to the credit of the flexible Lions management that Guscott did not crack at an early stage.

It broke all the democratic rules of the Lions, but Guscott was treated with kid gloves. In David McLean's words, 'He did what he wanted.' Certainly the famous Guscott groin was used as an excuse when training became too tedious. As early as before the second match against Border, the centre could be seen lazily stretching his groin away from the war zone that was opposed training with Allan Bateman and Scott Gibbs as opponents. I walked past him and laughed, 'Good tactical injury, Jerry' – to which he responded with a knowing wink.

In bygone days such privilege would have elicited jealousy and anger, but while the muse was with Guscott, everybody remained content. Guscott himself was surprised by the degree of warmth he received from the locals. 'The South Africans have been very warm and welcoming. I have been taken aback by their attitude; the crowd have even applauded us. But the hardest thing is the media, with their "wait until you get to . . ." comments.' (This is a legacy of the South African rugby fan who cannot believe a single South African team can be beaten unless *they* are weak, hence the 'wait until you reach . . .' philosophy.)

He was more enamoured still of the 'non-old-school-tie' management. Given responsibility, Guscott had responded sensibly. 'One [drinking] session a week is not too bad for me at my age' – although the overflow of joy hardly carried on to the training park, where the length of the sessions forced Guscott to compare Jack Rowell's notoriously long and rambling sessions to a quick sprint.

The edge of discontent was never totally missing, and Guscott would travel to some weird lengths to maintain his inner harmony. 'I have to make myself relax, and one way I do that is to wander around annoying people. I do what I want, when I want, and I am not going to conform.' There is more than a hint of arrogance in the words, but for too long the moderate British have been afraid of a characteristic around which teams like South Africa and Australia have nurtured great teams. The behaviour of Guscott and his sympathetic handling by management was as good a testimony to the benefits of professional management as anything on this tour.

Another beneficial side-effect of the new professionalism was the acceptance that nothing should hinder the mental preparation for a match. This resulted in small-scale delirium on the Thursday before the Lions faced Northern Transvaal. The Lions were booked for an Embassy evening, but to the joy of the 15 starters, McGeechan excused them. Jason Leonard positively bounced around the courtyard pool area of the Holiday Inn Crowne Plaza, Pretoria, where the Lions and media had set up base for 12 days.

A combination of settling into one hotel for a reasonable duration and a commanding, kaleidoscopic display in Witbank distinctly changed the atmosphere surrounding the tour party. The relationships between players and press were as relaxed as I can remember. There was no hint of the siege mentality that has afflicted the nation's travelling cricket teams. Scottish-Provident-clad athletes sat in the endless winter sun of the high veldt, sipping tea, coffee or juice and smiling contentedly. The mood was excellent. Tough and focused, with some medicinal relaxation thrown in. One thing missing from the Lions' itinerary was a sightseeing agenda. I wondered how players like Guscott, who were producing ghosted books, could discuss the general nature of Africa when all they had seen was the inside of a hotel that could have been in Jakarta, London, Paris or Pretoria. Even the food was carefully monitored. Nothing as exotic as kudu or zebra would pass a Lion's lips. (Zebra, by the way, is even worse than horse meat – not bad curried, but not much good in any other dish.)

The diet was important. Not only would the right food keep a player's tank fuelled in the dying minutes, but it would help fight the unseen germs and viruses encountered during a tour of a country as vast as South Africa. While the ship sailed serenely on, Dr James Robson and his crew worked remorselessly. The odd stomach bug that forced players from a team made a headline or two, but the majority of illness was unknown to the outside world. Far more players were being undermined than anyone realised. It was not the poison scare which Laurie Mains of New Zealand alleged occurred in 1995, but something as simple as the water. 'South Africa is so vast that all the different types of bugs in the water, which are normally harmless, can affect a player who is constantly travelling.' While Ian McGeechan, Jim Telfer and Andy Keast mused over videos of South African players, James Robson waged a silent war with the bacteria which were seeking to do what none of the first four opponents had done and lay the Lions low.

The Lions were well aware that their next opponents could prove as dangerous as even the most belligerent microcosm. Next up were Northern Transvaal. The Lions were to have their first taste of a Super-12 opponent. Like all the South African provinces, the famous Blue Bulls had struggled against the power of New Zealand teams, but the fact that mighty Auckland had been held to a 40–40 draw at Loftus Versfeld served as a reminder that this was a team capable of raising their game. Traditionally Northern Transvaal has been at the epicentre of the South African game. The entrance to the main stand is a shrine to the glory of a magnificent playing record. Pretoria is a town that has the whiff of rugby and racism in equal measure. The team's supporters are as partisan as any in world rugby. Although such luminaries as van der Westhuizen, Kruger, Dawie Theron and Krynauw Otto were missing because of Carel du Plessis's ill-judged decision to bar his best players from provincial encounters with the Lions, this would be another step up.

McGeechan knew it. 'There will be an increase in the intensity of the rugby. Super 12 has given them a different experience from us in some respects. We will have to find a new level if we are to do well tomorrow.' The Scot looked even further over the rugby horizon and saw 'the hardest month of rugby that any of us have been involved in'. To win the series, the Lions would have to make the most of every single opportunity, on and off the pitch. To achieve that the selectors would have to be as precise as the players.

Cotton was talking the 'there is no midweek side, dirt-trackers, call them what you will' line, but the nature of the team to face Northern Transvaal revealed a consistency with the other 'tour toughie' so far, Western Province. The Howley and Townsend combination teamed up with Guscott, and, more importantly, the coaches placed their faith in the big men of England. The entire front five were English, together with the consistently excellent Lawrence Dallaglio, whom most pundits had already penned into the Test team. Scott Quinnell was in pole position for the number eight slot, and the talented Irishman Eric Miller was granted a chance to stake a claim for the open-side position.

Under an eternal blue sky, the Lions train slipped off the fast track along which it had been rumbling. It was exactly what the tour needed. The ambition and skill of much of the Lions' play had been exceptional in the first four games, but the basics needed to win the first Test were all wrong. If the Lions had limped to Cape Town unbeaten, McGeechan and Telfer may not have been forced to make the radical selection which would carry them to glory.

This seems a harsh verdict when you remember that the Lions only lost by five points and finished on the attack. But, and it is a substantial but, Northern Transvaal were severely under strength and, as John Williams, the Blue Bulls coach, said, 'We had seven or eight players who had been out for a month and just ran out of steam.' There was, however, much he did admire about the Lions. 'If you allow them to run with the ball you will be in a hell of a lot of trouble.'

The Lions backs were devastating. Townsend, as maddeningly wild as ever, gave a try away but scored or created three. Howley sniped dangerously and Guscott was as lethal as a rattlesnake with ball in hand. The character of the team was proved in adversity; it was only the restarts and the scrums that needed work – areas in which the Lions knew improvement was possible. Unfortunately, without these foundations, McGeechan's effort to take British and Irish rugby from its ten-man mud hut to futuristic skyscraper was doomed to crumble and collapse. The England front row could compete with France, but against Western Province they had been catapulted and in Pretoria they were again outplayed at vital moments. The dynamism of the southern hemisphere game is less suited to the endurance of the English prop forwards. The scrummage in Britain is a ten- to twenty-second battle; in South Africa the war is won on the initial hit and drive. Rather like a tug-of-war contest, two teams may be evenly matched, but once one side gains a slight edge and a bit of momentum it becomes nigh-on impossible to halt the progress. The heavy-limbed English were finding the initial drive of the South Africans difficult to contain.

The southern hemisphere also applied the new rules far more stringently than their northern counterparts. The law states that back rows must stay bound on the scrum until the ball emerges from the base of the scrum. As a result the scrum becomes a fundamental weapon of attack and defence. Northern Transvaal were to teach the Lions a lesson. By wheeling the Lions pack with impunity on the 15-metre line, they moved Dallaglio out of the game and enabled Conrad Breytenbach a half-metre in which to break. That 50-centimetre window of opportunity ended in a try for the impressive Blue Bulls skipper, Adrian Richter. In defence the Bulls produced a drive and wheel that enabled Roland de Marigny to use his favoured left foot to clear. Under pressure, he would have been forced to kick with the weaker right foot. The difference was approximately 50 metres and a psychological hammer blow.

The positions of Leonard and Rowntree, doubtful after the previous two games, emerged as black and white. If Wallace and Smith held their form, the Celts, so battered in the northern hemisphere, would play in the Tests. Nobody was certain if they would bear the brunt of power from Adrian Garvey and the mammoth Os du Randt, but the inadequacy of the England pair's early form, added to the Celts' tremendous work rate and skill in attack and defence, made their case a strong one despite the incumbent risk involved. The other major beneficiary of the day was Neil Jenkins. Tim Stimpson kicked his goals, but in general play he was a gangling, slow-witted disaster. He missed high balls and tackles and hit the line with the intelligence of a cow. His counter-attacking lacked any sophistication bar 'Where is the next bloke for me to run over?'. Such subtlety might work in Wakefield, but not on the merciless fields of South Africa. Jenkins had not covered himself in glory either on his one start at full-back, but the problem with the restarts made his case irrefutable. Watching in London, Tony Ward reckoned that the forwards had not been given an incentive to chase restarts because Townsend 'is not a natural kicker'. He considered Neil Jenkins at fly-half, but, for all his faults, Townsend remained one of the Lions' few matchwinners. Neil Jenkins, who had been drifting away from the serious action, had suddenly been thrust back towards the centre stage without taking the field. That can only happen on a tour; thus has it ever been.

The Lions camp were philosophical in defeat. Telfer thought the pack improved on their Cape Town performance, but Gavin Hastings reckoned 'He will be seething inside. The forwards are in for a torrid time.' The Telfer magic seemed to work better on his fellow Celts; perhaps their ears were more sensitive to the Caliban style of his magic. McGeechan touched on the casual nature of the first half. 'We were too slack; we gave ball away too easily and allowed Northern Transvaal a lot of possession for which they did not have to work.'

But the pessimism was partially blunted. Guscott, outstanding again, echoed John Williams's sentiments. 'When we received the quick ball we require as three-quarters we were devastating.' Cotton also smiled with his handful of long straws. 'If we had controlled possession better and received quicker ball we could have won, because we have tremendous runners outside.' Even Adrian Richter refused to dismiss the Lions. 'They are preparing for a Test series and they will be a different team come Cape Town.' There were echoes of Dave Alred's comments after the first match of the tour: 'Don't judge me on today, judge me on the first Test.'

Despite the setback, the Lions stayed positive. The sheer quality and ambition of their game was lifting their backs to new levels of excellence, but the pressure was growing on the pack. John Williams was right to say 'If they want to play this game, they must scrum well and start driving. Scrumming is not a question about the strength of the Lions, it is a state of mind.' Those forwards who were on McGeechan and Telfer's wavelength had stolen a march as the tour moved inexorably towards the first Test.

The Lions had lost a battle, but this defeat might just have been the one that set them on course for a famous sporting conquest. Telfer looked back on this day as a crucial moment of the tour. 'Northern Transvaal gave us a shake because we thought that we had cracked it after Mpumalanga. The attitude was a shade lax against Northern Transvaal and we leaked tries too easily. We knew after that game of the level of tiredness we will reach and the level of concentration needed. It's the mental bit, what is between your ears, that matters at rugby's highest level.' The tour had reached a watershed. The 15-man flamboyance of the Lions was about to don a shield of quite extraordinary mental hardness that would end all the nostalgic talk of 1974 and finally bring the British and Irish game out of the past and into the present.

The Professional Lions:… To Glory
at Sea Level

The immediate future was grim for a man whose name stirred images of both eras. Scott Quinnell, son of the '70s Lion Derek, did not train on the Monday. He would not train again with the 1997 Lions. A long-standing groin injury was the official story, although reports of alleged disputes with the management whispered their way around South Africa. It is difficult to believe the management would consider sending the number eight home, because Quinnell's ball-carrying skills and raw power were a foil to the rapier threats out wide. If Quinnell played, it would be impossible for the Springbok back row to concentrate solely on the clairvoyant trickery of Townsend. He was a balance in the attacking plan. The blow was felt not only by Quinnell, but by the entire press corps, who had failed to trace even a scent. As Chris Hewett of *The Independent* said, 'Thank God we were not involved in Watergate. Nixon would have remained President until he died.'

As Quinnell departed, injured and not dismissed, the Lions looked forward to the Test match, only three games distant. Cotton, growing more Churchillian by the day, elaborated. 'We did not want to peak on 7 June, but on 21 June.' There were only 12 days remaining. McGeechan continued with his development theme. 'It's important that we are still developing the momentum and the way we want to play. The way we have to evolve is the key to the Test match.' The Lions were no longer unbeaten, but the Lions management refused to panic. It was onwards and upwards – with the exception of the front row in the scrum.

The cast of Lions continued to grow as Tony Diprose of Saracens and England joined team-mates Richard Hill and Paul Wallace. Three Saracens in the Lions – it was another sign of the changing order. When Kyran Bracken arrived to make them a clique of four, we entered a surreal world in which I feared losing all grasp of reality. A British team playing with flair and conviction, plus *four* Saracens – it was almost too much for my red-wine-addled brain to comprehend.

So too would be defeat for the Lions at Ellis Park, where they faced Gauteng Lions (formerly Transvaal). The matches were becoming as much a matter of personal performance as team development, as 35 players strained to prove that theirs was the chest to fit the shirt come 21 June. The side to face Gauteng contained few Test certainties. The one banker was Guscott, who was forced to play because of a slight hamstring strain for Allan Bateman and a one-match ban for Scott Gibbs. At this stage the chunky Welsh centre, later christened the fastest prop in the world by Guscott, was not enjoying his tour. Injury had delayed his start and such was his fierce determination to make an impact when he came on as a replacement against Northern Transvaal that he was immediately penalised, first for a short arm jab and then for a stiff arm tackle. In response to the Lions' justified demand for a citing of Mpumalanga's dirty duo of Marius Bosman and Elandre van der Bergh, the South Africans made a similar protest and Gibbs received a one-game ban. If Bateman had not been injured at this juncture of the tour, Gibbs may never have been offered a chance to terrorise the Springboks. Once again, luck may have been riding with the Lions.

Guscott was promised a break from training and playing if he could raise his game for a second time in four days. McGeechan was using his cutting weapon more than he wanted; the least he would do to correct the balance was allow him a complete break, both physically and mentally.

His Bath team-mates, Catt and Redman, were selected to make their debuts, but from a Test perspective all eyes were on Tom Smith and Paul Wallace. If they could stand up to a front row including a Springbok and an Argentinian international, they would be 90 per cent *en route* to forming one of the most unlikely front-row units in the history of the Lions. It was also another big game for Tim Rodber at number eight. He, more than any other Lion, summed up the growing importance of each fixture. 'When the crunch comes, that is when we have to be honest with one another. That's when the red shirt matters.' Telfer had an obvious acolyte in the Northampton skipper, and Fran Cotton was playing an almost identical tune of integrity. 'Nationality does not enter into anybody's head when you are a British Lion.' The midweek front five of 1993 may have lost their Lions' pride, but the '97 Lions were growing with every game.

The Gauteng game was crucial. All the confidence developed during the opening three weeks of the tour would vanish into the thin night air of Johannesburg, should the Lions lose a second match in succession to a Super-12 combination. The British and Irish inferiority complex would become a dominant dark thought. Cotton knew it. The smile was totally false as he paced up and down the touchline as kick-off drew near. If the pre-match dancing of the respective Lions, the large British and Irish one and the squatter Gauteng beast, was any indication, the Lions from overseas were in for a torrid time. The home Lion cavorted to the music like Michael Jackson, while the more staid British creature moved with all the grace of Prince Charles at a rock and roll party.

The early signs were ominous. Gauteng, honed by the ball-retention skills required to compete in Super 12, kept possession for the first ten minutes. The Lions defence was stretched to and beyond breaking-point and only an amazing handling blunder by Springbok winger Pieter Hendriks prevented an early try for the dominant home team. For the first time the Lions looked outclassed. The Springboks were growing into imaginary giants by the second in the minds of every British and Irish supporter, but somehow the Lions held out and reached half-time with the game still in the balance.

The second half will remain famous for the hallucinogenic John Bentley try. Few better solo scores can ever have been dotted down across the line by a British Lion. It was a sweet moment for Bentley, who had been substituted after an indifferent effort against Northern Transvaal. 'I was down after being substituted against the Blue Bulls, so this try was great for my confidence. I have never been greeted with anything like the elation I received from the rest of the squad.' The modest John Bentley then took command. 'Mind you, if I can't go around a hooker, I ought to be on the next plane home.' For the record, the hooker was the ultra-competitive James Dalton. After beating him, Bentley swerved beyond Dieter Krause, a flanker, before weaving infield and past four tackles for a try that any old Superman could have scored.

Cotton was ecstatic. Asked whether the Lions were back on track, he beamed, 'You should hear that changing-room right now.' The second half was described by the manager as 'the defining moment of the tour'. Two and a half glorious weeks later, he would be proved spot-on. Bentley's weave will be the memory that lingers, but the strengths that would be the Lions' bulwark in the battles to come were falling into place. Until Ellis Park, it had been the backs who had been grabbing the headlines. This win changed that. Gauteng scrummaged the Lions with a fearsome ferocity for five minutes when a score early in the second half might have carried them into an irretrievable lead. Wallace and Smith did not budge. Fran Cotton believed the Lions 'outscrummaged Gauteng tonight'. Kobus Wiese, the opposition captain, noted that the 'scrums went down a hell of a lot tonight'. The short Lions props would not allow any front-row unit to cause the mayhem inflicted by the Western Province front row. They would be penalised frequently in the next three weeks, but they would never buckle and they would never allow South Africa to assert a platform from which to unleash their monstrous running force of forwards.

It had been a heroic effort. That was the first time the word had been used. It was about to become *the* tour word. Austin Healey was in awe. 'They worked like I have never seen a pack work before . . . it was the forward effort that got us back into the game.' Ian McGeechan picked up another future byword for the successes to follow, claiming, 'The self-discipline in the second half was very important,' while the Gauteng coach Ray Mordt put his finger on the final piece of the jigsaw, admitting, 'In the last 20 minutes they had our guys pretty tired.' All those long and gruelling hours of training, supplemented with quality rest time, were starting to pay dividends. The Lions left Pretoria for Durban with increasing confidence, inspired by the ringing words of most white South Africans: 'Gauteng were useless; wait until you get to . . .' Next up were Natal Sharks, the Currie Cup holders.

The challenges facing the team selected for the last Saturday clash before the first Test were numerous. The marketing of the sport in South Africa frequently borders on, or crosses, the gruesome. Waiting for the Lions on every lamppost in Durban were the big-match posters which warned the public: 'Just when you thought it was safe to go back on a rugby field' . . . accompanied by the imaginary tune to *Jaws* as a fearsome great white shark juts his jagged teeth towards the reader and any Lion stupid enough to consider taking on South Africa's finest.

There was also the challenge for the team to continue developing towards the impending Test and, no matter what the players stated publicly, there was the battle that had reached fever pitch for a place in the starting line-up. The Lions management held their line about starting places being available up to and including the midweek match to follow, but there is no doubt that this was the nearest the management had come to a statement of intent. Neil Jenkins was included at full-back alongside a first Test backline with the exception of the resting Jerry

Guscott. Up front Tom Smith and Keith Wood were one solid game away from a Test berth, while Simon Shaw and Eric Miller also had real chances to ink themselves into the team.

Dave Alred and Neil Jenkins worked at every available opportunity, sizing up the kicking conditions at King's Park with one eye on the Natal match and one on the second date, a fortnight later. There was real confidence, not only in the boot of Jenkins but in what had been the Achilles' heel of the team: the scrummage. Telfer had defended his forwards from adverse criticism in the early weeks of the tour, but it was not until the day before the game in Durban that he began to talk them up. Now he was praising their scrum technique in advance of another major test, despite Natal being shorn of their Springbok entourage.

The individuals would need to impress collectively to find favour with the Scottish guru, as the core unity and spirit of the party was reiterated in blunt terms. Although the media regarded this as a dress rehearsal for the first Test, Telfer was adamant that it had not been discussed. 'The player who lays his body on the line for the team will be considered in front of the guy who plays for himself.'

Martin Johnson, growing in stature as he neared the heavy line of fire, reiterated this point, 'You have got to play better than the guys did against Gauteng if you want to play in the Test team.' And as Johnson had already stated how well the team had played in midweek, the magnitude of the mission was clear to every Lion as they ran out, through the five ubiquitous Lion Lager banners that had followed the tour throughout South Africa, to an audience of 42,000 spectators.

The match was a bittersweet one. The Lions performed with less flamboyance and more organisation than at any time on the tour. It was a superb step towards the first Test, but the sight of Lions scrum-half Robert Howley leaving the field with an injured collarbone was almost as sickening a blow for the entire Lions party as it must have been for poor Howley's parents, who were packing their bags in readiness for a holiday in South Africa. The Cardiff scrum-half had been perceived as the most important player in the team. Not only was he the crucial link between forward and back, he was also a threatening runner in his own right. His presence allowed the erratic genius of Townsend an extra split second in which to think . . . and at his best that is all Townsend needs.

The media from Britain and Ireland were actually more downcast than the Lions management, who, like a trainer with a racehorse, cannot afford to be too sentimental. Nor could they allow themselves to rage against fate excessively; that would merely undermine the confidence of a replacement who already knew that he was playing by default. Howley was going home, but the Lions were rolling on.

There was immense encouragement to take from the performance. Ian McGeechan reintroduced the themes that a week later would seem to have been on the tongue and in the mind of every reporter and commentator forever. 'I thought that today we were very patient and we kept our continuity together. Our scrummaging was excellent, our defence was better, our restarts were improved and our discipline was one of the most gratifying elements.' The skyscraper which nobody believed McGeechan could build in a brief eight-week period was rising on the Durban skyline.

Jim Telfer, sounding more and more upbeat, rated the efforts of the eight as 'the best scrummaging display so far. We became stronger and stronger as the game progressed.' Back in London, Tony Ward saved his eulogies for the defence of the Lions. 'It was all hands to the pump stuff. The tackling at the base of the gain line was the best I have seen on tour.' In victory, Martin Johnson appeared to develop a previously unsuspected *gravitas*. The Lion King was keeping his team's feet on the ground as effectively as the likes of Bateman, Gibbs and Dallaglio were knocking opponents to the earth. A scoreline of 42–12 is a convincing win anywhere in South Africa, especially in Durban, yet Johnson was deadpan. 'We've won quite well, but it doesn't mean anything. We have to win two Tests. It is a good progression, though; it's better than losing and not playing well.' And if these words were not enough of a dampener, Big Fran chipped in too. 'It has done no harm to our confidence, but Saturday is a different day.'

Despite all the low-key words, a number of Lions were unable to hide their elation. The stars of the show had been the dancing feet of Ieuan Evans and the immensely muscular game of Lawrence Dallaglio, but Neil Jenkins beamed a redder shade than a Lions shirt. McGeechan would probably have liked to see Natal test him under some high kicks, but Jenkins escaped the fury of aerial bombardment and calmly kicked himself into the Test team. Bateman and Gibbs were vying for a place alongside Guscott. It was Bateman's guile or Gibbs's presence. The fact that Bateman had not played inside centre would also count against him. Dawson did enough as a replacement to edge ahead of a strangely subdued Healey (who probably found the self-imposed discipline of the Lions a tough act to follow). In the forwards, Keith Wood and the fast-emerging cult figure of Tom Smith cemented their positions with a couple of dazzling performances, while Richard Hill found yet another gear to hold off the persistently outstanding Neil Back. The other iconic effort came from Eric Miller. The 21-year-old Irishman has everything a rugby player could want, except the most priceless commodity of all: luck. There is no legislation for the whim of the lady.

The tour was gathering such momentum that it would have been no surprise for the Lions to have flown down to Cape Town under their own steam. South African rugby people still did not believe that the Lions could possibly beat their world champions, but the initial preconception that the visitors would be more lambs to the slaughter than roaring lions, mere preparation for the Tri-Nations, had been brushed aside since their excellent response to the defeat at Loftus Versfeld. The winning habit had kept the squad fresh and together; all rivalry was of the friendly variety. There are times in sport when the spirit, the heart and the guts pull you through as much as talent. We were unsure whether the Lions would match the skill of South Africa, but every rugby follower who had watched McGeechan's team develop knew that this group were nothing if not scrappers. Cotton's insistence that they were special men even before they left Britain was surely grounded in rhetoric, but as a chink of light appeared in the week of the first Test, a few began to take the assertion seriously.

What was taken less seriously was the assertion that nothing had been decided in terms of the team for the first Test. In hindsight we can see that this was a deception on a political scale. Only Dai Young, Eric Miller and Allan Bateman started in Durban and not Cape Town. Of those three, Miller was to be cruelly deprived of a starting place by a stomach bug and Bateman only played in Durban because Guscott had to be rested. Conversely, the Tuesday team selected to face the Emerging Springboks carried one solitary member of the first Test team. Jeremy Davidson of London Irish and Ireland had grown in stature since a disappointing opener in the mud of East London. His selection in front of Simon Shaw was the final repudiation of Five Nations power rugby.

It was ironic that as Ian McGeechan belatedly pushed British rugby into the future, his counterpart, the inexperienced and fiercely criticised Carel du Plessis, was apparently returning to a bygone age of ponderous one-dimensional rugby. His reputation is that of a visionary, but there was nothing futuristic about the South African training session on the Monday before the Cape Town Test. However, there was plenty about which to be intimidated. It was a good session for Paul Wallace and Tom Smith to avoid witnessing.

The giants in green were training at the Silvermine naval base, a half-hour from Cape Town's centre. The only thing in Africa that could tower over these brutes was the rugged range of mountains that forged a scenic backdrop to bring a tear to a pioneer's hard eye. The rocks reverberated with the guttural cry of 'Een Groote' (one big one) as Os du Randt, glistening with sweat, ignored the Springboks' forwards' coach Gerd Smal's command to take a break. The Lions pushed to the rhythm of '1, 2; 1, 2'; the South Africans to 'yes, yes, yes'. A positive statement of intent.

Most of the communication and direction came from the players. Du Plessis prompted and pointed but never seemed to drive the direction. The backs worked shiftlessly, without a pattern. The forwards knew what they wanted and were doing it themselves. The voices of command were those of Mark Andrews, James Dalton, du Randt and skipper Gary Teichmann. Rugby needs assertive decision-makers, but it also needs the objective analysis of the coach. The South Africans lacked that cold edge.

That did not detract from the impressive intensity that these men brought to their scrummaging. The new scrummage machine was shunted 150 metres in an hour, a snail on speed. It would have been no surprise for a traffic cop to have booked it for speeding. But these machines were unreliable. The South Africans had already broken one. Gerd Smal rated the one 100-scrum session on a scale of intensity at seven. The Lions would not shove their way to victory.

The South Africans trained for two and a half hours that morning and returned to their base at the Cape Sun, in the heart of the city. The hotel is predominantly a business centre and the theory was that a group of sportsmen staying in such an environment would blend into the wallpaper. Fat chance. Nineteen-stone Os du Randt and friends tend to catch the eye.

In the afternoon they trained on Newlands and the forwards worked obsessively on their catch and drive from the lineout. Combine the athletic jumping skill of Mark Andrews and the mean-machine power running of du Randt, Ruben Kruger and André Venter, and the basis existed for an almost unstoppable driving game. It would require organisation and heroism on a scale thus far unregistered in the annals of British and Irish rugby. It would also need something flawed from South Africa. In training, the flaw was the lineout throwing of Naka Drotské. If the trigger jammed, the bullets would not fire. The training finished as dusk descended. It had been a long four and a half hours.

The intensity and passion had been impressive, but the structure and variety was distinctly *Jurassic Park*. I left Newlands with the firm belief that if the Lions did not capitulate against the monster scrum, and if the back row could erect a brick wall on the gain line near the fringes of the maul, they might just win. A large 'if' indeed.

The Lions, meanwhile, were preparing for the midweek match with the Emerging Springboks. It was the first match in a fortnight where the odds had been in their favour, as the opposition had not gathered until 36 hours before the match. The Lions might still be using scratch combinations, but the style that McGeechan had implemented was by now grafted on to the heart of every Lion. A victory was important to maintain the feelgood factor which so often provides intangible support in a crisis. Cotton perpetually reiterated that 'Unity of purpose has been a key element of every person on this tour'. Rodber's pre-Mpumalanga quote about the Lions being in South Africa to do one job, win a Test series, was ringing true a fortnight after he spoke, even as the shadow Lions XV ran out to a noisy welcome in Wellington. There was a gathering of the red shirts as the Barmy Army battalions arrived. A few guerrillas had fought the war from the coastal campaigns of Port Elizabeth and East London, through to the unforgiving high veldt of Pretoria. Arriving in Cape Town, these tired heroes were joined by the cavalry that swept over the horizon, galvanised by the stunning swagger and *élan* of the squad nobody thought could win.

The Lions offered another superb show for their growing legion of support as they dispatched the Emerging side by 54–22. That was excuse enough for some more barminess, be it in the nearby wine town of Stellenbosch or on the increasingly British waterfront in Cape Town. A drunken English was the local language for the rest of the week in the Western Cape.

Nick Beal, Mr Versatile himself, scored a hat-trick of tries, one courtesy of a flaring spinning top of a break from the Barmy Army's hero, John Bentley. The travelling supporters identified with the honesty and passion which he brought to his game. Even 'Flower of Scotland' was sung in praise; it was developing into a collective effort in the stand as much as on the pitch. The Lions, inspired by Catt, Back and Bateman, played a wide game at a pace beyond their opponents. This side had fulfilled its role in the lead-up to the first Test; the squad was bubbling. So were the nerves of a host of men who had played superbly and were desperate for a Test spot. Once again it was Bentley who summed up the feeling. 'There is a Test match on Saturday and we have all come to play Test rugby. There are going to be some really big disappointments.'

The final calling cards from the selectors had been delivered. The team would be selected the next morning. The air of Wellington was thick with that air of resignation which sportsmen use to hide their gloom. 'I have given 100 per cent, that is all I can do . . . I am hoping to make selection, but it is up to the selectors . . . All I have tried to do is improve continually. I have done as much as I could. Our job is to give the management a headache.' So spoke John Bentley, Allan Bateman and Neil Back.

Together with 32 comrades, these men had a fitful night's sleep. The good fairy or the evil one would arrive with the news at eight o'clock the following morning in the form of a note slipped beneath the bedroom door. Heaven or Hell. The theory was that each player would have time to collect his emotions, be they high or low, and arrive in public in control. The team would not be announced until Thursday lunchtime and the tension was unbearable – for the assembled media. Any clues were hard to find as the team fled from Cape Town to Stellenbosch and a training session. Only the photographers were allowed to attend, and then only for a ten-minute spell. This amiable, shambling mass of humanity was the centre of attention on arrival back in Cape Town, as the scribblers searched for any hints. The snappers and their theory of body language became so many oracles as Dave, Keith, Igor and Moonchild described their visions. 'Dawse was really down; 'ee sat with his 'ands in 'is 'ead. Shawsie was devastated and Tim Rodber could barely make eye contact' – at which a journalist added his wordy weight: 'Yeah, he had a face like thunder when he got in the lift.' So that was Rodber out. But 'Austin Healey was bouncing everywhere and Neil Back was charging all over the place' – at which point another, newly arrived journalist mused, 'Yes, I wondered why Backie was so chatty when I saw him this morning.' Congratulations Neil. 'And I have never seen Jeremy Davidson smile so much.'

So much for the body-language theory. The team was announced Thursday lunchtime in front of 80 keen ears: Smith, Wood, Wallace, Johnson (captain), Davidson (one for the photographers), Dallaglio, Hill (whoops), Rodber (whoops, as many thought, until the truth about Eric Miller's terribly timed illness leaked), Dawson (whoops), Townsend, Tait, Gibbs, Guscott, Evans, Jenkins.

No Bentley, no Back, no Bateman and, most unfortunately of all, no Miller. The Irishman had played his way into the Test team against Natal only to fall foul of illness. That was the cruellest blow of all; even the happiest tours have their sad moments. The overall Test selection met with the approval of those who believed that British rugby's obsession with the comfort zone had stifled its development. The front-row selection epitomised the unwavering courage of the Lions management. We did not know whether Smith and Wallace would hold out against the power of the Springboks, but they had earned their chance. Davidson had played his way into the team and Miller too was a brave initial choice.

At half-back the selection was the Northampton combination. It made sense now that Rodber was at eight. But as that was the position in which the Saints finished in the Courage League, it hardly inspired confidence. Tait was selected in front of Mr Inspiration for the quality of his defence, the one area where Bentley was vulnerable, while Gibbs and Guscott revived their 1993 partnership. The most effective chalk-and-cheese combination on the planet. At full-back, Neil Jenkins was included, mainly by default. Tim Stimpson had failed to progress at the same rate as his colleagues and the more proven goal-kicking nerve of Jenkins gained the vote. The Lions were facing the Springboks with their third-choice number eight, a scrum-half rated a few light years behind Robert Howley and a full-back whom Carel du Plessis thought a weakness. On paper, there was nothing rigid about the spine of the Lions.

It was left to the most eloquent of all the Lions to state the foundations that had been laid for battle. 'We have picked a front row to get below the Springboks and a front row who are all ball-players. The whole pack are athletes. Teams that beat the Springboks rarely annihilate them up front . . . There is no room for someone who cannot take and give a pass well under pressure.' The total footballing mantra was being reiterated by Telfer, together with the determination not to let the South Africans blast the Lions front row into orbit. It is better to collapse a scrum as referees will generally award penalties on a fifty-fifty split. What the Lions could not afford was to be shunted backwards in the manner they had been three weeks earlier at this same ground.

And then there was the need for special men, those who transcend the 'good player' label. 'We will need to concentrate more than ever before, especially when tired. The ability to keep the game in place when exhaustion starts to kick in is essential.' Telfer, the silver-haired prophet, told it as it would happen. Andy Keast, the ultimate back-room boy with the square eyes from watching rugby videos, spoke infrequently, but what he said revealed that the Lions were confident that they knew the nature of the South African beast. 'People revert to type in the high-profile matches, and once the South Africans are in behind teams, then you are in a lot of trouble.' The storm would hit the Lions, but at least they had prior warning.

Inevitably the final press-conference question before the first Test was related to that most British of millstone dates, 1974, and Willie John McBride. Mark Andrews had stated how sick he was of that year being quoted and how he did not want his children to suffer endless talk of 1997. I knew how he felt – at least, I agreed with the first part of his statement. Telfer was not a man suffering from a stiff neck, either. 'Historians talk about the past, rugby players and coaches look to the future. 1974 and 1997 are worlds apart.' You tell 'em, Jim.

The '74 Lions were red-hot favourites; the '97 Lions were ice-cold outsiders. Even on the day of the Test, Sporting Index reflected the world opinion and installed South Africa as favourites, expected to win by a margin of between six and nine points. But these Lions were professional in every sense of the word. The back-up work and planning had been better than anything ever to have left the rugby fields of Britain and Ireland. After the gruelling domestic season and three Super-12 teams in seven days, experts had expected the Lions to arrive at Newlands with little bar adrenalin on which to survive. Instead they arrived confident of their ability to outlast their opponents. Fitness was a real foundation for the team.

Some teams will work as hard as this Lions party, but few will monitor the effects as well. David McLean stood on the Newlands touchline absolutely certain that stamina would not prove the undoing of the Lions; they were fresh. 'We have conducted a staleness test. We ask players to judge themselves on a scale of one to five in the following areas: sleep, fatigue, stress and muscle soreness. At one stage two guys were on the verge of becoming stale, so we ordered them away from rugby itself for a while.' One of them, Jeremy Davidson, was about to ignite the skies over the Western Cape. On any previous tour, he would have burned out before rugby's equivalent to 5 November. This professionalism was a potent weapon in the Lions' arsenal.

Newlands is one of the great Test-match venues. With a capacity of 51,000 it is a long way from being one of the biggest, but the stands seem to lean towards the pitch, lending a seriously claustrophobic atmosphere to the proceedings. The Lions heard the Welsh hymns, 'Flower of Scotland' and the loathsome 'Swing Low' as they stretched and limbered up in their changing-room. The decibel level was lifted by the entire British and Irish contingent singing the Oasis single 'Wonderwall'. Not many pop songs are appropriate rugby songs, but this one, lyrically, would prove to be exactly right. The voices of seven or eight thousand supporters, many fuelled by alcohol, took the edge away from the traditionally hostile home crowd.

Johnson led the visitors out to a crescendo of away support probably unrivalled in the history of the sport. There would be no anthem for the visitors because of the Irish (or some would say British) problem, but the host nation sang their dual anthems. 'N'kosi Sikeleli' provided the calm, 'Die Stem' the storm. The hard men of South Africa were ready. Across the half-way line the Lions stood, stone-faced. Andy Keast's words about reversion to type came true before our very eyes as the Welsh contingent of Jenkins, Evans and Gibbs locked arms in a defiant display of Celtic camaraderie.

Eighty minutes later, Neil Jenkins would deliver a beautifully weighted pass to send Alan Tait across the Springbok tryline and the Barmy Army into space. Tait touched the ball down and embarked on a quasi-gun-toting celebration. The Springboks, with all their heavy-weight firepower, had been beaten by the lightweight Lions. The rolling rugby themes that were gathering no moss on this downhill sprint through South Africa had exploded into full flowering life in front of a stunned audience. The fitness factor helped transform the South African lead of one point into a nine-point deficit in a mere ten minutes; the scrum, under the most intense pressure, did not buckle; and the tackling of every player, but especially the back row of Hill, Rodber and Dallaglio, was heroic. In fact, that was the word on the lips of every rugby watcher: heroic.

The organisation was magnificent. Scott Gibbs justified his inclusion with a mighty marshalling of the midfield. 'I was bellowing at the top of my voice to keep the defence tight, and, bang, we then finished stronger than South Africa.' Matt Dawson, the unlikely hero, talked of the outstanding defence, as did a gracious Gary Teichmann, while an elated but exhausted Ian McGeechan struggled to find words beyond 'Quite incredible, quite incredible. We have improved our game without the ball. The games leading to the Test were vital.' The grand attacking vision had been matched by the foundations so clearly missing in the early days of the tour.

The quality that had been evident from the first day in South Africa, the deep-rooted spirit, also played its part. 'At the end of the day it was tremendous spirit,' said Johnson. In his moment of triumph, Dawson had time to say, 'My thoughts are still with Rob [Howley],' while Cotton could only add, 'It is a 35-man effort, as simple as that.' Six weeks' planning had paid off. 'We have trained, slept and eaten; that is all we have done.' The sacrifice was worth it, Scott.

Tait's memorable moment seemed a lot further than 80 minutes away as Colin Hawke whistled the start of the series. In the commentary box, I stressed the need for the Lions to start well and douse the South African aggression. But Neil Jenkins, pumped to the eyeballs with adrenalin, fired the kick-off out on the full. The Lions were shunted a metre backwards at the next scrum and Henry Honiball fired an exquisite kick to within two metres of the Lions' line. That is Martin Johnson's territory, but he was muscled off the ball by Hannes Strydom. From the resulting pressure a scrum buckled and Edrich Lubbe kicked a penalty. South Africa led 3–0.

The Lions' riposte was immediate and involved many of the men who would play starring roles in the Lions' quest for glory. Keith Wood threw to the lineout, Davidson soared high above Andrews and, from the ensuing ball, Dawson darted elusively forward. The next wave of attackers were the titanic Wood and Martin Johnson, who would quite literally rise to the challenge of his life. The Springboks gave a penalty away and Jenkins levelled the score.

Any joy on the part of the Barmy Army was short-lived. The 'Boks stormed forward and laid siege. Rodber and Dallaglio tackled incessantly, but from a catch and drive – the fulfilment of endless hours of practice – Os du Randt piled over for a score. It emphasised the real difference between the two sides: sheer power. It was also a graphic illustration of why the bookmakers had made South Africa such firm favourites.

Logic demanded a home win, but the spirit and intelligence of the entire party cocked a snook at such beliefs. Another Davidson catch, followed by a Dallaglio and Smith charge, resulted in another penalty, before an appalling error by André Joubert was capitalised upon by Dallaglio and Johnson. The Springboks conceded another penalty and somehow, for all the home side's power and control, it was the Lions who were 9–8 in front. Neil Jenkins had taken his chances, while the South Africans had not, and, irony of ironies, the Lions were testing the great Joubert and finding him wanting, while Jenkins was high-ball free. Du Plessis had forgotten his critical thoughts about Jenkins as a fullback.

The second half started well, with three more points. Again Davidson supplied the ball and for once it was a back, Scott Gibbs, who made the inroad. It was 12–8 and we dared to hope. That flicker was nearly extinguished when Scott Gibbs, of all people, missed a tackle on Gary Teichmann. His skilful one-handed pass released Russell Bennett for a score that was unconverted. The pressure mounted on the Lions and, for a brief moment, the British and Irish were rattled. Paul Wallace conceded a soft penalty and the Springboks nudged themselves four points clear. Only muscular defence kept South Africa out for the next ten-minute spell, but as the match moved tumultuously towards its thrilling end, the Lions picked up the pace. Their fitness was a partner that aided the journey to rugby heaven. Jenkins narrowed the gap to one point after a wheeled scrum enabled Tim Rodber to batter himself across the gain line. Telfer had a right to smile; the scrummage had been turned from water to wine.

His satisfaction was replaced by ecstasy ten minutes later and ten minutes from the end. Another marvellous Davidson catch, aided and abetted by the Wood and Smith charge, set up a fine attacking position. The pace and the pulse of the travelling team and its supporters were being raised. Telfer, sitting next to Redman, had his head in his hands. All those scrums in practice, all that goading, abuse and encouragement – now was the time. The scrum was wheeled, but instead of Rodber picking up, Dawson swooped for what would become one of the great moments of British rugby. 'Tim just said, "Go, Dawse, go yourself." I made a break on the outside. There seemed nowhere to go, so I put the ball over my head and everyone thought that I would turn it inside. Then it opened up.' Dawson was alone in Aladdin's Cave. The wheel had taken Kruger out of the equation; the dummy was taken by Teichmann, Venter and Joost van der Westhuizen; Dawson strolled to fame. It was almost surreal as he sauntered to the fence and the delirious support. Union Jacks were being waved by men in green shirts.

The dream became a reality on the stroke of 81 minutes. Gibbs bashed through three tackles to set up the ball. Dawson found Rodber, who defied Keast's comment about reverting to type and threw out a tremendous miss-pass to Jenkins with Tait in glorious space outside. The defence, heroism and spirit had been the defining features of the match, but the development of the team as a 15-man unit found expression when it mattered most. The referee blew for time and while the Barmy Boys danced and sang, Martin Johnson clapped twice. No smiles; it was only 1–0.

McGeechan was not so cool. In the tunnel he hugged his Northampton protégé Dawson. He had been heavily criticised for the selection, but the sheer control of Dawson's performance had justified his coach's faith and helped cement what many had previously considered an overstated reputation. The match had been planned to precision. It was a tremendous triumph for the management, but the memories will be of the men who rose to their maximum height. The front row were unsurpassed in their valour, Davidson was an outstanding trigger, and Rodber, Dawson and Jenkins came from the shadows into the light. Cape Town disappeared from the face of the planet, to be replaced by London, Cardiff, Edinburgh, Dublin and Belfast rolled into one.

The Capetonians were relieved to see the travelling army pack their bags and head north. They were also stunned at the loss in Newlands. The Sunday headlines were all about the 'Boks, screaming ''Boks blew it' and 'What Went Wrong?'. The South African rugby nation is incapable of crediting teams that beat them. Defeat is always due to a fault within their own team. The arrogant assertion is that South Africa will always win if they play correctly. That arrogance suited the Lions. It would guarantee that South Africa would approach the second Test in Durban with an identical game plan. Carel du Plessis was talking about better execution and more passion as early as the Monday. He had not considered how the Lions, so much smaller physically, had nullified their game so consistently. The thoughts were coming only from the northern hemisphere. As evangelists intent on saving the northern hemisphere from secondary status, the coaching team had almost accomplished their mission. But to guarantee that the gospel of 15-man rugby would be taken back to each respective club and Union, the Lions needed to bag the 'Bok and claim a series win. And while every member of the management had a streak of Mother Theresa about him, all were primarily in pursuit of the more immediate prize. As Rodber said, 'One objective – a series win.'

The Lions were not about to sacrifice one of their great weapons, team spirit, purely because of 80 glorious minutes. The mood that would sweep them to the mother of all parties in Durban was further consolidated the morning after the Test. The midweek team were to face Free State on the Tuesday. It was regarded as the one match in which nobody wanted to play. The team would travel there and back in the same day. If ever a game could be sidetracked into a quiet corner it was this one. In 1993, the Lions Test team hardly saw the midweek team after beating New Zealand. The next two results were both crushing defeats as momentum faded. Not this time. The Test team actually requested that they train with the team due to face Free State on the Sunday morning. It was impressive team spirit, the 35-man effort of which Cotton had spoken in the tunnel of Newlands.

The sight of McGeechan hugging Dawson prompted tears from Phil de Glanville and Dewi Morris watching in Britain, but an even more satisfying sight was the long conversation being held between McGeechan and Healey during the Monday session before the Free State match. Nobody regarded himself as a dirt-tracker, and consequently the players respected themselves as well as each other. That self-respect is a powerful commodity. It made a sunny Durban day even brighter. A lot of players who ached with pain at missing out on the first Test were leading by example. Jason Leonard, a Test certainty at the start of the tour, clapped his hands in delight as Mike Catt flighted a series of superb restarts, another area of improvement (Alred did prove his point in the first Test). The pack were hugely impressive, as were the communication and encouragement. Not one kick-off was mishandled as the Lions focused on their next challenge.

Another inspirational decision was made at this juncture, as popular Nigel Redman was chosen to lead the team in recognition of his tremendous contribution to the squad. Ollie the dirt-tracker was now Ollie the leader, a further fine example of skilful management. The pride of this Lions squad ran through all 35 members. Bentley was another man bursting with healthy ambition. 'I despise being called a dirt-tracker, especially when there can be just this [he indicated a tiny gap between finger and thumb] between being in and out of the team.' Such a strong personality mishandled could have created an internal rift, but Bentley, for all his dejection, did not feel like a dirt-tracker. The Lions selectors were making loud noises about the constant search for improvement. Cotton promised that 'We do not pick the Test team until Wednesday morning. We are constantly looking for improvement, and if that means changes of personnel we will not be afraid.'

The midweek side finished the session and Bentley strode over to McGeechan and asked the Lions coach if he would just remind the team of when the Test side was to be selected. The tour was on fire with ambition at every level. Cotton wanted a series win, McGeechan wanted perfect rugby and Bentley wanted that cap. 'I would give anything to be involved on Saturday. To play as well as the man in possession is good, but not good enough. You must play better.'

And so this powder keg of a party sent 21 inland to Bloemfontein while those not involved cheered them from the team hotel. The match nobody wanted to play in became the performance of the tour. The Lions went a long way to fulfilling every level of ambition. McGeechan witnessed what Fran Cotton quite properly described as 'one of the all-time great Lions performances'. He added, 'I am so proud of them. That was a great squad effort.' The win boosted morale to a level where the team hotel in Durban must have seemed to be back at altitude, and Bentley scored a hat-trick to boost his hopes. He knew it had been a remarkable team effort. 'Within a good tour performance individuals can shine. I have done all that I can.'

Free State were generous in praise. Their captain Helhard Muller said, 'It is no wonder they won the first Test if this was their second team.' When an Afrikaner journalist asked him who would win the second Test, he paused before saying, 'Er, rugby football will be the winner.' The pause said it all. The national team may still have been underestimating the touring party, but nobody else did. Such was the quality of the win that selection would bring another welcome headache. Cotton admitted that 'The meeting went on for far longer than normal due to the quality of the Free State performance. We discussed a number of positions, but number eight in particular.' Among those up for discussion must have been Back and Bateman, whose creative partnership had reached new heights in the Free State performance. The final scoreline read 52–30. Anybody with enough energy left to scrutinise the training session the previous day would have seen this coming.

The dampener on the day was the concussion that forced Will Greenwood to end an excellent tour prematurely and a reminder that the tabloids are more interested in a cheap headline than a serious analysis. Greenwood, out cold for a few minutes, was unaware how close he had been to death until he saw *The Sun*'s headline . . . oh well. He was not the only Lion to suffer. Ieuan Evans's tour was to end with a groin strain that left him a distraught figure as the Lions closed in on their moment of destiny. That injury depressed Evans, but left Bentley elated. He was pushing Tait hard for the one wing spot, but Evans's injury made his inclusion a formality.

It was imperative that the Lions win this Test. Not only is Ellis Park South Africa's favourite ground, but the signs of wear and tear, both physically and mentally, were starting to show. The work required to reach the plateau set by the Scottish coaches had forced every member of the party to drive himself beyond any level of rugby intensity he had ever known. Guscott's eyebrows were starting to raise in clear irritation at the thought of yet another extra session; Gibbs, too, was murmuring beneath his breath. But with glory so close, these thoughts could be submerged until Saturday. Defeat in Durban would almost certainly result in a series loss.

As 15,000 or so British and Irish fans arrived in Durban, McGeechan prepared his men for the decisive battle. Fran Cotton reckoned that they would be 'twice as motivated as last week', while McGeechan was unusually colourful, joking, 'South Africa will throw everything but the kitchen sink at us.' Standing and smiling on my right at the back of a press conference attended by a staggering figure of over a hundred journalists was Jeremy Guscott, who added to McGeechan's remark, 'That's only because we have the kitchen sink and his name is Scott Gibbs.' Both men were to be proved dramatically accurate with their words.

What can be written about 28 June? The day started as a Hieronymus Bosch nightmare. Ambling down to a 7.30 breakfast I was confronted with a pyramid of Boddington's beer cans and that truly awful tune 'The Lion Sleeps Tonight'. Carrying my battered notebook I inscribed the hurried words, 'Not if they win tonight, they fucking will not.' Durban, famous as the last outpost of the British Empire in Africa, was transported back in time. The Barmy Army were in the Natal capital and 20,000-strong, according to *The Natal Mercury*. Like the Lions they were on the threshold of history. The comrades in arms who had followed the '93 Lions, the countless cricket tours to Australia and the West Indies, and the abortive soccer campaigns had never witnessed anything other than the odd battle won. Victory at King's Park would win the war. I did not think that this would be any more a motivating force for the Lions than the excellent effect they had produced for Sky Sports' viewing figures . . . even on a Test-match day the mind must wander occasionally. At 11.30 I looked from my room to the poolside to see Gregor Townsend immersed in a newspaper. Whether he was reading it or not I do not know, but it looked damned cool.

Durban was a few degrees hotter and the temperature was soaring at King's Park as the Barmy Army set up camp. The chants of 'Lion, Lions' started at about midday, five and a quarter hours before kick-off. They would not recede into the distance until the last charter flight left Durban on the following Monday. As the sun set in Durban, the volume rose. The drum beat of the Zulu dancers set a tone of intimidation that was to intensify as this bruising battle moved towards its coruscating conclusion. It was not a game of great technique, but it was sport at its very best. It dripped with tension.

The cold post-match analysis tells a tale of South African errors. Six kicking chances represented 15 points. Not one of them was taken. Tactically, through the sheer arrogance of believing that the same game plan with a better execution would be enough, the Springboks and Carel du Plessis contributed suicidally to their own downfall, and Didier Méné made one particular crucial refereeing mistake which may have turned the balance of the game the Lions' way. But to hell with the cold calculations. This was an emotional day worth reliving.

The Lions had as much territorial control in the match as the British Empire will possess by the turn of the century, but intangible strength pulled them through. The victory came thanks to the sheer 'team spirit and total dedication to keep playing', according to a breathless Ian McGeechan. The contest was a throwback to the great days of heavy-weight boxing and that Ali–Foreman fight in Zaire when Big George pummelled Ali against the ropes for an eternity before the great man, having absorbed all that the giant could throw at him, nailed him with a quick lethal combination. The Lions relied on the precision jabs of Neil Jenkins to keep them in the ring before Jeremy Guscott, the man who floated through the tour like a butterfly, stung South Africa like a bee.

In terms of sheer heroism, it left Cape Town for dead. That was a soap opera compared to this Homeric stuff. The scrum held, but only just; the Springboks surged across the gain line in a manner that had been beyond them seven days earlier; and Gregor Townsend lacked the platform to spark any three-quarter attacks. Defence and discipline of the highest order were the Lions' mainstay. Lawrence Dallaglio and Scott Gibbs made John Wayne and Richard Widmark look like craven shirkers in *The Alamo*. But if their contribution to the rearguard effort was sensational, the discipline defied description. Battered and bruised and rocking on the back foot for most of the 80 minutes, the Lions conceded a miserly eight penalties. When the South Africans threw every conceivable weapon at them in the last 25 minutes, not a single penalty was awarded against a Lion. The trust in one another was such that nobody panicked in the teeth of a monstrous onslaught. We were light years beyond rationality, as great sport invariably must be.

When the rugby was over and frayed nerves were settled, Jim Telfer would remind the listening throngs, 'We have done a lot for northern hemisphere rugby with the way that we have played.' But this game was about the moment. The Barmy Army's thoughts were a long way from the development of the game in the northern hemisphere when their hero John Bentley rushed towards their tumultuous throng after the final whistle, fists raised and pumping upwards, urging almost impossible lifting of the already deafening decibel levels. But for Bentley on this tour weird things had happened, and so, defying logic, the noise grew. The emotional charge was extraordinary. 'I had to congratulate and commiserate with my opponents. There were 34 members of our squad, the management and all those thousands of British people watching. I wanted to hug them all,' said Bentley. Martin Johnson, a rock incapable of becoming perturbed in the series, struggled to control his feelings. The eyes welled up and the bottom lip wobbled as he nearly blubbered out his pride and mentioned 'Rob and Doddie watching at home'. The spirit of these 1997 Lions could not be quashed.

Images of this day will live forever in the minds of the Lions and the army of raucous supporters. This is how I remember the match. The Lions burst through the Lion Lager banners. Most threatening of all was Scott Gibbs, two arms raised, invoking the spirit of Mars with a cold, calm, deadly intent. As they gathered together in a huddle, the squat tank of a centre, one tooth missing, tightened the team. His right arm chopped at the air at eye level before ascending towards the heavens – 'This is where we are; *that* is where we are going to have to travel.' As 'Die Stem' echoed its bloody challenge, Lawrence Dallaglio tightened his grip on Martin Johnson and Tom Smith. Eyes tightly closed, this stallion drew deep breaths as he summoned every ounce of resolve. Above all others, it would be Dallaglio and Gibbs whose armour would shine brightest.

South Africa, as Fran Cotton had warned, came out twice as motivated. From Neil Jenkins's kick-off, Mark Andrews towered above the fleet-footed Lions pack. The 'Boks pack powered into overdrive. André Venter, Naka Drotské, Big Os du Randt, Ruben Kruger and Drotské again, the most powerful storm-troopers in world rugby, stormed forward, sweeping 30 metres. The Lions could only stem the flow illegally. From 48 metres, Henry Honiball missed. The story of the day was unfolding dramatically before our eyes. South Africa, eyeballs popping to a man, charged into the heart of the Lions defence, but nothing creaked. Fifteen minutes had elapsed before the Lions secured a good scrum ball in enemy territory. That alone produced a verse of 'Swing Low'. The resultant attack was ended by a South African foul. Up stepped the King of Pontypridd, old carrot-top, and the ball, from a full 48 metres, bisected the posts with the precision of Pythagoras.

Back surged South Africa, but it would be the Lions who scored next, on 28 minutes. Again the catalyst was the mighty Irish combination of Keith Wood and Jeremy Davidson. The Lions drove the lineout with South African ferocity which the home side short-circuited with an illegal collapse. It was five metres from touch on the right-hand side, and Jenkins coaxed another three points from that imperious boot. The lump in the throat threatened to become a commentary problem as I realised that the chorus of 'Bread of Heaven' which so inspired the Welshman was coming from Edinburgh, Dublin and even the Home Counties. This was a united effort in every sense. Six minutes later it was the voice of the Afrikaners that roared as Joost van der Westhuizen, a rugby predator with a killer instinct, finally breached the barricades, selling Paul Wallace a dummy. The missed conversion from Percy Montgomery left the Lions desperately hanging on to a one-point lead.

At half-time the crowd's roar was continuous, stimulated by a gladiatorial contest of epic proportion. South Africa held a clear lead on points, boxing style, but missed kicks and tactical ineptitude were the straws at which the Lions clutched. When would Neil Jenkins and Alan Tait be tested under the high kick? One hundred and twenty minutes of high-octane Test rugby and Jenkins, the converted fly-half, had not been tested once. Within a minute of the restart Honiball belatedly asked the question. The Lions had the wrong answer and Percy Montgomery crossed for a second Springbok try. The kick was missed, but the South Africans were on fire and in the lead. We waited for the valiant Lions to buckle, but we had underestimated the power of the kitchen sink. Scott Gibbs's riposte to the Springbok try was the symbolic moment of the series. The Lions scrum wheeled itself into a position from which Rodber and Dallaglio could launch a rare attack. The second-phase ball was moved into midfield, Townsend scissored with Gibbs and the West Walian plundered yards. As the bullocking charge gathered steam, the giant shape of Os du Randt loomed into view. To the amazement of the 51,000 spectators, Gibbs veered off course towards 'The Ox'. The two collided, sparks flew, and Gibbs careered on, with The Ox lying in the dirt. The crowd roared in disbelief. The giant symbol of South African power was on his arse. The attack ended with another Lions penalty and three more points for Jenkins.

If du Randt was the Springbok talisman, the Lions equivalent was the demotic Bentley. He too was to receive rough treatment. Twenty-five minutes were left on the clock when Bentley, so forceful all tour, was shrugged aside by André Joubert, who brushed through the lame tackle of Jenkins for a third try. A touchline conversion would have opened up an eight-point gap. That could have galvanised South Africa to more confidence and possibly broken the tiring spirits of a Lions team that had taken intense physical punishment. Joubert fluffed the kick.

It was more of the same as South Africa attacked and the Lions tackled with rigid discipline. The incursions into South African territory were becoming rarer and rarer, but when Johnson's men established a foothold, the Lions invariably bagged points. Another straining scrum caught André Venter not binding. Jenkins walked forward. He struck it with less conviction than his first three kicks, and the crowd were quiet. Miles Harrison, a bundle of nervous energy alongside me in the commentary box, whispered like a snooker commentator, 'Ooh, it's stayed right.' Then came the roar that proclaimed otherwise. It was 15–12, and still the Lions were alive.

The fitness garnered through those long, gruelling sessions, supplemented by the professional advice on diet and rest, would now make its mark, together with the tremendous spirit of the team. Seven minutes remained and from some mysterious depth, Keith Wood and Lawrence Dallaglio found even more reserves of stamina to motor into offensive overdrive. Wood knocked on, but Didier Méné thought the spilling motion was a result of a South African hand playing the ball on the floor. It was a turning-point. The penalty kick was a metre outside the twenty-two and almost in front of the posts, but normality was a dead concept. Harrison strained his vocal chords. 'Everybody back home will be on their knees, hoping and praying that he can find one more kick.' The immaculate boot made contact, and as the easiest penalty of the day levelled the battle, he bellowed, 'Fantastic kick.' Balls to objectivity.

And still the Lions surged forward. A barnstorming forward charge carried them to within ten metres of glory with four minutes remaining on the clock. The slight frame of Townsend flew at the tryline, but South Africa held firm. The ball popped back to Dawson, bodies were sprawling everywhere . . . the only man in view was Jerry Guscott. Quiet for 156 minutes, the Bath man – the cobra from the Roman city – now struck. Calmly, he pulled back the trigger. The snap on the contact was perfect as the ball sailed gloriously over the flailing arms of Henry Honiball. The Lions were in front. The Barmy Army transcended a state of barminess.

This was no longer a rugby match; we had descended into pandemonium. The Springboks, in utter panic, threw everything bar the kitchen sink at the Lions. Joubert sprinted forward and the kitchen sink hit him, the ball being smashed from his grasp by the might of the Welsh warrior Gibbs. One minute was left as Telfer started to watch the referee and look for the whistle. Honiball fired another kick into the Natal night sky. It hung there for an eternity, or at least long enough for a frantic Miles Harrison to implore, 'Come on, Neil.' Jenkins could not gather the ball, though, and Danie van Schalkwyk was following it across the line when Austin Healey, on as a substitute, dived full length and regained the ball. The pack regrouped, the ball was recycled to Gibbs and, damn it, he missed touch. Another wave of attacks crashed into the Lions defence. Mark Andrews was floored by a monumental Dallaglio hit; Pieter Rossouw gasped as Gibbs hammered in another thunderous tackle. Honiball and colleagues could not go through this human barricade. Running out of ideas, he chipped over and Jenkins touched down in the sanctuary of his dead-ball area.

The camera framed three men as the Lions prepared to drop out: Jenkins and Guscott, the point-scoring heroes, and, most importantly of all, Gibbs, the Lion firebrand. To the horror of every British and Irish supporter, the restart sailed out on the full. 'What next?' I thought, as exhaustion kicked in in the commentary box. What came next was a shrill blast of Didier Méné's whistle. Against the most monumental odds, the Lions had won the series.

Guided by McGeechan and Telfer, the Lions had taken British and Irish rugby to heights not reached for a quarter of a century. The progression of a style for the professional age had fired the tour in the early days before Telfer grafted on the basics to give the foundation for victory. How appropriate, therefore, that it was Jeremy Guscott, once a bricklayer before his rugby flights of fancy carried him away, who should lay the final stone in place to complete the skyscraper, built with vision and inspiration in eight short weeks.

It was a monumental achievement but, more than anything else, we should thank Fran Cotton's first professional Lions for proving that the end of rugby union's amateurism was not, by definition, the end to the romance of sport. I will drink to that.